SLAUGHTERHOUSE

SLAUGHTERHOUSE

CHICAGO'S UNION STOCK YARD
AND THE WORLD IT MADE

Dominic A. Pacyga

The University of Chicago Press   *Chicago and London*

Dominic A. Pacyga is professor of history in the Department of Humanities, History, and Social Sciences at Columbia College Chicago. He is the author or coauthor of several books on Chicago, including *Chicago: A Biography* and *Polish Immigrants and Industrial Chicago: Workers on the South Side, 1880–1922*, both published by the University of Chicago Press.

The University of Chicago Press, Chicago 60637
The University of Chicago Press, Ltd., London
© 2015 by The University of Chicago
All rights reserved. Published 2015.
Printed in the United States of America

24 23 22 21 20 19 18 17 16 15   2 3 4 5

ISBN-13: 978-0-226-12309-7 (cloth)
ISBN-13: 978-0-226-29143-7 (e-book)
DOI: 10.7208/chicago/9780226291437.001.0001

Library of Congress Cataloging-in-Publication Data

Pacyga, Dominic A., author.
Slaughterhouse : Chicago's Union Stock Yard and the world it made / Dominic A. Pacyga.
pages ; cm
Includes bibliographical references and index.
ISBN 978-0-226-12309-7 (cloth : alk. paper) —
ISBN 978-0-226-29143-7 (ebook)
1. Union Stock Yard & Transit Company of Chicago—History.
2. Stockyards—Illinois—Chicago—History. 3. Slaughtering and slaughter-houses—Illinois—Chicago. 4. Chicago (Ill.)—History. I. Title.
HD9419.U4P33 2015
338.7'63620831—dc23
2015001104

♾ This paper meets the requirements of ANSI/NISO Z39.48–1992 (Permanence of Paper).

TO LEO SCHELBERT
Mentor, colleague, and above all friend

CONTENTS

PREFACE

Confronting the Modern in
Chicago's Square Mile

Roses are red, violets are blue,
the stockyards stink and so do you!

TRADITIONAL CHILDREN'S STREET RHYME,
Back of the Yards, Chicago

*

This is not strictly a business history, nor is it a labor history, an ethnic history, or a social history. It is the history of a place, a particular place in the history of Chicago, the Midwest, and the American West, the square mile that made up the Union Stock Yard and Packingtown. It is a place etched into the collective memory of the city and the nation. Even today, more than forty years since livestock handlers unloaded the last steers at the rail and truck docks of the stockyard company, Chicagoans call the area just southwest of the corner of Pershing Road and Halsted Street "the yards." Place matters; in many ways it defines the human experience. As writer Tony Hiss has pointed out, "We all react consciously or unconsciously, to the places where we live or work." The urbanist William H. Whyte studied urban places and pointed not only to their functions, but also to the memories and feelings they provoke. The Union Stock Yard is just such a place.[1]

The Union Stock Yard and Packingtown provided an economic and symbolic base for the neighborhoods and the city that grew around it. This place drew men and women, both native born and immigrants, from around the country and the world to find their future in the maze

Burnham and Root designed the iconic Stone Gate and watchman's building as an entranceway to the Union Stock Yard in 1879. It quickly became the symbol of the market and the meat industry in Chicago. Sherman the Bullock looks down on Exchange Avenue from atop the center arch of the gate. (Postcard, Author's Collection.)

of livestock pens and giant packinghouses. To be from Back of the Yards, Canaryville, Bridgeport, or McKinley Park, the neighborhoods surrounding the old stockyards, still implies a certain social class and even worldview. The American working class was formed by such places all across the nation's landscape. In the nineteenth and twentieth centuries, these places introduced Americans to the modern—that is, the new industrial economy that emerged after the Civil War. Over the years, the stockyards continued to define and redefine what was modern and what was not modern for many Chicagoans. It provided both spectacle and innovation to a public that saw its very life being transformed by industrialism.

When they hear the word "stockyards," most Chicagoans born before about 1955 recall the smell emanating from that one square mile of the city's South Side on a warm summer day. For years after the packers disappeared the stench seemed to linger. It was not a ghostly stink: the huge fertilizer plants owned by Darling and Company on both Ashland Avenue and on Racine Avenue continued to operate well after the cattle, hogs, and sheep had left. In the "Square Mile" at its prime stood numerous packinghouses, ringed by railroad lines adjacent to the tens of thousands of animal pens of the Union Stock Yard. Train tracks encircled the stockyard and delivered a constant flow of livestock to the Chicago market and then the world. Railroad docks stood ready to unload the massive quantities of animals, to be sold to packers daily in the huge fairground. During World War One—the height of its history—some fifty thousand people found employment in the stockyards and adjacent Packingtown. Tens of thousands of cattle, calves, hogs, and sheep changed hands every day in the market. Afterward, about one-third reboarded trains and headed to slaughterhouses further east. The rest met their fate in Packingtown.

Unloaded on the docks that could handle hundreds of livestock railcars at a time, the creatures were counted and accounted for, then driven to the sale pens. Once sold, employees weighed and then drove them to the abattoirs that sent them off as meat products from Armour's, Swift's, Morris's, Wilson's, or any number of smaller independent plants. Thanks to the by-products industry, various animal parts became combs, buttons, lard, fertilizer, or even pharmaceuticals as the packers used everything, as the cliché said, but the squeal of the vanquished hog.

By World War One, Chicago's meatpacking products were known, for better or worse, throughout the world. As the river of cattle, hogs, sheep, and horses flowed into the Union Stock Yard, it seemed that Chicago would never lose its title as packing industry leader, but the seeds of its decline were sown as the practice of direct buying and the emergence of the truck began to further transform the business. By 1930, technological change and new entrepreneurial systems ended the glory days of meatpacking in Chicago. While the city's meat industry continued to perform admirably during World War Two, as the war came to a close it continued to fade.

In 1952, Wilson and Company opened an up-to-date packing plant in Kansas City; two years later, it announced the closing of its giant Chicago operations. By the end of the decade, Swift and Armour also decided to leave the Chicago Stockyards. In the late 1950s and early 1960s, the Union Stock Yard and Transit Company updated its facilities and celebrated its one hundredth anniversary, announcing that, while the big packers had left, it would survive and thrive. Charles S. Potter, the president of the USY&T Company, proclaimed, "Chicago will not be only the largest livestock market in the world, but also the most up to date in facilities for both buyer and seller." Famous last words: less than six years after celebrating its centennial, the Union Stock Yard closed forever. The new McCormick Place and other venues eclipsed the nearby International Amphitheater as a target destination for trade shows, political conventions, and rock concerts. The Square Mile was a shadow of its former self.

It was not, however, the end of "the yards." Today, the Stockyard Industrial Park is one of the most successful industrial sites in the city, to some degree taking up where the old Union Stock Yard left off. Many different industries have joined the few remaining meat purveyors and the two slaughterhouses located at Forty-First and Ashland Avenue and Thirty-Eighth and Halsted Street. Park Packing still slaughters hogs within the Square Mile, and Chiappetti Packing butchers lambs and sheep just outside the formal boundaries of the yards. New industries, such as Testa Produce and The Plant, a food business incubator, have arrived and are developing new green technologies. Once again, tourist groups visit some of the plants now housing a vast array of industries. Again, the Southwest Side of Chicago is on the cutting edge of industrial change.

My family and I have had a long relationship with the Chicago Stockyards. My grandparents left the Tatry Mountains of Poland to arrive in Back of the Yards just before World War One. They worked in the meatpacking industry, as did many of their children. For us, the smells of the packing plants were a normal everyday occurrence, simply part of life in Chicago. As a child, I heard the stories of neighbors and relatives who worked in the yards. Occasionally, cattle would escape and make their way through our neighborhood streets and alleys only to be rounded up and sent back to complete their fateful journey.

In the 1950s and early 1960s, most of the people I knew no longer labored on the kill floors or in the various other departments of the packinghouses. The white ethnic residents of Back of the Yards had largely moved on to what they considered better jobs in cleaner industries, such as the huge Western Electric plant in Cicero or one of the many manufacturing workshops that dotted the industrial-residential landscape to the west and southwest of the neighborhood. For my neighbors, when the packers left it was not a catastrophe. It hurt racial minority groups who by then dominated the packinghouse workforce,

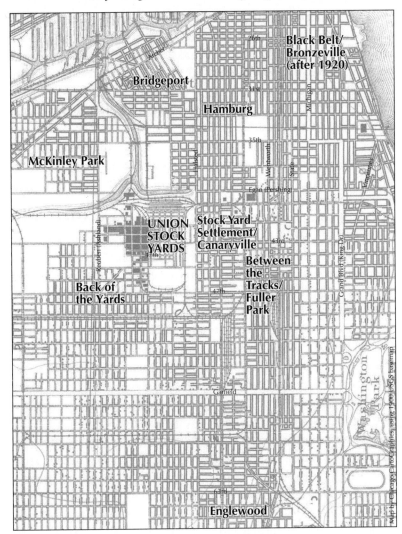

Map of the various stockyard neighborhoods, the Loop, and Bronzeville showing their relationship to the Union Stock Yard. (Chicago CartoGraphics.)

not the Polish, Czech, Slovak, Lithuanian, Irish, and German Americans of Back of the Yards. The then-small Mexican community in Back of the Yards and the African Americans in Englewood and Bronzeville more intensely felt the shuttering of the Armour, Swift, and Wilson plants in the stockyards.

In July 1969, I walked into the old Packingtown area of Chicago through the Forty-Fourth and Ashland Avenue entrance, wandering in the industrial district where most of my relatives had found work in the first half of the twentieth century. I had just quit a job that I hated in a steel fabricating plant on the Southwest Side and decided to seek summer employment somewhere in the old stockyards. I made my way east past abandoned packinghouses and had basically given up on my search when I crossed Racine Avenue and came upon what had once been the world's greatest livestock market. I entered an office under an old cattle viaduct on Exchange Avenue and asked about a job. That night I helped to yard (drive to sale pens) hogs delivered by trucks to the new hog house just north of Forty-Sixth Street. Thus began my fascination with the Union Stock Yard and its impact not only on Chicago, but also on the economic and industrial development of the United States.

Over the summer of 1969, I worked the 5:30 p.m. to 1:30 a.m. shift in the hog house and later in the cattle yard. I met men who had labored in the stockyards since the 1920s and listened to their stories. These tales began to merge with those I had heard around my grandmother's kitchen table and on the front stoops of houses in Back of the Yards. I began to think of ways the stockyards had shaped the lives of hundreds of thousands of people. I left that fall to return to college, but returned the following summer to work as a guard out of the Stone Gate. That autumn, I wrote an undergraduate paper on the 1921–22 packinghouse strike, a topic that I brought along to graduate school. My interest in that particular strike resulted from my work experience, but also from family history. What began in the fall of 1970 as a term paper developed eventually into my doctoral dissertation and then a book, *Polish Immigrants and Industrial Chicago: Workers on the South Side, 1880–1922.*

Over the years, I continued to study, lecture, teach, and write about Chicago's neighborhoods and their people. I always wanted to return to work on a history of that square mile of packinghouses and livestock pens that had so shaped three generations of my family from their arrival in Chicago. By the time I began this book, the Union Stock Yard had closed, almost all of the slaughtering plants that once made up much of Chicago's economic might had shut down, and the rendering plants that gave much of the stockyard smell to the city had moved on. In their place now stood the Stockyards Industrial Park, the most successful of Chicago's attempts to maintain and attract industry in the postindustrial world. What had once been a tourist attraction and the destination of over a billion head of livestock now served as an industrial park employing a mere fraction of those who once flocked to that section of the city looking for the American Dream — or at least the next month's rent. The Square Mile remained, however, and had once housed an industrial experiment that had much to say about the history of the American city and of the American West — not to mention capitalism, race and ethnic relations, and the struggle of labor in all its many facets.

Many Chicagoans before me have written about this place, from Jack Wing's original guide, published even before the stockyard opened in 1865, to a recent memoir by the late Larry Caine, the former general manager of the Union Stock Yard and the International Amphitheater. Various members of packer families have also left behind memoirs, some celebrating the family business, some trying to leave it behind. Government investigations provide much detail, as do journalistic accounts. Writers and celebrities as diverse as Rudyard Kipling, Sarah Bernhardt, and Max Weber joined the tourists on the kill floors and told of the fascination with the modern that drew them and countless others to the Square Mile. Over the years, both Armour and Company and Swift and Company provided different tour guidebooks for visitors to their plant. Several of these have survived and provide insight into what drew tourists to the packinghouses. Muckrakers, especially Upton Sinclair, painted a horrifying picture of the industry, which still haunts the American imagination.

Other historians, beside myself, too have written about the Union Stock Yard, the adjacent neighborhoods, and the labor movement in meatpacking. Louise Wade has written a history of the development of the stockyards and its neighborhoods in the nineteenth century. Robert Slayton and Thomas J. Jablonsky have produced studies of Back of the Yards and its pioneering neighborhood organization, the Back of the Yards Neighborhood Council. James Barrett has described the early years of the labor movement in the yards. Both Roger Horowitz and Rick Halpern have looked at the history of industrial workers and African Americans in Chicago's meatpacking plants. William Cronon has analyzed the economic and ecological impact of the Union Stock Yard in his distinguished study of Chicago, *Nature's Metropolis*. Robert Lewis has placed the Union Stock Yard and Packingtown within the

wider framework of industrial development in the city. The environmental historian Sylvia Hood Washington has looked at the effect of
the stockyards on the lives of working class Chicagoans. Various soci-
ologists from Charles Bushnell to Theodore V. Purcell have looked at
the industry and its bearing on the city and workers. All have contributed to an understanding of the impact of the livestock and meatpacking industry on Chicago and the nation.[2]

Numerous archives also document the history of the yards. Then, a
plethora of illustrations in the form of stereopticon cards, postcards,
trading cards, and memorabilia used as early forms of advertising
show us the stockyards and packinghouses. In all, the history of the
Chicago Stockyards is factually well documented and mythologized.
In this book, I will grapple with the industry's growth, its spectacle
for the wider public, and its decline and virtual disappearance from
Chicago. In its place other industries and a new entrepreneurial spirit,
on a smaller scale but well within the tradition of spectacle and innovation, have appeared. All of this occurred in one square mile, which
continues to shape Chicago's industrial future.

A note on usage: many Chicagoans have traditionally referred to
Packingtown and the Union Stock Yard as simply "the yards." While
I use that term, along with the Chicago Stockyards, the stockyard,
or stockyards, I prefer the official name, the Union Stock Yard, when
referring to the area between Halsted Street and Racine Avenue and
Pershing Road and Forty-Seventh Street. I use the term Packingtown
for the district to the west of Racine Avenue to Ashland Avenue. The
Wilson and Company plant, however, stood west of Ashland and
stretched to Damen Avenue north of Forty-Third Street and must also
be considered a vital part of Packingtown. Other independent packers
conducted business in Canaryville to the east of the Union Stock Yard
and in Bridgeport to the north, yet others operated in Back of the Yards
to the west and south of the stockyard and Packingtown. Much of this
area is now part of the Stockyards Industrial Park and related industrial districts covered by various city of Chicago programs designed to
encourage industrial redevelopment in the area.

In addition, the terms Big Six, Big Four, and Big Three are also used
when referring to the large meatpackers that controlled the meat industry until after the closing of the yards in 1971. The Big Six usually
refer to the Armour, Swift, Morris, National Packing, Cudahy, and
Schwarzschild and Sulzberger (S&S) companies. At times, Hammond

Packing, before the emergence of S&S, is also referenced as one of the Big Six. The Big Four or Big Three usually denote Armour, Swift, Morris, and S&S (later Wilson and Company) and then Armour, Swift, and Wilson after 1923. All of the members of this group, with the exception of Cudahy, maintained large facilities in Chicago until the 1950s.

1
SPECTACLE
Facing the Modern World

Cosmopolitan, indeed, is the sight-seeing throng that surges through the entrances of the Chicago Stock Yards. Ruddy-faced Germans jostle globe-trotting Englishmen, and the Japanese tourist, invariably armed with a camera, is a familiar figure. Every state in the Union, as well as almost every country on the globe, contributes its quota to the tide of humanity that ebbs and flows here with unfailing regularity, for the world-famed live-stock market enjoys unique distinction.

JOHN O'BRIEN, *Through the Chicago Stock Yards: A Handy Guide to the Great Packing Industry* (1907)

*

High above Packingtown, on the very roofs of the slaughterhouses, visitors gathered to witness the modern in all of its terrible efficiency. Thousands of hogs waited in pens. Livestock handlers drove roughly a dozen hogs at a time onto the kill floor as fascinated spectators watched the beginning of a process that helped redefine American industry and changed interactions between animals and human beings, as well as workers and management. Swift's massive plant killed thousands of hogs a day. Here animals met their fate at the hands of workers and machinery, creating a vast "disassembly" line that ended not just the lives of pigs but the age-old relationship between meat and mankind.

The "river of blood" that flowed just below the roof pen area attracted Chicagoans and tourist alike for most of the stockyard's existence. At the turn of the twentieth century, a reported five hundred thousand people visited the Union Stock Yard annually. To modern

Hogs waiting to be driven to kill floor at Swift and Company. Notice the pens of the Union Stock Yard in background. (Taken from F. W. Wilder, *The Modern Packing-house* [Chicago, 1905].)

sensibilities to take a tour of the stockyard and the packing plants—even to bring small children to the hog kill—might seem repulsive, but through most of its history the Union Stock Yard and the adjacent plants were major tourist attractions. Fascination with the new drew these visitors. Here people faced the modern head on with all its innovation and spectacle. For many people, Chicago's vast livestock market and packinghouses presented a compelling if somewhat frightening window to the future.

In this book, I explain how the Chicago Stockyards helped drag the world into what I deem "the modern": the industrial culture that appeared in the years after the Civil War, which eventually gave way to the postindustrial era we inhabit today. "The modern" is the frightening sense that something basic had shifted between man and nature. The modern was terrifying in that human beings seemed to be increasingly alienated from the age-old ways of creating goods. This was nowhere more explicit than in the changing relationship between man and food as seen in what Thomas Wilson, the president of Wilson and Company, almost lovingly referred to as the "Square Mile." All of the basic themes of modern industrialization soon played out in the Square Mile; the large corporation, the factory system with its merging of human labor and machinery, the mass marketing of goods, and a transportation system that collected natural resources from a vast hinterland and distributed goods internationally.

Machinery and the emerging factory system changed the essential relationship between people and food. People have killed animals for meat since the dawn of time. For centuries, the process was an everyday event on farms, in homes, and in butcher shops all over the world. But only in the nineteenth century did meatpacking emerge as a mass production industry. While this industry made meat more widely available and cheaper to purchase, its machinery, an enormous number of anonymous workers, and a massive marketing system came to stand between consumers and their food. The modern arrived in packing plants across the country, but especially in Chicago. Instead of taking eight to ten hours to butcher a steer, Chicago's packinghouses took about thirty-five minutes; hogs and sheep took even less time. Armies of skilled and unskilled workers, men and women, operated machines and disassembled animals as they passed by on endless chains into huge refrigerated rooms. Here carcasses waited to be shipped across hundreds and even thousands of miles. The modern sped up time. Everything seemed to move more quickly, more efficiently, even if not more naturally. This proved to be part of the spectacle, the fascination with the process as it played out in the packinghouses. The speed and efficiency of these plants provided a startling look into the future for the men, women, and children who came to see the marvel of industrialization in perhaps its rawest form.

The Square Mile, first officially mapped as Section 5 of the Town of Lake, became Chicago's entry point into both the new industrial economy and the modern world as it spurred the incredible growth of Chicago and the Midwest. It was here that the connection between meat and man was altered forever. If, as historian Perry Duis has pointed out, for many people Chicago represented a window to the future, then that future could be seen most explicitly on the kill floors of Packingtown, the western section of the Square Mile, which contained many of Chicago's major packinghouses. Over the years, this would be a contested image. Some Chicagoans looked askance at the kill floors as a symbol of their city, but in the beginning the city's boosters bragged of their speed and efficiency. Visitors agreed as they came to witness the spectacle provided by the packinghouses. The Union Stock Yard showed how ingenuity, greed, science, and industrialization created the modern world.

By the time the Union Stock Yard opened, machinery had been changing the nature of work, but mass industrialization in the form that would make over the Western world had only begun to emerge. The steam engine first altered humankind's sense of time and distance with its application to shipping and railroads. Before long, the manufacturing of cloth and clothing, shoes, and other goods still dominated by skilled artisans and their helpers felt the shift of new technological advances. Soon large factories emerged creating massive cities as rural people migrated to the emerging urban centers to seek work. The relationship between human beings and machinery quickly changed, as did that between entrepreneur and worker. The factory system emerged as workers' jobs were divided into smaller and more specific tasks. Large groups of individuals had always worked together, but now with machinery they could produce more goods and do so more quickly. Technology made everything different. Mass production and the factory system became the fascination of the age and the topic of both scientific and popular inquiry.

During the almost 106 years of its existence, the Chicago Stockyards epitomized the nation's livestock industry. Even before the market reached its centennial celebration, over one billion head of livestock had passed through its pens. The massive packinghouses transformed the industry and created modern consumer culture. In those plants, man and animal not only met the modern in the form of the factory system and technological innovation that altered the process of the killing, dressing, and marketing of meat, but also shifted the relationship between worker and owner, manufacturer and consumer.

The livestock market opened on Christmas Day 1865. As a tourist attraction, the stockyard defined Chicago to a fascinated public in the post–Civil War era. The rich and the poor, royalty and rubes traveled to see the maze of pens laid out across the prairie and then to be startled by the efficiency of the "disassembly" line of the packinghouses as they turned live breathing animals into hunks of pork, mutton, and beef in mere minutes.

Beyond the fascination with the killing floors, other marvels attracted visitors to the stockyards. The simple gathering of tens of thousands of animals to be placed on the market first insured a captivated public. Then the phenomenon of horse racing, professional baseball, the immensely popular International Livestock Exposition, and the myriad entertainment, political, consumer, and sporting events housed in the International Amphitheater all brought sightseers to the Square Mile. These marvels did not distract from the kill floors, but rather added to the attraction of the Square Mile. The yards presented "spectacle" to a city and a kind of industrial pageantry to the nation.

Visiting the Union Stock Yard

Visitors to the Union Stock Yard entered through the Stone Gate on Exchange Avenue, the main thoroughfare of the stockyard. As they proceeded west toward the Exchange Building, they passed the guardhouse and the cattle market. A guide might explain to the visitor that from midnight until eight in the morning trains unloaded livestock at the company's platforms. The animals had to be identified by owner, then yarded, fed, and watered. They would be sold, weighed, and delivered quickly in the best condition and without mistake to the buyer. As Arthur G. Leonard said in 1904:

> We do not buy and sell, we merely perform a service. For this reason our work can be systemized from top to bottom. And it has been systemized so that the executive work of a corporation handling three hundred million dollars' worth of goods in a year is concentrated in the hands of half a dozen men.[1]

The stockyard contained the makings of a city with its own water and light plants, a fire department, and a one-hundred-man police force. It had its own beltline railroad, the Chicago Junction Railway. In 1908, a branch of the South Side Elevated entered the Union Stock Yard circling the market and Packingtown creating a stockyard "Loop." On the first day, twenty-five thousand riders took the train to visit the stockyards or to work in the market and plants. In addition, the Union Stock Yard contained privately operated businesses including fruit stands; newspapers, such as the *Drovers Journal*; and stores. The Union Stock Yard and Transit Company (USY&T Company) was the landlord, leasing stables to horse commission merchants, and to various parties for mercantile, newspaper, and railroad purposes. It also owned the Exchange Building and rented out its offices. The company maintained the Transit House hotel and restaurant on Halsted Street, as well as various lunchrooms and a general store in the stockyard.[2]

Guides would explain that as trains approached the Union Stock Yard they rolled up to twelve platforms behind which were long rows of chutes and holding pens. The 450 acres of the Union Stock Yards were divided into three divisions with one devoted to cattle, another to sheep, and finally a huge two-story hog division. The pen area in all three sections was laid out on a grid with alleys or streets running between them marked so that each block and pen had a number, the equivalent of a city address. In that way the USY&T Company workers as well as commission men and buyers could easily navigate the vast complex of pens. The instant the train stopped with its load of cattle, hogs, and sheep, a conductor ran from it into one of two stations to give the bill of lading to a clerk. Operatives of the USY&T Company then unloaded the railcars, moving the animals into chutes where a checker noted which carload went into which holding pen. From there, the livestock handlers drove the animals to the pens of the commission companies. Here they were watered and fed. The receiving station kept a record of each lot received, of the consignee, the consignor, the number of animals, the car number, and railroad, the chute, and pen into which it was delivered. They created a complete paper trail for the thousands of animals delivered each day.

The separation between the packers and the yards was not clear to the public, but the distinction mattered. The USY&T Company operated and maintained the actual stockyard, which included the railroad docks, pens, chutes, and other facilities. The Chicago Livestock Exchange (commission salesmen) operated and regulated the market. The packers bought animals, slaughtered them, and then manufactured and sold a vast array of products. Once the market opened each day between 250 and 400 buyers bid on the animals. They represented both on-site packers and those located in different cities, as well as shippers who wished to ship livestock to other markets or abroad,

Unloading hogs at the rail docks of the Union Stock Yard, circa 1900. (Postcard, Author's Collection.)

speculators who held livestock for another market day when the price might go up, or feeders who wanted to buy calves to fatten for market.

Salesmen kept close to the pens assigned to their particular commission firm as buyers went from pen to pen to make purchases. Unless otherwise specified, livestock always sold on the basis of dollars and cents per hundred pounds live weight, except for milk cows, horses, mules, and purebred feeders, which sold per head. A buyer rode up on a horse to a pen and asked the commission man if he had any cattle of a certain grade. If so, he entered the pen to look the livestock over and ask the price and, if he agreed, would simply say, "weigh them." If not, he would make a lower bid. The salesman could let the stock go to the first bidder, or he might hold them hoping to get a better price later on. The next customer might want cattle at a different weight and grade, and he would purchase anything of that sort that the commission man had or they might not come to an agreement. The third man who came down the alley could have such broad orders from his packinghouse that he might bid on everything on hand. The process of showing the stock and arguing about the price continued until the seller disposed of his holdings at what he hoped was the best possible price. While there was no public bidding, it resembled an auction, as the agent kept showing the stock until he received a satisfactory price.

Nothing occurred to bind the bargain. In what may have been seen

Longhorn cattle in the sales pens, circa 1890. Notice the elevated ramp or viaduct in the background over which livestock were driven to the packinghouses. (Stereopticon, Author's Collection.)

as a rather premodern transaction, all buying and selling was by word of mouth and on the honor system; often buyers and sellers made their agreement by a nod of the head or the downward movement of a cane or whip. Such deals might involve whole trainloads of livestock costing many thousands of dollars, but rarely did either buyer or seller renege on a deal once made. Despite appearances, disputes concerning these dealings were dealt with in a modern way. If an infrequent dispute or misunderstanding occurred, it went before the Chicago Livestock Exchange for arbitration. Strict regulations guided the process from beginning to end in order to assure a fair sale. When dealing with tens of thousands of animals, these rules had to be in place in order to allow the maintenance of an effective exchange of goods and money. This was no small county bazaar where buyer and seller knew each other intimately, but rather a modern capitalist marketplace that brought producers from across the country together with buyers from large and efficient corporations. The fastidious record keeping spoke to the immensity of the yards and the complexity of the process. While the purchase agent was in the pen, the salesman could not raise the price he originally asked or refuse to sell at that price. As soon as a he left the pen, the offer was no longer valid. Later on, should the same buyer return, the seller no longer had an obligation to accept the original offer. The opposite also proved true, should the market for that particular grade of cattle slip. As a matter of courtesy—and professional gamesmanship—buyers refrained from entering a pen while another negotiated with a commission man.[3]

The commission men drove the newly sold cattle, hogs, and sheep to the scale houses where the USY&T Company weighed the animals and delivered them to the buyers. All of these transactions were made on a cash basis; a detailed report was sent to each producer-shipper listing the price his stock sold for, detailing all charges, along with the remittance. By three o'clock in the afternoon the market closed for the day, and the process began again the next morning.[4]

Touring the Packinghouses

After being weighed, those livestock sold to Chicago firms (like the human visitors to the stockyards) advanced to the packinghouses, driven over the huge elevated viaducts that led westward to the slaughterhouses from the pens. The French journalist Jules Huret wrote that the site of the herds of cattle, hogs, and sheep being driven to their destinies communicated "to the onlooker the melancholy like that caused by the departure of armies."[5] The 1903 *Swift & Company Visitors Reference Book* informed guests that the plant covered forty-nine acres with a floor space of over ninety-two acres and employed seven thousand men and women. The complex had a daily capacity of 2,500 cattle, 8,000 hogs, and 6,000 sheep.[6]

The tour of the Swift plant began at the "Visitor's Entrance," which included showcases of the company's finished products such as sausages, hams, and soap. Elevators then took the guests up to the roof of the pork house. Workers herded hogs, after being driven in some cases more than a mile, into holding pens on the roofs of the plants, where they rested overnight. Later this changed as it was felt that a much briefer cooling-off period was sufficient. Most packers felt that overheated hogs, or hogs overexcited after having been driven some distance, had to be allowed to "cool off" or to become perfectly quiet to prevent the meat from becoming "feverish." Swift and Company had a yard capacity of 5,000 hogs.

After the animals' night of rest, laborers washed them down and drove a dozen or so at a time into a pen where a worker, often a young boy, shackled their rear leg to the Hurford Wheel—a hoisting machine that raised the hog steadily until the shackle hook dropped unto a sliding rail. The animal would give out a loud shriek as the device suddenly pulled it into the air, on its way to the sticker, or dispatcher, who slit its throat. A cascade of blood gushed from the open wound. The sticker, covered in blood and standing in a pool of the hog's gore, stopped for a few seconds to let the blood drain. Every ten seconds another hog appeared before the skilled slayer. To many visitors, the sticker seemed a most repellant sight. He represented the most gruesome spectacle, one that remained with the tourist long after he or she left the stockyards. However impressed a visitor might have been by this moment, it was just part of a long day's work for the pig-sticker. The sticker, who was working rather than sightseeing, then pushed the hog carcass along the rail to the boiling vats.[7]

Men stood alongside the vat with poles to keep the hog rolling in the water until it reached the end of the vat, where an apparatus captured the carcass and dropped it on a table so that other laborers could take the hair from its ears, which was used for artists' paintbrushes and other such products. A machine then lifted the hog onto a scraper machine that removed most of its bristles, but even this process was part of the modern. The mechanical hog scraper first appeared in the 1870s. Before then, workers found the job grueling and very unpleasant as six men had to hand scrape the steaming carcasses. In 1876, William W. Kincaid of Fowler Brothers designed the first workable scraping machine. Later, in 1880, Armour and Company's Michael Cudahy and John Bouchard designed a superior scraper that adjusted itself to the size of the individual carcasses. The Cudahy-Bouchard scraper took off most of the hair, leaving the rest for workers to hand scrape. The skin was then shaved carefully, to remove remaining hair without scoring the hog. Guidebooks pointed out the fact that each of the workmen had a special duty as the hog carcass passed the army of men working in the killing department.[8]

Hurford Wheel at Armour and Company. Part of the spectacle of the packing-houses, a worker shackled the leg of a hog, which is then lifted into the air to begin the slaughtering process. (Postcard, Author's Collection.)

The hog then moved to the hog-dressing department, where men opened the bodies and removed all internal organs. Some men detached the fat for the production of lard. Two men wielding cleavers cut each hog carcass into two halves, which then passed to the hog-drying room. It took the hog twenty minutes to move from the shackler to the hog-drying room. In about two hours, the carcass dried enough to be placed in coolers.

Boiling vats used to prepare the hog for hair removal, circa 1890. (Stereopticon, Author's Collection.)

Visitors then moved to the first pork cutting station, where they observed hogs that had been in coolers kept at 32 degrees Fahrenheit for forty-eight hours. They saw the carcass subdivided into the various cuts—hams, shoulders, and sides—as demanded by the various markets across the country and overseas. Each pork cutter had his particular cut to make with a heavy cleaver. The men worked so quickly and accurately that the pork seemed to melt and vanish as it moved from block to block. As the guests progressed to the next pork cutting room, the cuts from the room above moved down chutes to be further trimmed, the pork loins removed, and those pieces to be cured and smoked prepared for those departments.

Touring groups then moved on to the smoked meat department, where they saw hams and bacon inspected, branded, and packed for shipping. The building consisted of five floors and held thousands upon thousands of hams and sausages hanging in a dense and almost

The hog scraping machine removed hog bristles. It is seen here in 1891. (*Scientific American*, June 19, 1891, Author's Collection.)

blinding smoke. They had been cured in a pickle of sugar, salt, and water for thirty to ninety days. Cured meat went into the washing room where it soaked in water three minutes for every day it had lain in pickling brine. Afterward, workers thoroughly smoked the meat in rooms heated to about 140 degrees Fahrenheit. Hams prepared for the American market stayed in the smoke rooms for thirty-six hours; those for export to Europe, two days longer.

At this point, tour guides took their charges outside and passed alongside the East Beef House. At the street crossing, the guides pointed out Swift's General Offices and described the five-story building that included executive offices, a telegraph department, file rooms, the general sales departments, and the accounting department as well as a 350-seat restaurant for office employees, reading and smoking rooms, and a barbershop. The one thousand office employees breathed air that passed through a curtain of running water warmed in the winter and cooled during the summer to maintain an even temperature. This was the first example of an early form of air conditioning for an industrial office in Chicago. Huret commented on the work ethic of the office employees: "The women were writing or working typewriting machines or attending the telephone. Some of them wrote rapidly. No one was unoccupied, not an idler in the room, not an eye raised to look at the visitors. I have never seen such an office in Europe."[9] Afterward, the tour group approached a busy loading platform. Here workers

At the right, busy men are loading refrigerator cars with meat products of all descriptions for shipment to every part of the known world. Refrigerator car service guarantees the delivery of these products in the same excellent condition in which they leave the plant at Chicago.

Illustration from the pamphlet handed out as a guide to visitors to the Swift plant in 1910 portraying the loading platform. (Swift and Company, *Visitors Reference Book*, Author's Collection.)

stocked a long line of wagons with the daily supply of dressed meat for retailers. Great piles of boxes, cases, and barrels containing products for shipment stood on the north end of the platform. Dressed beef in quarters wrapped in burlap for shipment swung on an overhead rail from the cooler to its destination in a wagon or a refrigerated boxcar. Men hurried along the platform to load the railcars and wagons with hand trucks filled with various Swift products.

Attendants then brought the tour groups to the sheep and calf cooler, which could hold 3,000 sheep and 1,500 calves. From there, they moved to the beef cooler, where dressed beef stayed for forty-eight hours in a temperature of 38 degrees Fahrenheit, chilled but not frozen. The room had a capacity 1,500 cattle or 3,000 sides of beef. Visitors soon proceeded to the wholesale market from which Chicago wholesalers and retailers bought their supplies of meats. From that market, visitors took another elevator to the floor on which the sheep and beef dressing took place. They passed by the enormous summer sausage drying rooms with a capacity of seven hundred thousand pounds of sausage, hung on racks. Workers made summer sausage out of cuts of beef and pork. The meat passed through a chopper, which cut it up into fine pieces, before it was seasoned. Employees put the meat in casings and hung the sausages in the smoke room for about twelve hours. Afterward, they took the sausage to the drying rooms where it hung to air-dry and remained from 60 to 125 days.[10]

Visitors stood on a balcony overlooking the sheep dressing department in order to witness the entire process from the beginning to the final inspection and weighing of the dressed meat. Workers slaughtered sheep in the same basic manner as hogs except that the wheels lifted two sheep up at a time. The animals met their destinies here at a rate of 600 per hour, as they passed by workmen. The sheep dressing took approximately twenty-six minutes from the sticker who killed the animals to the cooler.[11]

Guides next ushered the visitors to the beef dressing department. Livestock handlers drove cattle from the resting pens to the upper floor of the packinghouse. From the runways, cattle entered small pens where the knocker or stunner, a skilled employee wielding a four-pound sledgehammer, struck a blow to the middle of the forehead of animals. Machinery then raised the side gate, the floor tilted, and the cattle fell onto the dressing floor where men shackled one hind leg and a double-hoist lifted the animal into the air and sent it to the sticker who quickly dispatched it by cutting its throat. They then raised the carcass, bled it, and removed the head. Afterward, workers placed the beeves on the floor and removed the feet and stripped the hide. They then put the carcass on a spreader—technically known as a beef tree—where workers disemboweled it, finished removing the hide, and split the back. Then an endless chain took the sides and conveyed them through a set of washers.[12] The beef passed washers, trimmers, and weighers, and thirty-five minutes after entering the stunning pens, they arrived in the drying room. Machinery made the process move quickly, as did the veritable army of men who made up the kill floor line. Workers used fountain brushes to wash down the beef as trimmers used wooden skewers to lift the parts they cut off. They then dropped the various parts trimmed off down shoots to other departments for processing. Sides of beef stayed in the coolers for up to two weeks.

After visiting the beef kill, visitors entered the lard department, where workers cooked, filtered, clarified, and cooled lard that finally ran into pails, buckets, and barrels. Fresh lard made up from 13 to 15 percent of a hog's weight and provided a very important factor in the profit of any packinghouse. The refining of lard in large packinghouses dated from just before the turn of the twentieth century; before then, independent firms operated lard refineries.[13]

Guides continued to escort guests to Swift's soap factory. Thousands of boxes of Swift and Company's soap brands left this department everyday. Attendants explained that the company stored one hundred thousand boxes or 5 million pounds of soap in this department. Automatic machinery packed Swift's Pride Washing Powder on the floor above, the weight of the package to be filled determining the action of the machines that cut off the amount of powder at the moment the correct weight was reached. Further down the line, Swift's Pride Soap entered the department on wheeled trucks in blocks weighing 1,200 pounds. In making soap, employees placed tallow, a rendered form of beef or mutton fat, in large kettles and cooked it for about a week. They mixed a certain amount of caustic resin and lye with the tallow. From the cooking kettles, the mass passed through a mixing machine that gave it a consistent color and then flowed into iron molds to dry and harden for four days. Machines that cut more than ten thousand bars in an hour, then cut the slabs and distributed them on racks. The bars went from the cutting machines onto open racks to allow air to circulate around them. Workers then piled the bars into wheeled trucks to remain in the drying ovens until the soap dried enough to hold its shape when pressed. Finally, machines stamped the bars into final shapes, and workers packed them into boxes.

After passing through the soap department, guides escorted the visitors to the Libby, McNeil and Libby plant, a Swift subsidiary, to see the manufacturing and processing of canned meats. Meats for canning purposes came from lean cattle not suitable for dressed beef. The parts that could not be sold for a profit made up the bulk of canned corned beef. In the boning room, workers removed bones from the forequarters and cut the meat up into small pieces and placed it in sweet pickle for about thirty days. Next came a cold-water washing and thirty minutes of cooking in the boiling vats; then the meat was stuffed by machinery into cans. Women painted and labeled the cans and packed them into shipping containers.[14]

Changes over time in different industry publications illustrate the evolution of the process, as well as company attempts to control depictions of the meatpacking plants. Swift and Company issued various guides over the years including *A Glance at the Meat Packing Industry in America*, probably published in the 1920s. This pamphlet stressed scientific management and emphasized the fact that modern mechanical equipment and human expertise combined to create Swift products. While the 1903 *Visitors Reference Book* began in the Swift plant, the 1920s guide started in the Union Stock Yard itself, explaining the role of commission men, buyers, and government inspectors. Photographs of the plant showed modern techniques in hog dressing. These pictures portrayed a much more sanitized and modern plant than those of the earlier time period. Obviously, Swift and Company hoped to counter previous bad publicity, especially in the aftermath of the publication of Upton Sinclair's novel *The Jungle* and subsequent journalistic and government investigations. Once again, the writer of the official guidebook emphasized machinery, especially in the packaging of Swift's Pure Leaf Lard. The leaflet reads, "The machines that fill the containers seem almost human. Cartons and pails receive just the right amount, and in the case of cartons, mechanical fingers tuck in the edges and close the tops." One large difference from the 1903 tour guidebook is the appearance of the chemical laboratory where Swift employed one hundred chemists and assistants. They scrutinized products to ensure quality control, and finally they looked at finished products to guarantee high standards of quality and uniformity.[15]

In 1933, Swift and Company handed out a *Visitors' Bulletin* at the beginning of a tour of the plant that commenced in the reception room with a good view of the stockyards. From the observation roof on top of the building, tourists could see the Swift General Office. Guides took visitors to see the usual sites, beginning again with the hog kill. Now, however, perhaps reacting to changes in the sensibilities of visitors, attendants warned about the bloody process, and those who did not wish to see the hog slaughter could avoid the kill floor. The 1933 tour also included a visit to the experimental laundry unit, home economics kitchen, sausage products kitchen, and experimental bakery. In these places, guides explained that the Swift research laboratories conducted scientific studies to insure the highest possible degree of quality. The visit to these sites contrasted with tours in the early part of the century, and promised that Swift was a modern and up-to-date food company providing only the highest quality products to the public. At about the same time, Armour and Company also published a pamphlet to be handed out to visitors explaining its plant. While it did not take visitors step by step through the plant, it did stress many of the same points as the Swift pamphlet. These guidebooks emphasized meat inspection and the cleanliness of the plants. Much of this was in response to earlier stories in the press of unsanitary conditions and of government scrutiny. In all such tours, managing the image of the industry was paramount. The image the companies hoped to portray was one of modern, efficient, and sanitary conditions providing healthy meat products and useful by-products to the public.[16]

Visitors from Far and Wide

The first guidebook to the new Union Stock Yard appeared even before the livestock market opened. Jack Wing, an itinerant journalist, wrote a pamphlet describing the Union Stock Yard in December 1865, prior to the actual Christmas Day kickoff. For months, Chicago's newspapers had covered the building of the stockyard, and Wing found himself a frequent visitor to the site, in the then-suburban Town of Lake. He first went down on Friday September 1, 1865, as part of a Board of Trade excursion to see the construction firsthand. Two weeks later, he returned with a group of Englishmen, including Sir Morton Petoe, the English entrepreneur, civil engineer, railroad developer, and member of Parliament. Wing wrote an article for the *Chicago Times* based on this visit. In November 1865, James H. Goodsell, the newspaper's city editor, assigned Wing the task of writing a complete account of the Union Stock Yard. Wing's relationship with Goodsell was strained, and he feared that he would be fired as soon as he handed in the article, so on November 24, he conceived of the idea of a tract that he could write to make extra money if he lost his job. The next day, he returned to the Union Stock Yard and pitched such a brochure, but to no avail. The reporter persisted, and on November 28, William Tucker, one of the owners of the Briggs House, a hotel on the corner of Wells and Randolph Streets, agreed to buy five hundred copies of the proposed booklet. Several railroad men also agreed to purchase one hundred copies each. Wing felt that if he could obtain some advertisements, he would be able to self-publish the piece.

The next Friday, December 1, Wing went out to the Union Stock Yard to get information on the several old stockyards that were soon to disappear. Four cattle dealers agreed to place advertisements at twenty-five dollars a piece in the proposed publication. At that point, the editor of the *Chicago Republican* offered Wing a job. That Saturday, he signed up two more cattlemen in the stockyards to advertise in his pamphlet. He then went back to the *Times* offices, took his stockyard article, and quit the newspaper.

His printer delivered *The Great Union Stock Yards of Chicago: Their Railroad Connections, Bank, and Exchange, The Hough House, Water Supply and General Features also, A Sketch of the Live Stock Trade and the Old Yards* on December 12, and Wing went about happily gathering the money promised to him by advertisers and those interested in copies. The booklet sold well, and soon another edition was needed. Colonel Rossel M. Hough, the superintendent of construction of the Union Stock Yard, said that he would take two hundred copies. Other orders poured in, and Wing put out a second edition with even more advertisements than the first edition.[17]

In the tradition of Chicago boosterism, Wing's guide lauded the great engineering feats, such as pipes to drain the swampy area, the accommodations for railroads, noting that five hundred railroad cars could be unloaded at any one time. Wing also proclaimed the market's Hough House the finest hotel in the West. The author suggested that the view from the south veranda of the guesthouse was unequaled and worthy of a landscape artist. Wing's hyperbole would not be the last time exaggeration would be used to describe both the Union Stock Yard and Packingtown.[18]

News of the Union Stock Yard spread quickly, and it became a sight to see in Chicago. In the summer of 1866, delegates from the Cincinnati City Council—the city that had only recently lost the title of "Porkopolis" to Chicago—arrived. They traveled by train to the Town of Lake where P. R. Chandler, the president of the Union Stock Yard and Transit Company, welcomed them. The Cincinnatians visited the new tunnel crib and waterworks, various breweries, and grain elevators, and called Chicago a "wonder of the world." Chandler explained the market's facilities as the visitors toured the stockyard and dined at the hotel.

The next year the Civil War hero Major General Philip H. Sheridan visited. Several notables escorted Sheridan from the Tremont House in downtown Chicago to the stockyard by carriage, where they inspected livestock along with the alleys and streets of the complex. Sheridan and his company then met with drovers and commission men in the Exchange Building. Afterward, the entourage proceeded to the Hough House for lunch before visiting Cullerton's packinghouse on Eighteenth Street to see the butchering of hogs. Sheridan saw the modern industry being born as six hogs were butchered per minute at the plant.[19]

Packers were not the only promoters of such tourism. In 1869, the *Chicago Tribune* suggested various sightseeing drives around the city and suburbs and included the Union Stock Yard. The newspaper recommended a carriage ride down Michigan or Wentworth Avenues to Forty-Seventh Street and then over to the Dexter Park racetrack adjacent to the stockyard. The "fashionable" time for driving the route was early on a Sunday morning, in order to see the horses at Dexter Park. While the new racetrack attracted the "better" classes with a day of "sport," or rather gambling, for many tourists the lure remained the adjacent livestock market.[20]

In 1871, Grand Duke Alexei Alexandrovich, the fourth son of Czar Alexander II of Russia, toured the United States. Mayor Joseph Medill, who presided over the city as it recovered from the Great Fire of 1871, called for a committee composed of Chicago's business leaders to manage the details of the Russian visit. Chandler announced that the Union Stock Yard and Transit Company would provide lunch for the visitors at the renamed Hough House, now the Transit House. The grand duke spent New Year's Day 1872 visiting the sights of Chicago, then the livestock market and a large packinghouse. His party arrived by carriage to the horse stables adjacent to Dexter Park. Here the general manager, John B. Sherman, met them and showed off his menagerie including finely bred livestock, Mexican hogs, and other "curiosities of the animal kingdom." After visiting the stockyard, the Russians explored the Hutchinson Packinghouse. The new plant, located to the west of the stockyard, had the largest capacity in Chicago, and the packing process fascinated the Russian royalty. The grand duke's entourage then visited Dexter Park and went on to the Transit House where Sherman greeted them for lunch, with abundant toasts. Mayor Medill saluted his visitors and said, "May the rivalry between Russia and America be in the future what it has long been in the past, a rivalry to feed a hungry world." After the festivities, the party again visited Dexter Park to take part in a pigeon shoot, another stockyard tradition.[21]

American politicians soon saw a visit to the Union Stock Yard as a necessary campaign stop. Here they met average working people and paid homage to the modern as it transformed American society. It gave politicians a gritty populist appeal while endorsing modern industrialism and the new American economy. They witnessed the latest innovations in industrial production along with the vast market that brought the produce of the nation's prairies and farms to the table of the public. Industrial capitalism along with crowds of possible voters provided an irresistible campaign stop for any politician. On October 23, 1894, Thomas R. Reed of Maine, a powerful Republican who served several terms as Speaker of the House and had presidential ambitions, arrived in Chicago and spoke at a noontime rally in the stockyards. Some five thousand people greeted Reed in the Exchange Building courtyard. Stenographers, clerks, and typists hung out of windows to watch the political spectacle. Men stood on the pen fences and waved as the party rode down Exchange Avenue. Gus Swift met Reed and took his party into his plant for a tour.[22]

While Russian royalty and American politicians might get an extensive visit and lunch, others visited the stockyard in a less formal way. In 1889, an estimated fifty thousand "transient" visitors—what we would call tourists—came to Chicago annually. The Union Stock Yards attracted many of these. Packinghouse owners invited many to inspect their plants as they fought to have their chilled beef accepted in markets across the country. Members of the Pan American Congress visited the Swift, Libby, and Armour packinghouses in 1889. In 1890, a group of businessmen, disappointed because they could not visit the yards due to inclement weather, were shown instead a papier-mâché model in the dining room of the Richelieu Hotel downtown. Large groups such as the Knights of Pythias often arranged to tour the stockyards and Packingtown.[23]

Moreover, since the Union Stock Yard was open to the public, Chicagoans and others visited the complex daily. Many sought out the advice of "Old Man" Hildreth, the caretaker of the Chicago City Railway station in the stockyards. Over the years, he directed visitors in their search for one attraction or another. Boys often led curiosity seekers on excursions. The individuals involved determined the cost, but young guides usually charged twenty-five cents for a tour of the Union Stock Yard—fifty cents for both the stockyards and packinghouses. The packinghouse owners soon opened their plants for inspection by the public, and the larger packers organized formal tours led by trained and uniformed guides, putting the young streetwise entrepreneurs out of business. Eventually, visitors would be met in elegantly appointed lounges. The large packinghouses invested in catwalks and balconies from which guests could witness their industrial operations, explicated by signs.[24]

By the early 1900s, regular tours of the stockyards and packinghouses were commonplace. In 1903, to celebrate the one hundredth anniversary of the building of Fort Dearborn, an event that signaled the American arrival in the area, Chicagoans held citywide celebrations. By that time, Swift and Company passed out its own "Visitors Reference Book" to guests, which described nineteen stations with illustrations that visitors would stop on during their tour of the massive plant. Several years later, Swift and Company handed out a well-illustrated guide, *A Visit to Swift & Company, Union Stock Yards, Chicago* as a souvenir that could be mailed off to friends describing the "Clean—wholesome—efficient" characteristics of the company's Chicago plant. The pamphlet also depicted the "system" that made the company and the industry so efficient. In addition, these souvenirs gave proof to the folks back home that one had actually made the trip and witnessed the spectacle of the modern.[25]

In August 1910, the packers prepared to receive the most visitors they had hosted since the 1893 Columbian Exposition. Ten thousand Knights Templars, in Chicago for their annual meeting, visited on August 10. Women made up more than half of the sightseers, and guides took them through the plants in groups of one hundred. Every packinghouse opened its doors, and excursions began every ten minutes. A mounted detail of stockyard employees spread out over Packingtown and provided information to the throngs.

For visitors, the spectacle contained in the Square Mile began even before reaching the main gate as the stench of the stockyards immediately affected those not accustomed to them. Chicagoans complained of "curdled" air. One description had trolley riders entering the "odor zone" and young women covering their faces with handkerchiefs as even hardened laborers attempted to protect themselves from the stench. The writer complained, "The combined smells seemed to focus in a crescendo of coagulated putridity." Grand Duke Boris, the cousin of the Russian czar, exclaimed in 1902, "I never smelled such an awful smell, but the stockyards are greater than my imagination conceived."[26] That was the smell of the modern, a modern that was paid for by Chicagoans, as they had to put up with the odor and the obvious ecological impact of this great industry.

Russian grand dukes, French journalists, Japanese businessmen and their wives, British trade unionists, Irish nationalists, Texas cattlemen, and everyday Americans all visited the Union Stock Yard and packing plants. Rudyard Kipling's account of his visit to the Square Mile remains among the most graphic. Touring the complex in 1889, he described the hog kill and its victims, "They were so excessively alive, these pigs. And then they were so excessively dead, and the man in the dripping, clammy, hot passage did not seem to care." The stockyards fascinated Sarah Bernhardt, the famous actress, who described it in vivid terms in her memoirs. She wrote of "an abominable smell" and of the "almost human cries of the pigs" being slaughtered. The German sociologist, Max Weber, visited in 1904 and also described the plants in vivid terms:

> From the moment when the unsuspecting bovine enters the slaughtering area, is hit by a hammer and collapses, whereupon it is immediately gripped by an iron clamp, is hoisted in the air, and starts on its journey, it is in constant motion — past ever-new workers who eviscerate and skin it, etc., but are always (in the rhythm of work) tied to the machine that pulls the animal past them.

For Kipling and the others, this terrifying spectacle portrayed a modern world that shattered traditional relationships and pointed to a frightening future. It stank of barbarity despite the fact that it harnessed man and machine in a new industrial economy. Chicagoans often did not feel this way. They were proud of the stockyards and Packingtown. In 1908, Mayor Busse proclaimed the Union Stock Yard as one of the "Seven Wonders of Chicago" that should be visited by any tourist and certainly by all Chicagoans. The Chicago Association of Commerce, on the other hand, in contesting the views of the mayor and much of the public tried to rid the city of its cattle town image, and attempted to direct visitors away from the stockyards, but still the square mile of packinghouses, pens, and chutes attracted tourists and Chicagoans alike. The stockyards were Chicago.[27]

Stereopticons, Postcards, Trading Cards, and the Art of Advertising

Those who could not visit the Chicago Union Stock Yard or Packingtown in person could purchase the various illustrated guides or use a stereopticon or stereoscope to explore the area. These were a popular form of entertainment, allowing people to see the world from their living rooms. Photographers took a picture with a special camera that had two lenses and printed the photographs side by side. When viewed through a special device, the pictures blended into a three-dimensional image. By the end of the nineteenth century, many middle- and upper-class people owned these devices. They were praised for their accurate depictions of the world, bringing to the average person sights often unobtainable without a good deal of expense and travel.[28]

Stereopticon photographs of the Chicago Stockyards and Packing-town covered just about every phase of the process, and they provide a fascinating historical record of methods and conditions in the Chicago packinghouses. At times, the stereopticon cards contained a written explanation of the scene depicted on the back. Others simply left the explanation to the photograph. In either case, images of the pens, chutes, and packing plants found a ready audience in the stereopticon trade. These images were not only sold in the United States; Europeans and others could view the sights of Chicago's meat industry no matter how far they lived from South Halsted Street.[29]

Postcards too brought the scenes of the Chicago Stockyards to individuals around the world. Their images, like the stereopticons, depicted not only the market, but also the packinghouses. Views of cattle in the pens seemed to be among the most popular, but others showed the Transit House hotel, the horse market, and the various draft horse teams owned by the packers and the USY&T Company, as well as the Exchange Building and the various packinghouse general offices. Still others featured the packing process, including the Hurford Wheel, the sheep kill, the cattle knocking pens, coolers, beef dressing and cutting departments, and aerial views of the packinghouses.[30] Jules Huret explained that the packers realized the value of publicity and never failed to take advantage of it. The stereopticons and color postcards allowed them to amaze a large public with the size and complexity of the industry, and to convince the skeptical potential customer of the cleanliness of their methods.[31]

Some packers even produced the meat industry equivalent of baseball cards. Libby, McNeil and Libby issued colorful trading cards depicting the images of literary characters such as Shakespeare's Falstaff enjoying canned Libby, McNeil and Libby meat. Others extolled their cooked corned beef as valuable for explorers and travelers by portraying a frontiersman walking into the wilderness with his gun, his dog, and a huge can of corned beef under his arm. The back of the card contained statements by various chemists as to the quality, smell, and

Libby, McNeil and Libby trading card, circa 1890. (Author's Collection.)

taste of the canned meat. Yet another card had two children playing with an empty corned beef can using it as a toy boat with the caption "Even the children make a toy of an empty can." During the World's Columbian Exposition in 1893, Swift and Company greeted thousands of tourists to their plants and distributed colorful cards depicting their exhibit at the world's fair. These included an elegant depiction of an exhibit of a Swift Refrigerator Line Express railcar made out of glass so that the product lines could be easily observed. Other Swift products surrounded the picture of the faux railcar exhibit. On the interior of the two-fold card was a list of all of Swift's exhibits at the Columbian Exposition and an aerial view of the Swift plant with all the major buildings marked including viaducts for moving livestock from the pens. The back of the folded card pictured an elegantly dressed young woman sitting on a fence trying to shoo hogs, sheep, and cattle away with her parasol. The cards could easily be used to decorate the visitor's wall back home and to remind them of the "excellence" of Swift products.

Swift and Libby were not the only firms to dabble in the art of advertisement. Armour and Company put out calendars often depicting beautiful young women. These calendars carried the Armour name, and the company also distributed trading cards with these images each embossed with the packer's name. Armour even issued vanity boxes or women's compacts with the Luxor soap name on them and marked

Armour & Company on the bottom. The company issued advertising ink blotters with Armour's Magnolia Oleomargarine depicted on the card. In addition, the company published recipe books in order to promote Armour products.

Not to be outdone, the Union Stock Yard and Transit Company produced its own memorabilia. Images of the Union Stock Yard decorated teacups, glass paperweights, letter openers, and other advertising materials. Coin savings banks made in the form of hogs or the Livestock National Bank appeared throughout the stockyard's history. Comical postcards depicting visitors to the yards looking hungrily at livestock were distributed to remind visitors, and their friends back home, of the importance and purpose of the World's Greatest Livestock Market.

The various commission firms also used such promotional methods to entice producers to ship livestock under their care to the stockyard. Commission men distributed bullet pencils, notebooks, and printed materials imprinted with their company names. The Wood Brothers commission firm circulated an illustrated biennial report of the statistics important to shippers to the Union Stock Yard. These also featured portraits of employees of the firm and photographs of the Union Stock Yard, as well as the other stockyards in which the firm traded.[32]

The *Drovers Journal*, published within the gates of the Union Stock Yard, not only disseminated news of the market and the livestock world, but also put out other publications for producers, commission men, and packers alike. The newspaper supplied a vital means of communication and advertisement for the Union Stock Yard and the meatpackers under various titles from 1873 until the closing of the stockyard in 1971. In turn, the *National Provisioner*, a trade journal of the meatpacking industry, also supplied news of the Union Stock Yard and the packers around the nation.

Beyond newspapers and trade journals, other publications promoted the Union Stock Yard and Packingtown. In 1896, W. Joseph Grand published his *Illustrated History of the Union Stock Yard*. Grand explained that his book included sketches of familiar faces and sights as well as humorous stories, facts, and figures. O. Benson Jr. provided extensive photographs for the heavily illustrated book that told the story of Jack-Knife Ben, Willie the Telegraph Messenger, and other colorful stockyard characters. Grand began a tradition of tall tales of the stockyards, which embedded the myths of the Union Stock Yard in Chicago's history, and the history of the rural hinterland beyond.

Memoirs and "histories," often self-published, appeared, and even as late as 2011 a former member of the management of the Union Stock Yard self-published yet another memoir.[33] The Union Stock Yard and Packingtown produced images and texts for public consumption alongside food, leather, lard, and the other by-products of the industry. These celebrated the spectacle by portraying both the human and familiar side of the industry along with a demonstration of the industrial process.

And to think it all began in a swamp.

2

GENESIS

From Swamp to Industrial Giant

Chicago in giving the world cheaper meat will do more for health, happiness and culture than a whole nation of Mathew Arnolds. Under the stimulating influence of the roast beef of Chicago Ohio will cease its hungry scramble for office, the bloody shirt of the South will show nothing more sanguinary than gravy stains, the gamblers of New York will play for nothing worse than porterhouse steaks, the economical skins of New England will fill out, and every one of its women will be a Venus. Even St. Louis will become enterprising.

"CHICAGO BEEF FOR THE WORLD,"
Chicago Tribune, October 14, 1882

*

On Christmas Day 1865 Chicago's business elite gathered to celebrate the opening of the Union Stock Yard. Its promoters clearly thought there could be no more appropriate way to observe a festive Christian holiday in the midst of America's capitalist hothouse than to open the greatest livestock market the world would ever see. The first animals arrived the next day, but the holiday opening marked the end of what had been a lengthy and somewhat difficult process. Chicago had long hosted various small stockyards, often associated with a particular railroad and serving that line's geographic reach. The term *Union* Stock Yard implied the unification of these various markets as Chicago's capitalists attempted to centralize the livestock business not only for the city, but the nation.

Of course, in 1865 the term "Union" meant more than uniting businesses; it symbolized unity with the North's victory in the Civil War
and the creation of a national market that would be assured in four
years as railroads connected the city to both coasts. It also suggested
the victory of a particular kind of economic system. Modern free market capitalism, dependent on a vast cheap labor supply, emerged as the
dominant system after the Civil War. The Union Stock Yard symbolized
this new corporate America, as it emerged out of the crises of battle.
In January 1865, even before the guns of war had fallen silent, the *Chicago Tribune* stated that "'Union' is not alone a good thing in national
affairs, it is good in civic undertakings, in individual enterprises." The
newspaper claimed that centralization was an essential element of
commercial development and national growth: "it is only where ener-
gies are focalized, that great results ensue from human action." A new
corporate world emerged out of the battle between the North and
South. The Union Stock Yard implied concentration and the efficacy
of a modern marketplace; it promised large-scale efficiency and Chicago's domination of the nation's livestock trade. The experience of
war had taught its lesson.[1]

Beginnings

Chicago's livestock industry had begun nearly forty years earlier when
Gurdon Hubbard drove about three hundred hogs from the Wabash
Valley to Chicago in the winter of 1826–27. Hubbard found ready customers among the army garrison at Fort Dearborn and the small surrounding yet unincorporated settlement. That same year, Archibald
Clybourn established the first slaughterhouse in what would become
Chicago. At about this time, some crude hog pens were built, estab-
lishing what might be considered the settlement's first stockyard near
the main branch of the Chicago River. Farmers often held cattle on the
adjacent prairie, where buyers came to inspect the herds before taking
their purchases by hoof to be slaughtered. In 1832, George W. Dole
slaughtered 152 head of cattle and 332 hogs, packed them in barrels in
his establishment near the corner of Dearborn Street and South Water
Street (Wacker Drive), and shipped the meat to Detroit the following
spring. This was the first time that meat packed in Chicago was sent
east, beginning a trade that eventually made Chicago the center of the
nation's meatpacking industry.

The small riverside settlement officially incorporated as a town in 1833, and Sylvester Marsh slaughtered cattle on the prairie, swinging them up by tackle to the limbs of an elm tree. In 1834, the industry grew, slaughtering 4,400 hogs and 1,000 cattle. Archibald Clybourn, as the government butcher for the Pottawatomie Indians, operated a log slaughterhouse on the North Branch of the Chicago River where he packed about 250 head of cattle and some 2,000 hogs. By 1836, the year before Chicago's incorporation as a city, Marsh alone processed 6,000 hogs in his packinghouse on Kinzie Street near Rush Street (now site of the Trump Tower). Three years later, he partnered with George W. Dole, and they remained in the business until 1855. The by-products industry developed as well; John Miller opened the future city's first tannery in 1831, and various entrepreneurs marketed the raw material for making soap and candles to eastern markets.

The market for beef slaughtered and packed in Chicago continued to grow. During the winter of 1842-43, Clybourn slaughtered and packed about 3,000 head of cattle for shipment via the Great Lakes and the Erie Canal directly to New York City. In the 1844-45 season, Wadsworth, Dyer and Company shipped the first barrels of beef for the English market. According to Board of Trade statistics, local packers slaughtered 28,972 head of cattle and 74,000 hogs during the 1855-56 packing season. In 1857, after railroads had connected Chicago to the East Coast, the city's livestock drovers sent more than 25,000 head of live cattle to eastern markets, along with more than 110,000 hogs.

By the 1840s, Chicago's packing industry began to move to the South Branch of the river in what was then suburban Bridgeport. The firm of Wadsworth, Dyer and Company occupied about a half acre of land and opened a slaughterhouse in 1843 along the South Branch. The company employed over one hundred men in 1850 and killed more than 200 cattle a day, while a little further down the South Branch William B. Clapp employed forty men and slaughtered 100 cattle each day. The Reynolds Company engaged about thirty men and slayed about 90 head of cattle a day. The Hough brothers built a packinghouse on the South Branch in 1850 at a cost of $3,000 ($90,909 in 2014), and a mere three years later their success led them to build a stone packinghouse costing $20,000 ($606,061). It burned down in the fall of 1856, and the firm rebuilt it at a cost of $25,000 ($694,444). The successful industry attracted outside investors, and in 1854 the Craigin Company of New York built a large $45,000 ($1.3 million) packinghouse on the

South Branch. By 1858, Chicago's many packers had a daily capacity of 1,765 cattle and 9,000 hogs, even as the lack of refrigeration limited the packing season to the cooler months.

The first cattle market for drovers who purchased stock on the prairie and brought them to Chicago for sale opened in 1848. The Bull's Head Stock Yard, located on the West Side near Ashland Avenue and Madison Street, was a rather makeshift establishment, but it was the seed for the creation of the leading livestock market in the world. In 1855, John Sherman leased the yard, and the following year he also leased the Merrick Yards at Twenty-Ninth and Cottage Grove Avenue on the South Side. In 1852, railroads had initiated the transport of livestock for the first time; by 1860, they began to move large numbers of animals, and this shift in transportation changed how animals were sold. Rail lines connected the Sherman Stockyard on the South Side to both the Illinois Central and Michigan Central Railroads, and Sherman's establishment quickly developed as Chicago's premier livestock market with a daily capacity of 5,000 cattle and 30,000 hogs. The rail connection would prove to be central to the future of the industry in Chicago, as they expanded the hinterland of the quickly growing city on Lake Michigan. Stockyards without rail connections, such as the Bull's Head Stock Yard, became obsolete. Sherman's market had made a giant leap into the future.

Suddenly, Chicago's markets were a national concern. Until the railroad came to Chicago in 1848, the city had exploited a rather limited hinterland, with the majority of fed cattle coming from Illinois, especially McLean County, although drovers brought smaller numbers from Indiana and Iowa. Cattle, hogs, and sheep arrived in the city "on the hoof." But the defeat of the Confederacy in 1865 and the triumph of the railroads unlocked Northern markets for Texas cattle. The disappearance of the buffalo opened the vast ranges of the West to cattlemen. As the white man displaced the Native American, so cattle, hogs, and sheep replaced the bison. Beef profits soared and attracted Texans to the cattle business because of high Northern prices. In the spring of 1866, herds set out from Texas for the new railheads to the north and east. The next year, the Kansas Pacific Railroad reached the plains of central Kansas. Illinois cattle buyer Joseph McCoy built a stockyard in Abilene, Kansas, at the end of the Chisholm Trail to ship cattle to Chicago and points east. Many considered Texas cattle a lower grade product and regarded the meat as tough and stringy, but the market responded to the vast western herds. The number of cattle shipped from Abilene grew from 35,000 in 1867 to 700,000 in 1871. This so-called cattle boom enticed investors across the continent and as far away as England. The *Breeder's Gazette* explained, "A thousand of these animals are kept as cheaply as a single one. So with a thousand as a starter and with an investment of but $5,000 [$96,154 in 2014] in the start, in four years the stock raiser has made from $40,000 to $45,000 [$769,231 to $865,385]." The news of these lavish earnings spread across the Atlantic, and the British Parliament sent two members on a fact-finding tour; they reported a typical return of 33 percent per annum. Europeans gladly entered the industry not only as investors, but also at times as ranchers.

Eventually, railroads reached the Texas cattle country, and after about fifteen years the great drives to Abilene ended. The railroads entered other cattle areas and herds roamed from Colorado, Wyoming, the Dakotas, and Montana making their way to Chicago and other central markets. Western cattle arrived at Chicago as did prime midwestern beef cattle. Midwestern hogs remained a major source of profits for farmers and packers alike. Sheep also arrived from as far away as Colorado and even California as the railroads expanded across the continent.[2]

As livestock receipts at the various Chicago area stockyards grew, having various yards located across a wide part of the city proved to be less than efficient for filling orders. Buyers often had to travel to two or more stockyards to purchase the number and quality of livestock they needed. This often meant driving animals back and forth through increasingly crowded downtown thoroughfares, and Chicagoans complained about livestock running over city streets. In 1863, cattle crossing the Rush Street Bridge in downtown Chicago had destroyed the iron structure, which had been built seven years earlier: it fell into the river, breaking two of its turntable wheels and three of its trusses at a cost of $50,000 ($943,396 in 2014). While many Chicagoans worked in the livestock trade, it presented an annoyance to many other businesses and to the routines of daily life in a city quickly leaving behind its frontier roots. A modern city needed to control such encroachments on its day-to-day life. As Chicago grew, the divide between the urban and rural increased, and while city dwellers welcomed industrial development and the livestock trade, they wanted to control the nuisance of having thousands of animals moving down their streets and across the city's bridges. If the city was to become more than another western cow town, it would have to deal with the problem.[3]

A New Stockyard

The city of Chicago grew in part due to its ideal geographic position on the Great Lakes and near the Mississippi watershed. In 1825, the Erie Canal opened, providing an opportunity for Chicagoans to tie into newly developing east-west trade patterns that focused on New York City and the East Coast. The Illinois-Michigan Canal, along with the Galena and Chicago Union Railroad, increased these connections. The city's preeminence only increased with the rise of the railroads, and it made more and more sense to centralize the various livestock markets around the railroads.[4]

The Chicago Pork Packer's Association and other businessmen, including John B. Sherman and Samuel W. Allerton, as well as various livestock drovers and buyers, began to argue for the construction of a central market. Railroad owners supported consolidation of the various yards as well. The Chicago Pork Packer's Association moved to raise funds in July 1864, and a prospectus in the fall of that year resulted in an initial stock subscription of $1 million ($15.1 million in 2014), of which nine railroads had pledged $925,000 ($14 million).[5]

Upon the organization of the Union Stock Yard and Transit Company, Timothy B. Blackstone was chosen president, F. H. Winston secretary, and Robert Nolton assistant secretary. Plans took form by the following January to build the stockyard to the southwest of the city in suburban Town of Lake. Some feared that a centralized market would work against the economic interest of farmers, and used the fear of monopoly to rally rural opposition. These qualms resulted from the traditional American dread of largeness and of market fixing. Some feared that farmers would lose control of their products and be swindled by large faceless corporations. Concerns regarding the construction of new railroad lines also appeared in the Illinois legislature. These apprehensions revolved around the real dangers of trains speeding across the landscape and presenting a hazard to human beings and animals alike, as well as a fear of the railroads that symbolized the new industrial society after the Civil War. Despite these obstacles, the process of planning the Union Stock Yard continued and drew support from the majority of livestock producers who saw value and efficiency in the

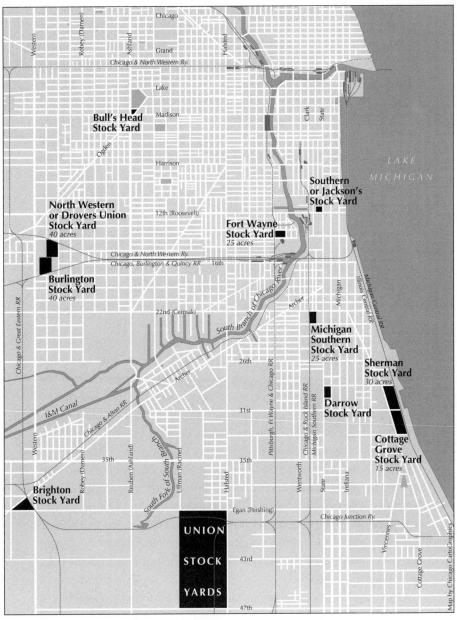

Map showing location of the old stockyards and their relationship to the new Union Stock Yard. (Chicago CartoGraphics.)

proposed Chicago market. On February 13, 1865, Governor Richard J. Ogelsby signed the law authorizing the creation of the new stockyard.

Plans called for the new market to be built on land previously owned by "Long" John Wentworth, a legendary political figure in the early history of the city. Wentworth speculated in land and championed the railroads. This part of the Town of Lake was marked as Section 5 and covered the area from Ashland Avenue on the west to Halsted on the east, and from Thirty-Ninth Street (today Pershing Road) on the north to Forty-Seventh Street on the south. Wentworth and his father-in-law, Riley Loomis, had purchased the 320-acre tract in the eastern half of Section 5 in 1852, for $7,400 ($224,242 in 2014); thirteen years later, they sold the land for $100,000 ($1.5 million) to a committee made up of the chairman, Homer Earle Sargent, along with H. H. Porter, the general freight agent for the Lake Shore and Michigan Southern Railroad, and John Houston who represented the Pittsburgh, Fort Wayne and Chicago Line. The purchase occurred before the actual incorporation of the Union Stock Yard and Transit Company, Sargent went on to serve as one of the directors of the new corporation.[6]

Skeptics felt that the marshy land was not useful for the new livestock market, or much of anything else. The Board of Directors hired engineer Octave Chanute to design a system of sewers to drain the property. Chanute's friend W. H. Civer served as resident engineer, and both worked under the general direction of Colonel Rosell Hough, superintendent of construction. Chanute devised an intricate system of pipes and sewers to drain the 320 acres. The original plan called for 40 acres of pens, an office building, a hotel to serve shippers and visitors to the Union Stock Yard, and rail lines heading east and west to connect to the railroads that would serve the market. After three other railroads joined the enterprise, the Board of Directors of the USY&T Company purchased another 25 acres and raised more cash for a larger pen area. Chanute left the remaining land to the south open, to be built upon later if necessary.[7]

Construction officially began on June 1, 1865, with the breaking of ground for a box sewer on Halsted Street between Egan Avenue and Forty-Third Street to serve as a discharge for the vast number of drains and sewers designed to make the land suitable for construction. Like much else connected with the new enterprise, the box sewer was immense and costly, it ran north and south on Halsted Street for a half mile and cost $15,000 ($217,391 in 2014) exclusive even of some materials. Eventually hundreds of smaller pipes ran throughout the site and connected with the box sewer. At Egan Avenue (Pershing Road), several sewer lines dropped into a large drain, which carried the water into the South Branch of the Chicago River. Once the land had dried, wagons brought lumber and other materials to the prairie, and workers laid a railroad track to deliver more building materials. More than one thousand men began planking the livestock pens. Workers placed large sills of timber on the ground and laid three-inch joists upon which the men laid the planking. Cattle pens required three-inch pine planks nailed into the joists, while two-inch planks covered the hog pen floors. This system allowed water and waste from the animals to drain into the pipes that led to the massive box sewer.

Chanute laid out the new livestock metropolis in a familiar manner to Chicagoans. Like the city itself, the Union Stock Yard followed a strict grid pattern. North toward Bridgeport and through the center ran E Street (later named Laurel and then Morgan Street). Seventy-five feet in width and divided into three lanes for livestock and pedestrians, it was paved with Nicholson blocks manufactured from the ends of pine timber used to plank the pens. Lesser streets and alleys ran parallel to E Street and led to the railroad docks. Other east-west arteries crossed E Street at right angles. The sixty-six-foot-wide principal east-west street, Broadway (later Exchange Avenue), ran from Center Avenue (now Racine Avenue) to Halsted Street and provided the main entrance to the stockyards. A sidewalk on the south side of the street paralleled the avenue, and led past the new Exchange Building and the hotel, christened Hough House after the superintendent of construction. At first, visitors felt lost in the labyrinth of pens; but Chanute marked each as part of a particular block, and numbered the pens, it soon proved fairly easy to find one's way. The numbering system proved to be an effective way of bringing order out of chaos. Workers and visitors alike could easily move between the pens and not get confused. Even in the maze of pens the modern desire for order and efficiency could be seen.

Initially, laborers constructed some five hundred pens covering sixty acres. Varying in size, they all shared an oblong design, and included connecting gates so that larger pens could be created as needed. The pens varied in size from twenty by thirty-five feet to eighty-five by one hundred and twelve feet. Other pens were precisely the size of a railroad car, situated near the various railroad docks. Covered hog pens protected the animals during the winter and prevented them from piling on each other to stay warm. The USY&T Company offered cattle sheds for prime cattle. A Worthington steam pump sent water into five huge tanks near the center of the yards. Some sixty miles of pipes originally provided fresh water for the pens from the South Branch. Fairbanks scales located throughout the yards weighed livestock and made sure that shippers received proper payment.

Chanute divided the stockyards into various divisions, each controlled by a railroad. The Union Stock Yard provided water tanks for engines, wood yards, turntables, and everything required of a railroad depot. Nine railroads initially served the new market on fifteen miles of tracks operated by the USY&T Company. Along with switch tracks and side runs, each railroad had one thousand feet of unloading tracks and chutes. As many as five hundred railroad cars could be unloaded or loaded at one time, and Chanute's design made it easy to transfer livestock from one railroad to another. Also, each of the railroads could petition to use another road's tracks. The original design included a slip that would connect to the Chicago River and allow the creation of a harbor at the Union Stock Yard, but this proved unnecessary due to the dominance of the railroads. At the outset, developers saw the stockyard as a transfer yard at which the majority of animals would be purchased and then shipped to eastern packers and markets. The lack of refrigeration technology meant that most meatpacking operations were local: they slaughtered for nearby butchers who sold in their neighborhoods.

One month after the beginning of construction, crews broke ground for Hough House. The six-story white-brick structure cost $150,000 ($2.2 million in 2014) and included a double veranda, 263 rooms, and an artesian well to provide water. The two-story Exchange Building, made of the same Illinois white brick as the Hough House, stood to the west, in the yards. Frederick Baumann and Edward Burling, designers of Chicago's Chamber of Commerce Building, designed both structures. The Exchange Building housed offices for the USY&T Company, dealers, and commission firms, as well as massive telegraph headquarters so market news could be sent and received across the country. The quick transmission of information, as well as physical efficiency, was crucial for modern capitalist enterprises.[8]

The Union Stock Yard

The first hogs arrived at the stockyards on December 26, 1865, on the Chicago, Burlington and Quincy Railroad. Competition immediately broke out as to who would have the honor of purchasing the first lot. Livestock buyer John L. Hancock, Esq., won the contest; Peter Notingham made the second purchase of five carloads for Wooster, Hough and Company. D. Kreigh and Company made the third purchase. The Union Stock Yard was now open for business. The following day, the Chicago, Burlington and Quincy Railroad instituted daily commuter service to and from the new stockyard for a fare of twenty cents.[9]

Due to the holiday season and a slow market, cattle receipts at first trickled into the new stockyard. The market for cattle and sheep proved dull, but hogs provided a livelier market; the Union Stock Yards attracted 17,764 hogs during the first week of operation. On Saturday, December 30, the cattle market began to liven up, and the numbers for the first five days of the market reached 613 head. The *Chicago Times* mentioned that as news of the opening of the new stockyard spread, buyers from both Cleveland and Pittsburgh entered the market to purchase cattle for packers in those cities. Both the Northwestern and Rock Island Railroads agreed to run trains into the new yards on or after the following Tuesday. In 1866, the first full year of operation, receipts included 392,604 cattle, 980,864 hogs, 209,737 sheep, 1,122 horses, and 244 mules. Shippers sent 263,693 cattle, 482,875 hogs, and 75,447 sheep to off-market packers.[10] Soon the old yards disappeared to be redeveloped as part of the expanding city.[11]

On New Year's Day, his admirers held a dinner and testimonial to honor Colonel Hough. Hosted by William F. Tucker and Charles Baldwin, proprietors of Hough House, the staff of George H. French of Chicago's Briggs House catered the elegant affair five miles from downtown, on what had recently been lonely marshland. Roughly one hundred men representing the various business interests of the city arrived by a special train. The architect Edward Burling presented Hough and his wife with gifts of silver dinner settings created by silversmith A. H. Miller at a cost of about $2,500 ($37,313 in 2014). The sumptuous dinner applauding Hough's achievement of the construction of the modern livestock facility lasted until midnight. It celebrated the continued growth and importance of Chicago and its industrial base and heralded a brave new future for the city, the region, and the nation recently reunited by war.[12]

Despite the fact that the Union Stock Yard had opened, construction continued. The hotel was not yet ready for guests that January, and the pen area already had to be considerably enlarged. Costs escalated and increased expenditures had to be made during 1866. When the market opened in 1865, the privately funded cost for the land and construction reached $1.5 million ($21.8 million in 2014). During 1866, the USY&T Company made an additional outlay of $180,000 ($2.6 million) to complete the market and make changes and enlargements.

The growth of the stockyard soon outstripped its natural resources. The South Branch of the Chicago River proved to be inadequate source of fresh water, and so the USY&T Company dug an artesian well between May 14 and October 30 in 1866, finding water at a depth of 1,032 feet. Because of its high mineral content, the water could only be used for livestock. The company then sunk six artesian wells with an average depth of 1,300 feet, to produce six hundred thousand gallons per day. These wells also proved to be inadequate, and eventually the stockyard company laid a water intake line to Lake Michigan in 1878.[13]

Human resources mattered as much as land and water. John B. Sherman proved crucial to the success of the new livestock market. Like many of the city's early entrepreneurs, Sherman grew up in New York State. Born in 1825, he spent his early years on the family farm in Dutchess County in the Hudson Valley where he received only an elementary education. He went to work in a retail store at the age of nineteen, but the 1849 Gold Rush attracted Sherman to California. After making several thousand dollars there, he briefly returned to New York before moving west and purchasing a farm in Kendall County about forty miles southwest of Chicago. A few years later, Sherman moved to Chicago and ventured into the livestock business. He seemed an obvious choice to run the new Union Stock Yard, but railroad politics interfered. Some feared Sherman's friendships with James F. Joy of the Burlington Railroad and James Walker of the Michigan Central Railroad would cause him to favor those two lines over others, so the general superintendent position went to Frank T. E. Bryant. But when Bryant died, the Board of Directors turned to Sherman to fill the position on June 1, 1867.

In a career that stretched from 1867 until his retirement as president

in January 1900 at the age of seventy-five, Sherman became synony-
mous with the Union Stock Yard. As one of the original incorporators of the USY&T Company, Sherman had been involved with the
enterprise since its inception, and he proved a good choice to run the
operation. By all accounts a well-organized and charming man, Sherman epitomized business culture in the stockyards, with its thousands
of daily face-to-face transactions. When he took control, Sherman
dismissed men associated with Colonel Hough and Bryant, both of
who were identified with the interest of the meatpackers, and replaced
them with the team he had earlier assembled at his old stockyards. The
new superintendent quickly established control over the collection
of pens, docks, and chutes and reached out to livestock growers by
banishing any hint of secrecy. Commission men and meatpackers had
wanted little or no market information published in the newspapers so
as to keep livestock producers in the dark, but Sherman hoped to make
trust a constant watchword in stockyards dealings. He saw that transparency would prove vital to the successful operation of the stockyard
and in maintaining the confidence of livestock producers who feared
being swindled by "big city" operators.[14]

In another move against his predecessor, Sherman renamed the
Hough House the Transit House and hired William F. Tucker, who developed one of Chicago's finest restaurants in the hotel. The USY&T
Company regarded the Transit House as a service to the shippers who
brought their livestock to the market. These men often coming off of
long cattle drives and then following the herds by rail to the Chicago
market proved difficult to manage in the "civilized" atmosphere of a
major urban hotel. The Transit House offered a fifty-cent meal served
by Irish immigrant waitresses who knew how to handle the rough
western crowd. But Sherman could not control all aspects of food,
drink, housing, and entertainment in the district. Quickly, a row of
saloons and several cheaper hotels, some of a rather dubious reputation, appeared across the street from the Transit House to serve the
cowboys, shippers, and others who came to the yards. Nonetheless,
the stockyard management did its best to keep order on Halsted Street,
and especially in the Transit House, where the management prevented
prostitution by strictly enforcing the rule of "no women above stairs,"
the few shippers' wives and other female guests visiting the Transit
House being exceptions.

The Union Stock Yard continued to grow, and in 1867 further con-

Transit House about 1890. The building fronted on Halsted Street and provided a first-class hotel for shippers to the Union Stock Yard. (Postcard, Author's Collection.)

struction costs equaled $34,434 ($546,571 in 2014). Adding to the spectacle of the yards, the new superintendent that summer opened the eighty-acre Dexter Park racetrack on company property just south of the Transit House, between Forty-Second and Forty-Seventh Streets along Halsted Street. The entrance to the track stood to the north on a street paved with Nicholson blocks, and wooden horse stables lined the park on its west, while to the east stood a row of sheds for the carriages and horses of visitors. A large octagonal edifice with a saloon and betting parlor stood nearby, and an observatory topped off the structure for the use of "gentlemen of note and distinction" to watch the races away from the crowds. Just south of this building stood a long grandstand facing west with a capacity for about 1,500 spectators. A smaller grandstand, reserved exclusively for ladies, could accommodate 200 female horseflesh enthusiasts and faced east about fifty feet from the main stand. A smaller stand accommodated judges. Well-designed Dexter Park provided an unobstructed view of races from every point in the stands and observation deck. The stockyard company opened the track on July 4, 1867, and Dexter, the legendary trotter owned by Robert Bonner and namesake of the park, visited at the end of the month.

Dexter Park soon also became a center for baseball in Chicago. In fact, the history of Chicago professional baseball began there with a team that would eventually evolve into the city's "North Side" club. On April 9, 1870, the newly formed Chicago White Stockings, now the Cubs, played their first practice game at Dexter Park against a select group of amateurs before going on tour. On June 8, they beat Cleveland's Forest City team 15 to 9 in their first professional game. The games of the newly created National League provided yet more pageantry in the stockyards.

In August 1871, the Dexter Driving Association leased the park for ten years at a cost of $35,000 ($673,077 in 2014), with Sherman as one of the trustees. For the USY&T Company, Dexter Park provided an entrance into the world of sport and entertainment. The track also provided a gathering place for many in Chicago not only to admire and bet on horses, but eventually for other livestock and sporting expositions. Sherman proved himself an expert entertainer, as well as an adept businessman and stockman, and until the end of its nearly 106-year existence the stockyards maintained that tradition. In the barn behind the hotel and Dexter Park, Sherman kept a zoo that included a six-legged hog and a camel-backed horse, just part of the carnival that the stockyards provided Chicagoans. While today such a menagerie might seem peculiar, it was well within the tradition of spectacle in the nineteenth-century city. Animal oddities often attracted crowds familiar with the dime museums and freak shows of major cities. It developed as part of the showmanship that would mark the stockyards from Sherman's time forward. Chicago enthusiast and booster John Wright quoted the *Chicago Post* as recording that 164,416 passengers rode the South Division street railway to the Union Stock Yard in 1867. Others came to the market on the daily commuter trains that made their way from the downtown. While many of these worked in the yards, many more came to visit the new livestock market and the Dexter Park racetrack.[15]

Sherman also saw the value of creating a bank in the stockyards to facilitate sales and money transfers. The Union Stock Yard National Bank opened for business in 1868 as a clearinghouse for Chicago's live-

Men loading cattle onto a cattle car for shipment to Chicago, circa 1890. (Stereopticon, Author's Collection.)

stock trade, and nearly all of the drovers and commission men opened accounts in the bank. By the end of 1873, the Union Stock Yard National Bank commonly paid out over $2 million ($39.2 million in 2014) per week to customers. In 1885, the bank had $200,000 ($3.9 million) in capital with another $100,000 ($1.9 million) at rest.[16]

Packingtown

Originally most livestock men saw the stockyards principally as a shippers' market to supply eastern slaughterhouses. Nevertheless, the land immediately to the west of the stockyards, from Center Avenue (now Racine Avenue) to Ashland Avenue, attracted the attention of investors. Town of Lake pioneer Samuel Beers originally owned some of this land, and real estate dealer James B. Goodman sold much of it. Land syndicates purchased the western half of Section 5 in 1865. John F. Tracy and Martin L. Sykes, who were among the incorporators of the USY&T Company along with attorney Henry H. Porter, owned the northwestern section. In 1868, they placed the land between Forty-First and Forty-Third Streets on the market as the "Packers' Addition." Henry H. Walker, Briggs Swift, James D. Lehmer, and Nathan Powell held title to the southwestern quarter.

In 1868, Benjamin Peters Hutchinson decided to move his meat-packing establishment from the South Branch in the northern section of Bridgeport to the west of the stockyard. He purchased land in September and began construction of a large packinghouse, other industrial buildings, and a boardinghouse for his employees. Meanwhile, Hutchinson bought up several smaller firms and incorporated the Chicago Packing and Provision Company. By 1870, as Chicago's largest packer he handled nearly 200,000 hogs annually. At that time three smaller plants and several slaughtering sheds also appeared in the area west of the stockyards. In addition, Nelson Morris and Samuel Allerton purchased property, but did not enter the packing business until later in the decade. A livestock reporter predicted that within a few years all of Chicago's meatpackers would abandon the South Branch and settle in this area.

By the mid-1880s, twenty-nine major packinghouses and several small firms located near the stockyards, with most situated just to the west. Packers locating there had several obvious advantages. South Branch packinghouses drove cattle, hogs, and sheep over a mile to their plants. This resulted in frequent accidents and the death of valuable animals. In addition, packers had to follow Chicago's laws prohibiting the driving of livestock on city streets between 8:00 a.m. and 5:00 p.m. Hutchinson's men, on the other hand, simply drove livestock through the pen area and across Center Avenue to his own holding pens. The pens, alleys, and rail lines of the Union Stock Yard presented the only headache for these men. In 1879, the USY&T Company solved that problem by opening the first overhead livestock viaduct, which crossed the pens and railroad tracks and led to the emerging packinghouse district to the west. In this manner, livestock purchased by firms located adjacent to the yards avoided both other herds being driven to the train docks for shipment, and also crossing the dangerous railroad tracks. Eventually, the viaduct system developed into an intricate three-level maze of overhead passages serving most of the on-market packers and reaching west of Ashland Avenue. It connected all parts of the market with the packinghouses enabling men and animals to move about freely above the crowded stockyard.[17]

One of the most important of the entrepreneurs who arrived in the Chicago Stockyards was Philip Danforth Armour born in 1832. He grew up near Stockbridge, New York, and, like Sherman, went west to join the California Gold Rush. Armour's biographers, Harper Leech and John Charles Carroll, claimed that Armour was more a merchant than a butcher: "There is no tradition, much less authentic record, that Armour ever stuck a pig, slit the throat of a sheep, or stunned a struggling steer." Prior to the Civil War, Armour became a pork packer in Milwaukee when he went into the provision business with Frederick B. Miles. The young capitalist saw a growing market as the country moved west, and the two partners outfitted wagon trains in the Wisconsin port. The sale of salt and pickled meat to these travelers made up the bulk of their business; they then began to slaughter hogs to assure they had adequate supplies. In 1862, Armour partnered with John Plankinton forming Plankinton and Armour meatpackers.

During the Civil War, Armour saw that Chicago would become the great emporium of the West, and in 1863 he helped his younger brothers set up a provision firm there. Chicago attracted the capitalist because of its entrepreneurial spirit, but also its rail connection and growing livestock trade. The city had become a great supplier of goods to the Union Army and to settlers moving west. In 1848, the establishment of the Chicago Board of Trade made Chicago a center for trade with the quickly developing Midwest and West. Four years later, the Armours rented a small packinghouse, the "Old Bell House," on the South Branch, and slaughtered 25,000 hogs. They formed Armour and Company in 1868 and purchased a larger plant, the "Griffin House," on the South Branch just west of Halsted Street. The firm added cattle killing in 1869, and sheep slaughtering the next year. Over the next three years, they averaged an annual profit of $75,000 ($1.4 million in 2014). By the winter of 1870–71, Armour and Company was Chicago's sixth largest packer, and in September 1871 they purchased 21 acres in the Packers' Division for $100,000 ($1.9 million), equal to the price paid for the original 320-acre purchase from Wentworth a mere seven years earlier. Yet observers considered the sale price as low for the market. The company built an immense pork house, and in 1874 a large storeroom surrounded by an icehouse, the first large chill room in America. Philip Armour finally moved to Chicago in 1875, where the original investment of $160,000 in the South Branch site had become worth $500,000 ($10.8 million). Michael Cudahy, who worked for Plankinton and Armour in Milwaukee, arrived to manage the packing operation, while Philip Armour took care of sales and finances.[18]

Gustavus Franklin Swift soon joined Armour in Chicago. Born in 1839 in West Sandwich, Massachusetts, Swift, took a job in Sandwich with a butcher. After learning the trade, he opened his own shop in Barnstable in 1862 and operated a small packinghouse. Seven years later, he moved to Brighton, a suburb of Boston and the center of the livestock trade in the area. In 1872, Swift formed a partnership with James A. Hathaway, and the new firm moved to Albany, New York. Swift often visited the Buffalo and Chicago Stockyards in search of cattle. Finally in 1875, attracted by the quality and quantity of the cattle at the Union Stock Yard, Swift and Hathaway transferred their firm to Chicago to work as cattle buyers and shippers, and began slaughtering cattle there in 1877. Three years later, Hathaway and Swift dissolved their partnership and Swift's brother, Edwin, came to Chicago to help organize Swift Brothers and Company. In 1885, the firm incorporated as Swift and Company and employed about 1,600 men.[19]

Like Swift, Nelson Morris entered the business as a livestock trader. His roots in the Union Stock Yard went back to the Sherman Stockyard. Born in 1839 as Moritz Beisinger in Hechingen, Germany, he came to the United States at the age of twelve and arrived in Chicago in 1853. While working for a man named Nelson, he became known as Nelson's Morris, which he adopted as his American name. John Sherman hired Morris as a watchman at his stockyard. The young man got his start purchasing crippled and smothered hogs in Blue Island and selling them to renderers. Sherman encouraged Morris and loaned him money to try full-time cattle dealing. In 1859, Morris and Isaac Waixel, another German Jewish immigrant, formed a partnership that developed into the first livestock commission firm in Chicago. In 1865, Morris moved to the new Union Stock Yard, and over the next decade, he entered the meatpacking business. Known as a shrewd judge of cattle, Morris often acted as his own purchasing agent. Like his friend Gus Swift, Morris had been an expert butcher. He and Swift both entered the Stone Gate daily at 6 a.m. and walked to their offices in Packingtown. Others often recognized Morris by his diminutive size and heavy German accent and knew him for his "rough and ready sack suit of clothes." By the end of the 1870s, the three men who would become Chicago's major meatpackers had all arrived at the Union Stock Yard. The Chicago Stockyard site attracted these men and others. The location of the yards close to the growing source of livestock as well as the size, efficiency, and reliability of the market and the railroads that served it made Chicago an obvious choice for the packers as they modernized and transformed the industry.[20]

In 1882, Gustavus Swift wrote an old friend, Lucius Bowles Darling, to ask him to join him in a rendering business in Chicago. Darling had discovered that rendering proved to be a more profitable business than meatpacking. Originally, meatpackers offered waste products such as offal free to anyone who would haul it away. Darling concentrated on fertilizer and other animal by-products. In response to Swift's request, Darling sent his son Ira to Chicago. Ira Calef Darling had already spent his young life in his father's company and proved to be an energetic and knowledgeable partner for Swift. By 1885, the business had proved so profitable that Swift offered to buy the Darling family out; they declined, and instead bought out Swift's interest in the company. After the premature death of Ira C. Darling, the family incorporated Darling and Company in 1891, and it became the largest fertilizer producer in Chicago. Darling and Swift created an important spin-off from the meatpacking business as the industry continued to transform Chicago's economy. Armour, Swift, Morris, and Darling put their stamp on the Chicago meat and by-products industry making the Square Mile the leading packing center in the United States.[21]

Threat of Fire

Like Chicago, the Union Stock Yard and adjacent packinghouses were largely made of wood, and the ancient threat of fire constantly endangered the stockyards. Hot summer days made the collection of wooden pens planked with pine and bins filled with hay a tinderbox for any spark from a passing train. On June 14, 1866, the roof of the water tank house on the western edge of the stockyard caught on fire from the sparks from its own smokestack. The blaze destroyed a nearby building, which ironically included machinery to dig an artesian well. Employees labored to put the flames out with water buckets and contained the conflagration.

A more tragic fire occurred on February 22, 1873, when an inferno broke out in the second story of a distillery located just north of the stockyard. Several explosions occurred in the four-story wooden frame structure and spread the fire to the nearby pens. The blaze soon overwhelmed a bucket brigade of stockyard employees. The 700 cattle in the nearby pens panicked, and efforts to save them failed. Fire engines arrived from Bridgeport, but a lack of water hampered the firefighters. Cattle piled themselves on top of each other, and those that could leap the pens rushed across the prairie on fire. Upward to 150 head of cattle perished, while others scattered across the grassland at a loss of some $25,000 ($490,196 in 2014). The damage to the distillery, machinery, and contents amounted to upward of $90,000 ($1.7 million).

In part to fight such fires, in 1874 the Town of Lake and the Township of Hyde Park opened a jointly owned waterworks at the lakefront. Water mains were cut across to the Union Stock Yard at Forty-First and Forty-Seventh Streets and tied into the grid of pipes that supplied the livestock market. The stockyard company replaced its huge water tanks with large stone reservoirs and installed larger mains into the various divisions and new pumping machinery along with a one-hundred-foot-high standpipe to insure enough water pressure for routine uses and firefighting. In 1874, the stockyard company established a full-time fire brigade and built a fire station with a first-class Silsby fire steamer christened the "Liberty." The engine fought blazes in the stockyards, Packingtown, and across the Town of Lake and Hyde Park.

Of course, the Liberty engine did not always prove adequate to fight fires. On July 23, 1879, the hay barn in the shipping division of the Fort Wayne Railroad in the stockyards was set afire by a spark from a passing locomotive. Despite the efforts of both the stockyard and Town of Lake fire companies, the fire grew. Finally, a city of Chicago engine arrived from Thirty-Fifth Street and helped to douse the blaze. The next day, another fire broke out in the Northwestern Company's hay barns and spread to the Chicago Packing and Provision Company and several freight cars. Armour and Company's private fire department responded until the stockyard firefighters arrived. Earlier in January, a similar fire had broken out at the Armour plant, causing the company to dig an artesian well and create a large reservoir. That winter, ice paralyzed the suburban waterworks and Armour's warehouse caught fire and again threatened to destroy the Union Stock Yard.

Both stockyard officials and the packers begged the local suburban government to replace the pipe, but Hyde Park trustees balked at the expense. Fire haunted the stockyard throughout its history, but in 1889 overwhelming majorities in both Hyde Park and the Town of Lake voted to join the city of Chicago. Suddenly, the Union Stock Yard could benefit from Chicago's water system and fire department.[22]

Growth

The twenty years from 1865 to 1885 saw amazing expansion that foreshadowed future growth. While 1867 and 1868 had seen slightly lower numbers of cattle arrive at the stockyards, 1869 saw cattle receipts top 400,000; they soared to 1.9 million in 1885. Hog receipts far overshadowed the numbers of cattle, reaching 2 million in 1867 and more than 7 million in 1880. Sheep market receipts topped 1 million in 1885, while horses numbered 19,356 that year. The packers matched the growth of the Union Stock Yard with over 1 million cattle packed in Chicago in 1883, 1884, and 1885, and over 4 million hogs packed from March 1, 1884, to March 1, 1885. For John Sherman, the success of the yards vindicated his leadership.[23]

Sherman's Union Stock Yard continued to improve. By 1885, 2,600 cattle pens accommodated the massive bovine runs, along with 1,600 covered hog pens to add to its capacity. The stockyard already had a capacity for 35,000 cattle, 200,000 hogs, 10,000 sheep, and 1,500 horses. Three-quarters of the livestock that arrived in Chicago came from out of state, proving the market's wide appeal to livestock men across the nation. The USY&T Company alone employed one thousand men, in addition to the thousands more employed by the commission firms, buyers, and packers.

Sherman symbolized the stockyard and the business to the public. He arrived on horseback daily at 6:00 a.m. and usually stayed until dark. His cluttered desk sat in the middle of the huge office of the USY&T Company, accessible to all visitors. Sherman thrived on what others saw as the chaos of the vast market that surrounded him. In addition, he conducted animal breeding experiments and maintained a "laboratory" on a farm near Washington Heights to the south of the city. On occasion, he displayed his own fine cattle, and during the Christmas season in 1882 Sherman had six of his choicest shorthorn cattle slaughtered and the beef distributed to his friends.[24]

Sherman had solidified his position in the company after a scandal involving the management of the Union Stock Yard in 1872. President Peyton R. Chandler borrowed $75,000 from the company with the help of Treasurer Frederick H. Winston. A special board meeting replaced both men. Sherman's old friend and supporter James Walker became the new company president, but he had various other obligations and relied heavily on Sherman, who in turn served as permanent superintendent. Sherman's ally George T. Williams became company secretary, and despite the scandal, investors received 10 percent dividends during the depression-wracked decade, and 15 percent in 1879. The USY&T Company proved profitable despite economic conditions.

Sherman nonetheless led a modernization program that transformed the stockyard. The company spent approximately $1 million ($22.2 million in 2014) in the 1870s to upgrade and enlarge facilities; paving alleys in cinders and macadamizing the main roads. Sherman added additional pens, chutes, and scales, and oversaw the expansion of the Exchange Building, doubling the amount of office space in 1873. A new separate bank building opened next to the Exchange Building. Not even a decade old, the livestock market boomed.

In the mid-1870s, the USY&T Company shifted its architectural business to the new firm of Daniel H. Burnham and John Root. After the firm designed Sherman's new family home on Prairie Avenue in 1874, Burnham married Sherman's daughter Margaret. The next year the company employed the architectural firm to construct several buildings on Halsted Street, and in 1878 added more space to the Exchange Building. Burnham and Root also persuaded the company to erect a water tower around the one-hundred-foot standpipe with a lookout platform for a watchman to check for fires. This also gave visitors a startling panoramic view of the sea of cattle, hog, and sheep pens. In 1879, Burnham and Root then designed a lasting symbol for the stockyards, a large neo-Gothic stone gate constructed out of Lemont limestone to replace the recently erected wooden entranceway just west of the tracks on Exchange Avenue. The architects designed the substantial structure with three arches, a massive central arch flanked by two smaller pedestrian arches. The center section rose to an imposing height of almost thirty feet and a steeply pitched roof covered

View from the Union Stock Yard water tower looking southwest to the sheep house and Packingtown about 1890. Notice the smoke rising from the huge plants. (Stereopticon, Author's Collection.)

in sheet copper crowned the entrance. Maintained in the center of the arch, a bust of Sherman, the prize bullock, named after the general manager of the Union Stock Yard, presided over the entrance. The gate could be closed at night by lowering a heavy iron grille housed in the roof. Next to the portal stood an attached two-story security station also made of rough-faced limestone. The gate remains today as a symbol of the industry.[25]

The Transformation of an Industry

Chicago's meatpackers embraced new technology as the market grew. The invention of a tin can making machine in 1847, and Gail Borden's success with condensed milk, popularized the idea of buying food in tin containers. Preserved meat, however, did not come out well in the cans: the canning process created an unappetizing mixture of water, grease, and tired looking meat. A process devised by William J. Wilson, and the introduction of steam pressure autoclaves in the winter of 1873–74, solved that problem, and Wilson soon had a thriving business based in Chicago. A small packer founded in 1868, Libby, McNeil and Libby, secured Wilson's permission to use his pyramidal can and started producing corned and roast beef in cans. By the 1880s, sales soared, and Libby, McNeil and Libby had a huge modern plant and canned two hundred thousand cattle a year. Other packers quickly joined the canned beef trade.

The hot and humid Chicago summers caused the early packinghouses to shut down for the season. During the 1850s, the vast majority of live hog receipts arrived in Chicago during November, December, January, and February, with about half the winter capacity being carried out through March, April, May, and perhaps half of June if the weather remained cool. A small number of hogs arrived during the rest of the year, but these tended to be slaughtered for immediate consumption in the city. It cost between eighty cents and a dollar ($22 to $27 in 2014) for the ice to keep a hog carcass cool in the summer months, and this prohibitive expense resulted in pork packinghouses sitting idle. But idle factories are an inefficient use of capital, and packers sought solutions.

As historian William Cronon has pointed out, the Chicago packers, with the help of the railroads, manipulated the seasons of the year. For half a century, ice cut in ponds near New York and Boston in the winter and stored in insulated warehouses supplied the needs of East Coast urbanites for ice over the summer. In Chicago, local ice had been cut from the Chicago River and ponds since the 1850s, used primarily by the city's brewers to store and chill lager beer. In 1858, local ice cutters stored some winter ice to pack pork during the summer. The coming of the railroads allowed ice to be shipped over long distances to supply businesses such as the Chicago meatpackers. Soon ice came

on railroads to Chicago in larger amounts from nearby shallow glacial lakes in Wisconsin and elsewhere. The presence of new sources
of ice allowed the packers to reduce the fluctuation in the seasonal
market and take better advantage of their costly investments in physical plants, and so packers and farmers could now count on a yearlong
market at Chicago. Foreign markets purchased most of the summer
pork, but increased summer packing caused a jump in hog receipts
at the Chicago market. Still, even as late as 1882 seasonal fluctuations
and the European market determined whether or not packinghouses
remained open during the hot months. Philip Armour explained that
year that poor economic conditions meant low European demand and
prevented the lower classes from eating pork, while the European rich
did not care for hog meat.

Advances in refrigeration had an even greater impact on the beef
trade just as the cattle drives of the post–Civil War era changed the
sources and numbers of beef cattle. Americans preferred their beef
fresh rather than packed, and as late as 1871 the vast majority of cattle
arriving at Chicago were shipped to eastern packers. In order for Chicago packers to extend their reach into the nation's beef market, they
had to find a way to ship fresh meat east. Chilling beef in Chicago was
easy; but keeping that meat fresh until it could reach eastern markets was another thing. Refrigerated railcars were the answer. Detroit
meatpacker George H. Hammond Company shipped the first chilled
meat in an ice-packed boxcar to Boston in 1868. William Davis had
designed Hammond's refrigerated car the year before as a simple device, basically a boxcar insulated and packed with ice. While the meat
arrived in edible condition, the cars had to be filled with new ice daily,
and the meat became discolored by contact with it. In addition, the
beeves hung from a rack tended to sway; this shift in a railcar's center
of gravity could cause derailments when going around turns at a high
speed. Despite Hammond's initial success, meatpackers still lacked
the ability to transport commercially viable beef over long distances.
Hammond's limited achievement, nevertheless, induced him to move
his plant from Detroit to the Chicago area next to an ice-harvesting
plant. His operation in Hammond, Indiana, began to introduce the
nation to chilled beef.

Chicago packers knew refrigerated railcars could be a major break-
through that might give them control over the national market. Railroads had changed the meatpacking industry, with livestock railcars

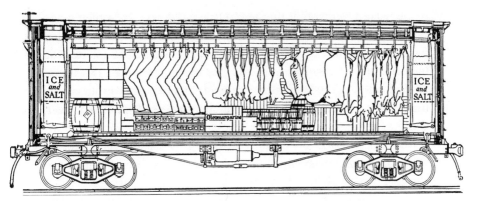

Swift and Company refrigerated car sketch. Notice the various kinds of products carried in these cars. (Swift and Company, Author's Collection.)

crossing the country and eliminating many of the long and arduous cattle drives. Shippers disliked the system, however, since less than 60 percent of the animal's weight resulted in edible and saleable products. The railroads charged for transporting the entire live animal. In addition, the transport of live animals resulted in more shrinkage and death. If Chicago packers could successfully ship chilled meat, they could save over 40 percent of shipping costs, make by-products with all parts of the animal, and set prices lower to capture eastern markets.

In 1877, two years after arriving in Chicago, August Swift suffered losses shipping cattle east to New England butcher shops. In response, he attempted an experiment, sending two carloads of dressed beef east during the winter. Swift shipped the meat in stripped down express railroad cars with their doors left open to keep cold air moving across the beef. The success of the venture convinced Swift to continue his experiments. The next year, Swift hired engineer Andrew Chase to design a refrigerated car. Chase came up with a simple solution of placing boxes filled with ice and brine at both ends of the car, venting them so that chilled air passed throughout the car. Soon all major firms in the dressed beef trade started using refrigerated railcars.

Maintenance of the ice cars necessitated an entire new infrastructure, and the demand for ice soared. By the 1880s, Swift and Company alone consumed 450,000 tons of ice. Eventually, Chicago firms reached all the way north to Green Bay, Wisconsin, for ice. Swift established a series of icing stations to refill the railcars as they made their way to the East Coast. Each car required an average of one thousand pounds of ice per station on a typical four-day trip. At first, the railroads balked at carrying the new refrigerated cars since they made greater profits moving live animals, but Swift and Armour arranged for the Canadian Grand Trunk Railway, a railroad that had done little business in the livestock trade, to carry the cars. By 1885, the Grand Trunk hauled 292 million pounds of beef east annually. Despite a hard fought battle by local packers and butchers against "embalmed" beef, Chicago packers won the minds, taste buds, and dollars of East Coast consumers. In 1882, Swift built a massive cold storage warehouse in New York City to make his company's products available in the prized Gotham marketplace.

Swift's competitors were not far behind. Philip Armour remarked in Chicago that his company planned to go into the chilled beef business on a large scale. He stated, "At our packinghouses we kill from 800 to 1,000 cattle per day, and we shall enlarge our capacity as fast as demand increases." Armour and Company planned a fleet of refrigerator cars at a cost of $1,800 ($41,860 in 2014) each with a capacity of twenty thousand pounds of beef. Roughly six tons of ice would be packed into each car. Because of such expense, only large firms such as Hammond, Swift, Morris, and Armour could join the chilled beef business. During the 1883–84 packing season, the number of fresh beeves packed in Chicago exceeded the number of live cattle sent to off-market packers for the first time. Only after the invention of refrigeration could Chicago and other such centers be truly considered terminal markets rather than simply shippers' markets. Refrigeration proved vital for the growth of the meatpacking industry and for the Chicago packers' eventual domination of the nation's meat trade.[26]

Swift and Company also looked to the West Coast market. In 1890, Swift's agents bought the Baden-Lux estate in California. This property had long been associated with the land, cattle, water, and meatpacking firm of Miller and Lux, which dominated the San Francisco market, and was a final feeding stop for Miller and Lux cattle headed to that city. After the arrival of the railroad and the decline of California cattle drives, the property declined in importance and the 1,700-acre site was put up for sale. Peter Iler, on behalf of Swift, bought the property and the surrounding 3,400 acres. The following year saw the establishment of the South San Francisco Land and Improvement Company and the Western Meat Packing Company. Swift sent refrigerated meat from Chicago, entered the California cattle market, and built a $2.5 million ($65.7 million) state-of-the-art packinghouse at Baden that produced meat more cheaply than other San Francisco area companies could. As part of the vastly profitable Swift and Company, Western Meat could afford to take a loss until conquering the market. Chicago had extended its economic reach to the West Coast.

As on the East Coast, local firms resisted the Swift incursion, but to no avail. Miller and Lux organized the Butchers Board of Trade of San Francisco and Alameda Counties to fight the Swift subsidiary. In the 1890s, Western Meat slashed prices in its six San Francisco butcher shops and opened a wholesale market in the city. In 1898, the company then underbid Miller and Lux to supply San Quentin jail. It also received a contract to provide meat to the U.S. Army in the Philippines. After the 1906 earthquake, the Western Meat location south of the city remained standing and received a government contract to supply residents with meat. By 1913, Miller and Lux had lost a considerable share of the local market, and as livestock production costs rose in California it began importing hogs bought at the Chicago Union Stock Yard. Thus despite resistance on the part of local butchers who characterized the imports as "embalmed" beef, Chicago meat soon became an important staple for Californians, and by World War One the city's packers controlled much of the American meat industry from the Atlantic to the Pacific.[27]

The meatpacking industry expanded as it developed more innovations. New products and new machinery increased production and profits. The expansion of the by-products industry produced the cliché that Chicago's packers used every part of the hog except the squeal. New products such as oleomargarine, dried blood for fertilizer, lard, and even illuminating gas created from the fumes and odors from rendering tanks increased profits. The dressed beef trade quickly developed into the export trade with chilled beef carcasses easily shipped across the Atlantic in the refrigerated holds of ships. While getting less publicity, Chicago's pork packers expanded their business as labor-saving devices made hog packing among the most modern industries in the world. Fifteen years after the opening of the Union Stock Yard, the meatpacking industry accounted for one-third of Chicago's total value of manufactured goods.[28]

The Stench and Pollution Problem

Despite—or perhaps because of—its huge success, the industry presented serious ecological problems to Chicago. Any gathering of tens of thousands of animals on a daily basis in a confined area created obvious and irrefutable noise, waste, and odor. Packinghouses added to those problems. What Chicagoans called the "stench" nuisance had longed plagued the city and suburbs. Bridgeport's packing plants gave off smells that covered the city when the wind was from the southwest. In 1859, the *Chicago Tribune* complained of the odors coming from the polluted waters of the South Branch. The slaughterhouses contributed manure, offal, blood, tank water, and the offensive gases involved in rendering to the malodorous stream. All these merged into what Chicagoans simply called "the Bridgeport smell." In the 1860s, politicians saw the annexation of Bridgeport to the city as a way to deal with the stench, as Chicago's laws might then be enforced against the suburban meatpackers. This did not prove to be the case, as authorities often poorly enforced laws or judges and juries threw out cases due to packer influence or apathy.

In 1872, on the West Fork of the South Branch just north of Egan Avenue (now Pershing Road) stood a small dam that the USY&T Company had built to bring river water into the stockyards. That supply proved to be insufficient, but the dam remained. Above it the river stayed clean, below it the water turned foul, as a distillery on the north bank dumped its waste, and manure from cattle pens on the south bank ran into it. Meanwhile, just north of the stockyards two sewer lines ran through the district and emptied into a ditch off of Egan Street. Several packinghouses operated just to the east of the yards, and the blood discharged from these plants flowed freely into a gutter along the east side of Halsted Street; conditions unimaginable today prevailed.

The pollution caused by the stockyard and packing plants and the subsequent contamination of the West Fork of the South Branch, commonly called Bubbly Creek, has long remained an issue in Chicago. At the industry's height, the river became so encrusted that small animals would make their way across it walking on the solidified mass floating on its surface. Residents reported large bubbles resulting from decaying matter in the creek rising to the surface with diameters measured in feet! At times the South Branch would turn red with blood flowing into it from the packinghouses. Environmental historian Sylvia Hood Washington has explored this issue in great detail and its danger to the health of Chicagoans living near Bubbly Creek.[29]

With the coming of a new city charter and the passage of a strict antipollution ordinance in 1877, Chicago could reach into the suburbs in an attempt to deal with the unhealthy stench. First, the city cleaned Bridgeport's notorious Healy Slough, located just off of Lyman Street and the river and the Ogden Slip near Archer Avenue; then it moved against the packinghouses. Dr. John H. Rauch proved crucial in the early fight against the stench problem. His successor, and head of the newly organized Chicago Department of Public Health, Dr. Oscar C. DeWolf, armed with a new tougher ordinance and city charter, carried on the crusade. Under the new charter, the city had the power to license packers and renderers within one mile of the city's boundaries. The Chicago Department of Health survey of the Town of Lake found forty-four pork and beef packing establishments, thirteen fertilizer plants, three glue works, and two blood drying companies. These various firms ran 292 rendering tanks, only 11 of which were equipped to eliminate odors. The others omitted noxious fumes into the air. Chicago's new "stink" ordinance gave DeWolf the power he needed to attack the problem, and it led to various court cases. The Illinois Supreme Court finally ruled in Chicago's favor, stating the city had a right to protect its citizens, and in early 1878 a grand jury indicted twenty-seven companies including Chicago Packing and Provision and Armour and Company. After the grand jury ruled against the Scanlon and Sherwin fertilizer companies, the others pleaded guilty and appealed for leniency. With the city's authority legally established, the packers began to install equipment to deal with the dilemma. Pollution and the smell nuisance continued, but Chicago had exerted some control over its environment.

A further issue complicated relations between the city and the Town of Lake and Hyde Park, prior to annexation. In the "Perfumery War," they fought over the transportation of offal across Hyde Park to rendering and fertilizer plants in Ainsworth (now South Chicago). Hyde Parkers tried to eliminate the offal and cattle trains that passed through the town, but the courts stymied them. Ironically, Chicago took the side of the packers. Technological changes and the opening of nine new rendering companies, two in Indiana and seven in the stockyard area, finally solved the problem. Some of the stockyard plants

THE GREAT UNION STOCK YARDS OF CHICAGO.
THE LARGEST LIVE STOCK MART IN THE WORLD.

This aerial view of the Union Stock Yard from the east in 1877 shows the packing-houses to the west and Dexter Park racetrack to the south (Courtesy of Library of Congress.)

scattered their offal over the open prairie outside of Commissioner DeWolf's reach, but he convinced the Town of Lake to prohibit the practice and aided the suburb by loaning five Chicago inspectors to help police the problem.[30]

Like fire, the smells and pollution of the packing and rendering process provided tremendous problems for the packers and the city. Some of this would be dealt with over time through the growth of the by-products industry, but the industry's growth cost Chicagoans through the degradation of their environment. The modern obviously came at a price for the larger community.

By 1880, the Union Stock Yard had established itself as the prime livestock market in the West. Its location proved advantageous to meat companies as they moved their operations near the stockyard in what became Packingtown. Easterners flocked to the city on the lake looking for quick and easy profits. Packers devised technological advances that gave them greater profits and eventually created a worldwide market for Chicago beef, and the Union Stock Yard emerged as one of the wonders of the post–Civil War era. The packing industry was the avant-garde of industrialization and so remade the face of both agricultural America and Chicago. The city, which had taken the title of "Porkopolis" from Cincinnati in the early 1860s, dominated the national and international market.

The future and the modern mass market had been born at Forty-Seventh and Halsted.

3

WORKING IN THE YARDS

The Move to the Modern

We care nothing for their union. They can make as many unions as they please and demand what wages they please. If we can afford to pay what they ask we shall do so; if not we will not.

B. P. HUTCHINSON, president,
Chicago Packing and Provision Company, 1879

*

While important packinghouse owners such as Hutchinson, Swift, Morris, and Armour or stockyard notables such as John B. Sherman seemed to shape the history of the Square Mile, it was workers who made the industry profitable. They flocked to the site, built the stockyards, and manned the packinghouses. As the packing industry moved next to the new livestock market, workers and their families came to the Town of Lake to find work and make their homes. The original plan for the stockyard called for worker housing. Some critics felt that the market was too far away from the city to draw laborers, but the draw of so much work ensured that the USY&T Company never needed to build lodgings. Benjamin P. Hutchinson's Chicago Packing and Provision Company did erect a boardinghouse for workers, and later Armour and Company built several cottages near its plant. These minor attempts at company housing proved to be temporary, as the plants needed that space to expand operations. Private developers and individuals soon built permanent housing for the thousands of workers and their families, creating neighborhoods on what had been prairie.

Canaryville and Between the Tracks

The years leading up to the eight-hour strikes and the Haymarket affair saw many disputes break out between the packers and their workers. As the modern was being born, it was obvious to everyone that workers had fewer legal rights and little recourse against capital. The nature of the technological and organizational changes in meatpacking meant that employees found themselves regarded as cheap labor easily replaced, like so many interchangeable parts. These men and women sought to get some control over their lives. In response to the overreaching power of capital, they created a sense of community in the neighborhoods that surrounded the stockyards, an ethnic communal response centered on churches, fraternal organizations, and neighborhood institutions, especially the ethnic tavern with its attached hall that could be used for meetings. Then they reached out to other working-class communities to create unions and involve themselves in the political structure of the city. The political and economic elite that ruled Chicago resisted this extra-communal response.[1]

The Town of Lake was sparsely settled before 1865, but soon boomed as the new stockyard increased demand for nearby properties. The first neighborhood to develop stood just east of the main entrance on Halsted Street; its residents originally called it the Stockyard Settlement. This locality eventually became known as Canaryville, while the district farther east was "Between the Tracks," until later in the twentieth century when it began to be called Fuller Park. In May 1866, Butters and Company sold lots on Halsted Street, which quickly developed into a teeming business district of bars and restaurants, including the Farnsworth House, a large wood-frame, low-cost hotel and restaurant, situated directly across Halsted Street from the Transit House. The population of the Town of Lake grew as quickly as the stockyards and Packingtown, and the settlement east of Halsted Street pushed south toward Englewood. The *Chicago Tribune* pointed out that development would soon reach Fifty-Fifth Street (now Garfield Boulevard). The horse railway between the city and Englewood, with its connection to the stockyards, improved the area, especially along State Street south of Forty-Third Street, which emerged as a central thoroughfare for the South Side.[2]

At first, Irish and German immigrants and their families predominated among the workers in both the stockyards and the packinghouses. As always, workers brought other institutions with them, especially religious ones. The Irish founded two important parishes, St. Bridget's (1850) on Archer Avenue at Arch Street in Bridgeport and Nativity of Our Lord (1868) to the north of the Town of Lake in the Hamburg neighborhood. This parish originally held Mass in a converted stable on Thirty-Ninth Street, hence its name, recalling the location of Christ's birth. By 1870, 3,370 residents called the roughly half-square mile area between Halsted and Stewert Street south of Thirty-Ninth Street to Forty-Seventh Street home.

The locale also attracted several packinghouse owners who wanted to live close to their investment adjacent to the livestock market, including Gustavus Swift, who lived on Forty-Fifth and Emerald and Ira C. Darling who resided at 4341 South Emerald, as well as packinghouse clerks, livestock traders, commission men, brokers, and others. The Swift family donated funds to organize the Union Avenue Methodist Church in 1877, and locals soon referred to it as Swift's Church. Elite stockyard personnel built homes south of Forty-Third Street and along three north-south streets, Emerald, Winter (Union), and Lowe. Further east stood more modest dwellings owned by bookkeepers, clerks, and tradesmen. Swift and other packers, along with the more successful of the packinghouse and stockyard employees, moved out of the neighborhood as the smells and noises associated with the Union Stock Yard became more of a nuisance. By the 1880s, the district took on a distinct working-class character.

As the packing business expanded, Irish Catholic families moved into the neighborhood in large numbers and in 1880 established St. Gabriel's. Father Maurice J. Dorney, later known as the "Pastor of the Stockyards," founded the parish. At first, the priest lived in the Transit House, where he also said Mass in a rented room. As the congregation grew, Father Dorney held services at Walsh's Hall at Forty-Fourth and Halsted. By July 1880, Catholics constructed a temporary wood-frame church, and the following year the Sisters of Mercy opened a parochial school in the parish as Canaryville took on a definite Hibernian flavor. Farther east, the Irish founded St. Cecilia's in Between the Tracks in 1885.

Germans tended to settle in Bridgeport and then later spread to the stockyard neighborhoods to the south. The establishment of St. Anthony of Padua (1873) and Immaculate Conception (1883), Catholic parishes in Bridgeport, along with the First Lutheran Church of the Trinity (1865) and Holy Cross Lutheran Church (1886) marked the establishment of a permanent settlement of German workers near the packinghouses along the river. German-speaking Catholics established the national or ethnic parish of St. George in Between the Tracks in 1884. The Irish and Germans often fought each other politically and at times in open street battles.

Many Czechs or Bohemians also found their way to the kill floors in the immediate years after 1865, settling at first in Bridgeport where they organized a Catholic parish, St. John Nepomucene in 1871. Reverend William Coka, ordained just five years earlier, celebrated the first Mass in the frame church at Twenty-Fifth and Portland Street (now Princeton Avenue) on December 3, 1871. The parish remained small compared to Czech parishes north of the river in the expanding Pilsen neighborhood. Eventually, wave after wave of immigrants and their children founded over fifty Catholic, Protestant, and Hebrew congregations that circled the square mile of packinghouses and livestock pens.[3]

Technological Change and the Modern

The work these men and women found in the meat industry changed as technology reshaped the industry and the relationship between owners and workers. The birth of the modern often meant fewer worker rights and greater profits for owners. Originally, hog packers in Chicago adopted the methods first perfected in Cincinnati. In the early 1850s, Chicago pork packers killed and packed a mere 20,000 hogs a year, while Cincinnati's meat plants slaughtered and shipped more than 330,000. In order to deal with this vast number of hogs, Cincinnati's packers had devised manufacturing techniques that transformed the industry. This method relied on the minute division of labor rather than technological change, but it transformed the nation's hog business. Originally, a butcher and his assistant would kill and cut up a hog performing all of the various chores. Now many men repeated a single task as the hog carcass moved from one worker to another. Employees dispatched and cut up the hog at incredible speed by using this method of the division of labor. Chicago packers embraced the new techniques and with the help of the railroad and the disruption of the river trade due to the outbreak of the Civil War surpassed Cincinnati in the slaughtering of hogs during the 1861–62 season. By the 1870s,

Hog sticker in Packingtown, circa 1890. The mass slaughter of hogs and other livestock transformed the relationship between man and meat. (Stereopticon, Author's Collection.)

Chicago companies packed well over a million hogs annually in the new "Porkopolis" on the banks of Lake Michigan.[4]

Technological improvements in Chicago's packinghouses further transformed the industry as the city stood firmly on the cutting edge of manufacturing innovations. Railroads rapidly transported hogs, cattle, and sheep over great distances. The use of machinery and the elevated endless chain, which propelled hog carcasses across the kill floor, sped up production. Workers who entered the increasingly larger packing plants saw themselves taking part in a revolution that resulted in what only could be called the "modern." At the center of this stood the hog, a staple of human consumption for thousands of years. One of human-kind's earliest benefactors became central to the arrival of modernization on a prairie outside of Chicago, in an irony worthy of some modernist literary writers, who valued that quality above all others.[5]

In the thirty years before the Civil War, hogs became a staple of midwestern agriculture. Frontier farmers raised hogs as a residual crop as they could fend for themselves and foraged in prairies and woodlands. They proved to be wonderfully productive animals. Razorback hogs scavenged throughout the Midwest and found their way to local slaughterhouses. Before the arrival of the railroad, farmers had a difficult time getting bulky Indian corn to market, so they turned corn into liquor or fed it to swine. Samuel B. Ruggles spoke the often-quoted line, "The hog eats the corn, and Europe eats the Hog. Corn thus becomes incarnate; for what is a hog, but fifteen or twenty bushels of corn on four legs." Both kegs of whiskey and hogs driven on the hoof to local slaughterhouses provided a practical way to profit from the ubiquitous crop. An enormous domestic market arose for bacon, ham, sausage, lard, and various forms of pickled pork. Hogs contained more usable meat and fat, as a proportion of their body weight, than a steer.

Many regional slaughterhouses appeared in small towns across the Midwest as hogs were more difficult to drive long distances to market than cattle. Drovers could herd steers easily over long distances and, before the railroad, often brought them on the hoof to eastern markets. Hogs, on the other hand, were smarter, more stubborn, and for the most part, could only be moved short distances. Thus packinghouses were built across the rural Midwest. Cincinnati, with its vast river trade, was the one large central market. Canal boats loaded with hogs made their way to the Queen City during the fall packing season from Ohio and Indiana in the years before the Civil War. Afterward, as we have seen, the railroads brought hogs in greater and greater numbers to Chicago.[6]

The double-deck railroad car proved to be a boon to Chicago's hog packers, as the expanding railroad system allowed the city to extend its rural hinterland. Drovers brought hogs short distances to their local railheads and loaded them on the cars for shipment to Chicago. Once they arrived, livestock handlers for the USY&T Company or the commission firms met them at the railroad docks and drove them to covered pens where they were fed and put on display for the morning's market. Off-market packers then had the hogs shipped to their plants again by rail.

Driving hogs roughly often caused them to pile up on each other and could injure the hams, and so the packers admonished men handling the animals to treat them with care, as any bruise might affect the meat. Men herding hogs were told not to use whips or sticks to goad the hogs. The packers developed canvas slappers that made an almost firecracker sound when they hit a hog, but did not leave a mark on the animal.[7]

Working Conditions

The packers' concern for the comfort of their livestock did not necessarily extend to their workers. Working conditions varied from plant to plant, but the modern came at a price, especially for those who labored in the plants. In the Union Stock Yard itself, those men who worked as livestock handlers faced difficult conditions. In dry warm weather, animals raised clouds of dust mixed with dung as they moved from the rail docks to holding pens and then to sale pens. Afterward, an army of men moved the animals back down the alleys to the scale houses and then off to the slaughterhouses breathing the unhealthy dust. In the winter, the snow and sleet could not stop the great packing machine. Livestock handlers worked all year and under all weather conditions. Laborers, including young boys, toiled irregular hours in the stockyards, performing tasks from cleaning stables to running errands for the commission men. While livestock drivers were perhaps the largest group of employees of the USY&T Company, others labored in the cleaning department, the feed department, or as maintenance men, while still others worked in the waterworks or carpentry divisions. Both male and female office personnel filled the massive offices of the Exchange Building, and some one hundred watchmen patrolled the stockyards. In addition, people worked for the many different commission firms as buyers, traders, and brokers. Employees of the various firms fed and watered the animals held over for yet another market. Railroad men and work gangs also toiled throughout the stockyards. The Union Stock Yard seemed like a city of its own with its own hotel, newspaper—the *Drovers Journal* founded in 1873—stores that provided whips, saddles, and other accouterments of the livestock trade. The Union Stock Yard even had peddlers who sold their wares on Exchange Avenue such as the legendary Jack-Knife Ben (Benjamin Chew) and Mary Valanta, the "Apple Woman."[8]

While work "out of doors" in the Union Stock Yard proper could be difficult, it nevertheless was work that most people understood. After all, animals and men had toiled together for thousands of years. The basic relationship between livestock handler and animal remained constant and seemed natural. Working in the packinghouses, however, meant confronting the new modern economy and workplace. For one, it meant being physically confined inside the plants until the kill ended. Before the 1920s and the advent of welfare capitalism, the workday, as well as the work year, could be irregular, as it depended largely on the number of animals available for slaughter.

Once the slaughter began, it seemed endless. In the cattle kill, which the owners greatly expanded after refrigeration and the invention of the refrigerated railroad car, the line moved with a ferocious speed never before demanded of workers. And management soon found ways to speed up the process. In 1884, five cattle splitters in a gang would process 800 cattle in ten hours or 16 cattle per man per hour at an hourly wage of 45 cents per hour. Ten years later, four splitters were putting out 1,200 cattle in ten hours, or 30 head per hour, an increase of nearly 100 percent. But the workers' pay fell to 40 cents per hour except for the "pacemakers" who made 50 cents per hour. These men were paid more to work at a quick pace to keep the line moving. Management paid such "steady-time" men a regular wage that did not depend on number of hours worked or the number of animals available each day. The "steady-time" men thus remained loyal to their employers, not only increasing profits, but also hampering labor organizations. By the 1890s, beeves passed a gang of nearly two hundred men who dispatched 84 head of cattle per hour.

From 1870 to 1900, unskilled wage earners made up a larger percentage of packinghouse employees as the companies split the disassembly process into simpler and more discrete tasks. By 1904, in one large Chicago packinghouse, two hundred and thirty workers killed 105 cattle in an hour. Three workers on the gang earned 55 cents per hour, and eleven others, holding skilled positions, earned 50 cents per hour. Eighty-six workers received 20 cents or more, while one hundred and forty-four earned less than 20 cents per hour. Management could rely on the elite skilled workers and disregard the concerns of others, many of whom they paid 14.5 cents per hour. These unskilled workers included washers and wipers who cleaned the carcasses of water and blood, truckers who moved material and supplies around the various departments, general laborers who assisted the penners,

Beef cutting department, Chicago, circa 1890. (Postcard, Author's Collection.)

knockers, and hoisters, and carried carcasses into the coolers and "squeegee" men who moved the blood off of the kill floors and into gutters with mop-like instruments. Management considered unskilled positions temporary, often filling the positions on a daily basis. When the kill tapered off, foremen let the unskilled go and moved skilled men who would otherwise be idle into those positions. While such laborers were then paid at a lower rate it beat being out of a job, and so created loyalty to the company.

The jobs had many built-in dangers. Packinghouse workers worked at fast speeds in dark rooms, often with little ventilation. Many of the slaughterhouses were ramshackle affairs, rooms being added to older structures as needed. Workers on kill floors stood in blood and grease, and in the summer they moved between hot conditions and chilly coolers. In the winter, men stood in pools of steaming blood and freezing water performing their tasks in unheated spaces. Packinghouse employees frequently acquired skin infections such as "pickled hands" (dermatoconiosis) and "cut worm" (tubular wart). Respiratory diseases infected workers in the wool and hair houses, fertilizer plants, and horn rooms. Pneumonia afflicted those in the refrigerated rooms. Packinghouse and stockyard workers also suffered from rheumatism affecting the joints and back. Damp conditions remained even after management installed concrete flooring or raised platforms. All of these circumstances could aggravate illnesses such as nervous disorders and tuberculosis.[9]

Women workers also appeared in the packinghouses, as gender became a factor in the new relationships transforming butchering. While by tradition managers did not allow women to use knives, long considered a man's tool, many women entered other divisions in the packinghouses. Women first joined the packinghouse workforce in 1875, in the canning division, where they painted and labeled cans and jars. They also canned beef and tended machines that chopped various types of meat. Fewer than one thousand women worked nationally in meatpacking in 1890. By 1904, however, some two thousand worked in Packingtown alone. As the twentieth century progressed, their numbers grew substantially. During an 1894 strike, management allowed women to "take up the knife" as pork trimmers, and immigrant women soon filled ranks previously held by men. Management often paid women by piecework; in theory the quicker they worked, the more income they would make. Most women, however, had to accept less skilled labor such as feeding cans into machines or stuffing sausages. In either case, women tended to be paid lower wages than men. Officials of one packinghouse explained that women simply could not do the heavy lifting that men could when needed, and thus merited a lesser wage. Women did not receive equal pay even when they replaced men at the same job, as the female pork trimmers did.[10]

In an era before strong child labor laws, children also made their way into the industry. In 1894, more than three hundred children, including eighteen girls under the age of sixteen, worked in Chicago's packinghouses. Most of these found employment with the large packers, Armour, Morris, and Swift. By 1900, just over five hundred children were known to labor in the plants. The quantities might seem small, but they did not reflect actual numbers. Neighborhood doctors or clergymen, especially ethnic Catholic and Lutheran priests, often forged documents to falsify birthdates and so allow children to go to work in the plants. Most of these children came from immigrant backgrounds and cultures that expected them to contribute to the family's income. Their fathers and mothers often labored as low-paid and unskilled workers, and so a child's income helped a working-class family survive. Many such children, once they entered the packinghouses,

Women in the sausage department, circa 1900. The packers paid these workers by the piece. While men ran the casing stuffing machines, women tied off the sausages. (Stereopticon, Author's Collection.)

spent their lives working in them. They worked as common laborers and at the lowest rates and often performed the tasks of shackling hogs or pushing blood and other materials into the gutters. Despite the passage of progressive child labor laws in 1893 and 1897, children continued to work in the plants and across the stockyards. In 1904, Jane Addams claimed that hundreds of children who should be in school labored in the stockyards. She stated, "The employers fail to look behind the certificate that the little boys bring. Although the papers indicate the child is of legal age to be employed, any person by a visit to the big establishments can see that the law is violated. The employers are to be blamed." This practice remained in place well into the 1930s.

Both reformers and local residents knew education as the only escape route for the children of the area. In 1898, Seward School, on Forty-Sixth and Hermitage Avenue in the area just to the west of

Packingtown in Back of the Yards, became a center for manual training. Edward Tilden, the president of Libby McNeil, and Libby and
of the Chicago school board supported a measure creating technical
schools to train boys in industrial crafts. The hope was to provide boys
with the competences to enter into more skilled industrial positions
thus providing upward mobility for the children of unskilled manual
laborers. Town of Lake High School, located in Canaryville, became
Tilden Technical High School in 1917 to serve the stockyard area neighborhoods.[11]

Early Labor Unions and Strikes

As the new industrialism arose, workers began to search for ways to
humanize the system. Primitive labor unions appeared among shoe-
makers as early as 1792 on the East Coast. In the West, workers had
little representation, and, although some early trade unions appeared
in Chicago, industrial workers remained largely unorganized. Chicago's reputation for labor agitation began soon after the Civil War. In
April 1867, agitation mounted for a strike on May 1 to gain a reduction
in the workday to eight hours without a decrease in pay. On that day,
strikes and demonstrations shook Chicago. By May 2, labor had come
to a general halt in the city, the strike enforced by flying squads of men
and their supporters who went from factory to factory calling fellow
workers out. They often moved about on wagons or horseback going
from plant to plant. In Bridgeport, riots broke out as crowds went to
the Union Steel works and various riverfront factories and lumberyards to enforce the citywide strike. The strikes did not affect the
packinghouses along the river or the stockyard itself, perhaps because
the packing season was coming to an end and the plants, which operated primarily through the cooler seasons, would soon be closed for
the summer. The eight-hour strikes effectively ended by May 8, 1867,
as most workers returned to their jobs. The first attempt at a strike in
the Union Stock Yard did not occur until 1869, four years after the livestock market opened.[12]

Ten years after the eight-hour strikes in Chicago, however, a much
more serious national movement appeared in 1877. The great railroad
strike that year spread across the country from the East Coast to the
Pacific. In Chicago, the most radical agitation took place in the railroad and lumberyards of the Lower West Side (Pilsen), just across the

South Branch from Bridgeport. Officials feared the strike would soon engulf the stockyards and packinghouses. The strike spread to Chicago on July 23, and by July 25 had caused most freight handling in the city to come to a halt. The packers adjacent to the Union Stock Yard closed down as a general strike broke out. At Armour's, workers prevented the resumption of work and secured written pledges from some plant managers that laborers would be paid two dollars a day and that skilled butchers would receive a proportional pay raise.

This was no peaceful dispute. Halsted Street from Maxwell Street south to Eighteenth Street, a half-mile stretch, provided the epicenter of the conflict. Persistent rumors floated that a mob from Bridgeport and the stockyards was on its way to fight the police, who called for aid from the militia and the U.S. Army. Soon, 750 law enforcement officials stood ready to face the crowds. On the morning of July 26, a mostly Irish group of packinghouse workers gathered at the Union Stock Yard and marched north on Halsted Street brandishing wooden gambrels (frames used for hanging carcasses in the packinghouses) and butcher knives. At Archer Avenue, they joined Czech lumber workers, and the crowd swelled to about 500 demonstrators as it reached Sixteenth Street. The throng clashed with mounted police who fired into the masses of workers. Between 20 and 30 demonstrators died; 150 were injured and more than 300 arrested. The exact numbers were not known because workers fearing police retribution took the dead and dying away from the scene to be buried quietly in their neighborhoods. Militia and police patrolled the area afterward, and soon freight began to move again on the railroads. Two companies of the Second Regiment of the Illinois Militia arrived at the stockyards and occupied the Transit House, while the Town of Lake swore in 150 special policemen to guard the packinghouses and the livestock market. By July 28, the strike had ended except for a few skirmishes between workers and police in the mostly Irish neighborhood of Hamburg, where packinghouse, railroad, and rolling mill workers still ruled the streets.

The 1877 strike provided proof to some radicals that workers needed to be better armed to resist the forces of the state militia, police, and army. For other workers, it meant that the working class should organize both politically and economically. While the newspapers and many observers referred to packinghouse workers as "rough" characters who worked in one of Chicago's "grosser" industries, one *Chicago Times* reporter described the men as eminently respectable people who wished it understood they were not ordinary railroad or city strikers: they were skilled tradesmen.[13]

The years after the 1877 strike saw more labor agitation in the stockyards. In December 1878, a strike occurred. Workers demanded higher wages, as a result the USY&T Company temporarily suspended the shipment of livestock to the market. While most of the packers brought in nonunion help, strikers continued to shut down the Chicago Packing and Provision Company. Management, however, defeated the union, and the men returned to work. That December and January, union men continued to meet informally and invited others to join their organization.

In November 1879, the union asked for a wage increase of fifty cents per day for skilled workers and for all other workers twenty-five cents. By the fall, enthusiastic crowds attended meetings at the union hall on Halsted Street in Hamburg. Supporters filled the hall and several nearby saloons to hear the charismatic orator Daniel O'Connell, president of the Butchers' and Packing House Men's Protective Union. He had turned the ad hoc organization into a trade union that appealed to unskilled as well as skilled butcher workmen, thus temporarily overcoming a traditional division among the workers. Of course, other rifts remained including those based on ethnicity, religion, and gender. These seemed to be overcome at the time, but remained important issues in the background. The packers, largely cooperating with each other, bought time by giving in to the union's demands by the November 5 deadline. While the packers could easily afford the increase, they feared that O'Connell wanted to create a union shop. The president assured them that all the union wanted was a wage increase and the organization held a big celebration at Nativity of Our Lord Church on Thirty-Ninth Street (Pershing Road).[14]

On November 14, 1879, the plant superintendent of the Chicago Packing and Provision Company, on the orders of Benjamin P. Hutchinson, the principal owner, discharged O'Connell along with his work gang. Hutchinson explained that he had ordered the closing of part of the plant to curtail the production of light cuts of pork known as Irish bacon. In response, about one thousand men walked off the job. Hutchinson exclaimed that he had the right to lay off whomever he wanted to and that O'Connell's membership and leadership position in the union had nothing to do with his dismissal. The owner flatly stated, "It is my idea that, so long as I pay the current prices for labor, I should be allowed to run my business as I see fit. It is nobody's business whether I employ Union or non-Union men." The next day, however, the company reinstated O'Connell and the strike ended.[15]

The struggle between Hutchinson and O'Connell continued, and the following month saw another strike. On Sunday, December 14, the union announced that its members would not work with nonunion men after December 17. Several packers allowed union shops and did not want a strike, but Armour, Anglo-American, and the Chicago Packing and Provision Company welcomed the confrontation and shut down operations. Union officials met with the packers on December 20, but came away with nothing but cigars for their trouble. The Town of Lake hired more police to patrol the stockyards and Packingtown as the three packers reopened on December 26 with nonunion workers.

On Monday, December 29, 1879, workers showed up at the Chicago Packing and Provision Company plant and encountered a notice pasted to the front door of the establishment, which read:

> To Whom it May Concern: We, the Chicago Packing and Provision Company, hereby give notice that on and after this date this firm proposes to run its own business. Men will be employed who want to go to work irrespective of any union or association.

Hutchinson declared an open shop: workers would not have to join a union, and so Hutchinson served notice that the union was finished in his plant.

The men discussed the notice, and all of them walked out, including sixty cattle butchers. The confrontation spread to other packers. Both the Armour and Fowler plants remained at work. Armour reportedly purchased two thousand hogs and planned to have 1,200 men working the next day. The company added 100 special guards to bring to 250 the number who patrolled the plant. Fowler Brothers' continued work with over 1,000 men employed. Many on both sides feared the outbreak of violence. Reportedly, some union men had harassed a former Fowler worker who intended to return to the plant during the strike. Conflicting rumors came from the various packinghouses. Several nonunion workers suddenly professed their loyalty to the Butchers' and Packing House Men's Protective Union. Some of the packers wondered if the Chicago Packing and Provision Company would hold to its open-shop stance. The sheriff and the military announced to the public that they were prepared for trouble in the Stock Yard District.

Yet workers soon turned against each other. Despite the fact that O'Connell had attempted to bring all laborers into the fold, the traditional divide between the skilled and unskilled rose again. Confidence in the union eroded, and some questioned the wages paid by the union to elected officials. A union officer then absconded with some funds fueling further division and mistrust. The pastor of Nativity of Our Lord, Father Joseph Cartan, even tried to convince O'Connell not to push for a union shop. Some unionists accused Michael Cudahy, Armour's manager, of bribing the priest to ask the union to back down. By January 11, the strike ended in defeat. Unions, as the name suggest, require unity, and stockyard and packinghouse workers were too divided by skill, ethnicity, and religion to form a lasting organization. Soon the men returned to work, and management looked the other way as assaults on strikebreakers proved common.[16]

1886 and the Eight-Hour Movement

A little known labor organization, the Knights of Labor, had benefited from the fiasco of the 1877 railroad strikes and emerged as a major labor organization in the following years. Nationwide, the Knights attracted some seven hundred thousand members after they discarded secrecy under the leadership of Grand Master Workman Terence V. Powderly. A child of Irish immigrants, he understood that Catholic prohibitions against joining secret societies hampered the organization in attracting immigrants and their children. Once the Knights gave up their Masonic-like rites, Irish and other workers flooded into the union. Perhaps surprisingly, the Knights organized women and African Americans as they sought to create a wide-based membership and to avoid ethnic, racial, and gender fragmentation. In many ways, this organization foreshadowed twentieth-century unions that would take up this approach. The Knights of Labor, although they displayed some characteristics of such later institutions, were not yet a truly modern labor union. Powderly and the Knights generally hoped to avoid confrontations that led to strikes. True to his Irish Catholic roots, Powderly believed the boycott and a cooperative society answered crises, which regularly saw workers outmaneuvered by capitalists and if not,

Sheep kill in Packingtown, circa 1890. Notice the number of young boys employed in this department. (Postcard, Author's Collection.)

then out-gunned by the police, militia, or regular army troops on the streets of America's cities. The Knights, moreover, never had the centralized control that more organized and disciplined unions used in the twentieth century. The violence of the 1877 strike had shaped Powderly, and he hoped to avoid such confrontations in the future. He knew that despite the success of the Knights, they still operated at a disadvantage against a united front of management and government. Notwithstanding these reservations, in 1885 the Knights led a successful strike against Jay Gould's railroads and witnessed even more growth nationally in their membership. In the stockyards, workers still angry over their 1879 defeat looked to the Knights for leadership.[17]

Michael J. Butler arrived in the Chicago Stockyards in 1879 just as that strike had ended in defeat, and he came to play a pivotal role in organizing the packinghouses seven years later. In 1885, a strike against the city's transit companies emboldened leaders, as had the growth of various European radical movements particularly among the German, Czech, and Polish immigrant working-class populations. Chicago had been the center of eight-hour agitation for some time, and most figured it would be no different in the future. In the Union Stock Yard and packinghouses, organizers found men willing to take up the cause yet again.[18]

In 1886, another attempt to bring about the eight-hour day emerged out of the national trade unions and again centered on Chicago. When the general strike for the eight-hour day took place on May 1, 1886, it seemed to be an immediate and overwhelming success, especially in Packingtown. As plant after plant shut down, Armour, Swift, Fowler, and the others decided to buy time and agreed to what they felt would be a temporary settlement. On May 3, some workers were killed by police at the McCormick Reaper Works, and an anarchist rally was called for the next day in Haymarket Square. At that rally, a bomb exploded in the middle of a group of Chicago police, killing seven, and an untold number of workers died in the ensuing melee. The tragedy resulted in an intense reaction against organized labor generally. Police shut down the radical press and detained anarchists and others across the city. Eventually, eight men were arrested and blamed for the bombing. Four men, known as the Haymarket martyrs, were hung for the crime in 1887.[19]

Despite the fact that Powderly and the Knights condemned the anarchists in a most vitriolic way, politicians, capitalists, and much of the public blamed the union along with all labor organizations, for the bloodshed. Yet even after the Haymarket tragedy, as the bombing and ensuing conservative reaction saw the return of the ten-hour day across most of Chicago, the eight-hour day remained in effect in the stockyards and Packingtown. Chicago's packers did not want an immediate confrontation and waited for the proper moment to move against the eight-hour day and the Knights. Rumors persisted that they would soon restore the old arrangement. On May 22, 1886, the *Chicago Tribune* noted that management wanted a return to the ten-hour day, but had not yet decided when to make the announcement. Several meat companies desired to go back to the old arrangement the following week, but others, fearing a violent confrontation, wanted to wait until the end of the month or the beginning of June. In either case, the resumption of the longer day seemed imminent. Packers offered to reinstate a fifty-cent pay cut imposed on skilled labor in 1884, if workers would accept the ten-hour schedule. The cattle butchers resisted because they already slaughtered as many animals in eight hours as they had under the old schedule. If they accepted the increase, they would have to continue to kill at the new rate, thus in reality losing two-hours of pay in relation to work performed. Packinghouse management stated that if the unskilled did not accept the ten-hour day, they would simply be replaced. The workers nonetheless rejected the offer.

Meanwhile, Powderly had his hands full with a second strike against the Gould railroad interests in the Southwest. The General Assembly of the Knights of Labor adopted stringent new strike rules and tried to centralize authority, but the nature of the organization worked against effective control. The Knights directed Chicago's South Side District Assembly 57 to solve its various internal disputes by electing new officers, and in July 1886, District 57 members elected Michael J. Butler as the district's new master workman. The Knights worked hard to organize more packinghouse workers that summer. In an attempt to win over public approval, the leadership condemned the Haymarket bombing and praised the packers for not rescinding the eight-hour day in its immediate aftermath. Meanwhile, the packers complained that plants outside of Chicago ran on a ten-hour schedule and this placed the Chicago's plants at a competitive disadvantage. Rumors of a return to the ten-hour day ran through the stockyards and packinghouses. In July, an unnamed, but "well-known" railroad switchman described a conversation with Armour and Company manager Michael Cudahy, who reportedly had stated that the packers had decided to make their move on September 1. Anyone who refused the ten-hour day would be dismissed, and Winchester rifles would protect those who returned. Still, nothing happened.[20]

On October 2, the press reported that an agitated workforce understood that management would soon move back to the ten-hour day. One packer stated that a reasonable amount of men would come to work, as many did not support the eight-hour day. He made the rather dubious claim that it was hard enough under the ten-hour system to allow the packers to remain in the Union Stock Yard and that "only pride" kept them in Chicago. It was becoming apparent that the packers had kept the eight-hour day in the beef kills in hopes of fragmenting the labor movement.

Finally, on Wednesday, October 6, while the Knights of Labor General Assembly met in Richmond, Virginia, Chicago's packers announced they planned to return to the ten-hour day on Monday, October 11. The Chicago Livestock Exchange called an emergency meeting of its board for the next day at two o'clock in the afternoon. The threat of the strike curtailed sales on Wednesday, when fully eight thousand hogs did not sell as only five packers purchased hogs. These remained in the pens with the hope of selling them the next day, causing increased costs for livestock shippers and commission firms. Workers understood that they had leverage in the new industrial system and could put pressure on the packers by hurting their profits and their suppliers' incomes. The modern did not leave workers without some agency.[21]

On Friday October 8, some 1,500 men marched to various packing-houses, attempting to rally support. They were the first of what would become 15,000 hog packinghouse workers throughout Packingtown who struck the Chicago Packing and Provision Company without approval from the Knight's District Assembly 57. The Chicago Live-stock Exchange restricted hog deliveries to the market. As the strike occurred during a General Assembly, it fell upon delegates to decide what to do rather than the Knight's General Executive Board and Pow-derly. The strike took Michael Butler by surprise, and he returned to the city immediately. The General Assembly voted to send Thomas Barry, a talented organizer and ally of Powderly from Bay City, Michigan, to help District 57, and he left for Packingtown on the evening of October 9. The General Assembly told both men that the Knights would not take responsibility for the unauthorized strike, and the organization refused financial assistance to the strikers. It was not even clear to Powderly how many of the roughly 15,000 men who had walked out were Knights.

The stockyards and Packingtown were a mass of contradictions and conflict, a powder keg. The workers agreed to negotiate, but blamed Armour for much of the stalling by the packers. Meanwhile, the stock-yards remained quiet. About 9 a.m. on October 11, Sylvester Gaunt of District Assembly 57, along with both Butler and Barry, met in the Exchange Building and then visited various company offices to discuss the situation and the workers' demands. The Knights planned a mass meeting at Walsh's Hall on Halsted Street across from the stockyards, but the crowd of about 5,000 proved to be too large for the venue, and they scheduled another meeting on the evening of October 12 at the new Germania Turner Hall on Thirty-Fourth and Halsted. Despite the postponement, organizers held an impromptu outdoor meeting in a vacant lot across from Walsh's Hall. Union leaders advised the men to stay away from strong liquor, and requested that stockyard area saloons close. Barry acknowledged the workers' desire to keep the eight-hour day and told them to leave the nonstriking beef operations alone, not wanting to make his task more difficult. The Knights' leader suggested a boycott against Armour and Company, the obvious chief of the packers. Meanwhile, a large gang of Armour clerks worked loading railroad cars and manager Cudahy himself labored in the freight department. Earlier that day, the *Daily Drovers Journal* quoted Philip D. Armour: "The day of Chicago's supremacy as a pork-packing center will soon be a thing of the past." The obvious threat was that the union and the constant fear of industrial warfare would force the packers to leave to some other location farther west. In the new modern industrial relationship between corporations and workers, businesses did have a greater ability to move their operations, in part because of the nationwide railroad system. While this was still a relatively empty threat in 1886, it would remain a factor in labor management relations from this point on in the Square Mile.

The rally at Germania Hall attracted about 1,300 union supporters. Nearby Burke's Hall, at Thirty-Fifth and Emerald, in the Hamburg neighborhood acted as headquarters for the strikers. Meanwhile, about 150 nonunion men found accommodations in the Fowler plant. While the union kept peace in the stockyards and Packingtown, the firms quartered about 300 Pinkertons, a notorious Chicago-based group of private guards often used to violently break strikes, in the Washington Butchers' Son's establishment. They drilled daily and had ammunition delivered as the plant began to look more and more like an arsenal. Captain Foley said that if any trouble started up, another 300 additional Pinkertons would be dispatched to the area. Railroad switchmen in the yards refused to work. Butler ordered them to return to work until they heard from the union, but a Rock Island train with sixteen cattle cars derailed under suspicious circumstances and two cattle died in the accident. The only firm slaughtering hogs, the Cragin Company, maintained the eight-hour day and did a thriving business.[22]

An October 13 meeting between strikers and the packers did not occur because owners neither showed up nor sent representatives. Armour brought nonunion workers in on trains from Milwaukee, many of them immigrant Poles. By October 13, the number of new Armour men amounted to roughly five hundred. The Lake Shore and Fort Wayne Railroads both ran trains filled with strikebreakers right up to the packinghouses. In addition, Pinkerton guards centered their attention on Armour and Company, the focal point of any clash. A spokesman for the Knights claimed that except for fear of Philip Armour's retribution, several packers would break ranks with the others. On October 15, Philip Armour sent a messenger to ask Barry to come and meet with him. Both he and Butler went downtown to meet with the leader of the packers and Samuel Allerton at Armour's office. The packer claimed that he had been singled out unfairly and had nothing to do with the hiring of the Pinkertons. Allerton explained that as chairman of the committee that had employed the Pinkertons, he did not feel that the packers could depend on either the sheriff of the Town of Lake or the governor to maintain order. Armour further said that his heart was with the men and he would like to keep the eight-hour day, but it put the Chicago packers in an unfair position vis-à-vis Kansas City and other western packing centers that worked the ten-hour day. Armour promised to return to the eight-hour day once the Knights obtained it in the other centers. Of course, Armour had had a plant in Kansas City sine 1871 and was not about to agree to the eight-hour day there either. Armour said that the beef trade, since it did not face the same competition that pork packing did, could continue on the eight-hour schedule for the time being. He further stated that while Morris and Swift had not moved against the eight-hour day given contractual obligations to maintain it among their beef butchers, they did support a return to the old ten-hour system and would follow in sixty days once the beef butcher contracts expired. Both meatpackers insisted on the unity of all of the companies.

At ten o'clock that morning, Armour's 1,300 cattle butchers walked out and joined the strike, preventing management's offer from dividing the workers. The striking cattle butchers took with them most of the carpenters, refrigerator car repairmen, mechanics, and even the firemen, when mangers asked them to load the refrigerator cars. This walkout further confused matters for Barry, who was furious with the men. Armour lashed out at Knights Local 7802 for breaking the beef butchers' contract and presented a signed testament by all the pork packers and John B. Sherman of the USY&T Company calling the Knights "unjust and unreasonable." Union representatives moved between the various Armour departments and called more men out on strike despite Barry's wishes. John Mulcahey and his "persuasion" committee stopped strikebreakers outside of Armour's plant. Fearing violence, strikebreakers often retreated. Armour waited out the strike, and he shipped twenty-five to thirty carloads of cattle from Chicago to

Cattle knocker preparing to stun cattle in Packingtown, circa 1900. Notice the meat inspector watching the process on the right. Two cattle were driven into the pens where the knocker waited above on a platform with a sledgehammer. Once the animals were knocked out, the pen wall lifted and workers shackled their hind legs to a pulley that lifted the stunned animal into the air on its way to the sticker. (Taken from F. W. Wilder, *The Modern Packinghouse* [Chicago, 1905].)

his plant in Milwaukee. The other packers threatened to bring in more strikebreakers.[23]

Barry informed Powderly that the workers, by calling out the beef butchers, had fallen into a trap set by the packers and that the strike faced defeat, as Pinkertons hired by the packers incited random acts of violence. The Town of Lake seemed under siege. Under orders from Powderly, Barry announced at Germania Hall in front of some two thousand men and their supporters that the men should return to work on October 19. When Barry claimed, "An honorable retreat is better than a defeat," bedlam broke loose, but the strike did end. The skilled workers received a fifty-cent-a-day winter increase, but had to work ten hours. Despite the settlement, clashes between workers and the retreating Pinkertons continued, with fatal consequences. On the afternoon of October 19, Pinkerton guards shot into a crowd and killed Terrence Begley, a self-employed teamster.

Barry settled due to his apparent belief that at least two packers might break with the others and agree to an eight-hour day. This opening could give the Knights a firm footing in the industry and allow them to later take on those packers who were refusing to treat with them at that point. Many workers hoped Butler would call a second strike after the November township elections, especially if he gained the sheriff's office or if he gained enough votes to give him a chance to be elected in the spring as a Town of Lake supervisor. Yet the *Daily Drovers Journal* proclaimed an unconditional victory for the packers, who told the strikers that the men who had replaced them would remain on the job. A member of the Knights claimed, however, "These men won't last long if we get back to work. When they see they cannot hold up their end with us they soon become ashamed and drop out. They would not feel very comfortable anyway if the regular men resumed their places." Many of the strikebreakers were hardly as skilled as those who had walked out, also obviously returning workers had ways of making the strikebreakers feel unwanted and intimidated in the plants.[24]

The eight-hour beef workers at both the Swift and Morris plants knew that management might emulate Armour and return to a ten-hour day. Gustavus Swift told reporters that both he and Nelson Morris stood with Armour and the other packers against the union. A delegation went to see both Swift and Morris, who informed them that their contract was null and void because of the cattle butchers' actions against Armour and Company, and that they would switch to the ten-hour day on November 1. The companies offered to increase skilled wages fifty cents and unskilled twenty-five cents per day, and were willing to try another contract if it included the ten-hour day and had a seven-day warning period on strike action. The workers agreed to the terms, and a contract was signed on October 28. The day the agreement went into effect, two butchers asked for more money, including one who had signed the compact, and Swift Superintendent Fred Wilder lost his temper and fired the signer immediately. The rest of Swift's butchers then struck the plant. Swift ordered Wilder to rehire the man and consented to wage increases on the unskilled level. As November 1 ended, rumors and confusion ran through the stockyards.

Meanwhile, Butler lost his bid for Town of Lake sheriff, but his United Labor Party elected some candidates to the state legislature. Critics condemned the party's radical call in its platform for the confiscation of the packinghouses, transferring their ownership to workers as the true creators of wealth. Not surprisingly, the *Chicago Tribune* told "honest" workingmen to turn their back on the Reds and to work hard and become involved in the business as entrepreneurs if they so wished. The newspaper restated the old charge, "The money paid in wages and wasted in the grogshops of Bridgeport during the last twenty years, if profitably used, would now amount to more than the fortunes of all the packers derived from their business in the region." The newspaper went on to say that Armour and the rest had acquired their wealth "by hard labor and patient industry." Of course, workers saw their situation differently and turned more to organizing than to taking the *Tribune*'s advice.[25]

Powderly, in New York, remained unaware of events in Chicago and did not catch up with news from the stockyards for some time. Barry could not contact the grand master and returned to the city without his permission. In the meantime, District Assembly 57 decided to flex its muscles. The assembly's leadership, including Edward Condon and John T. Joyce, proposed another strike. Several leaders opposed the move, as it violated the recent agreement with Morris and Swift, and this dissension split the union.

Events moved quickly thereafter. On Wednesday, November 3, the packers prepared for a possible confrontation and did not purchase hogs. The next day, the union held a mass rally and called for a general strike and the crowd shouted its approval. Butler issued the order for a second strike and wrote Powderly that now was the time to regain the eight-hour day. Nelson Morris proclaimed, "I am having cattle slaughtered at a dozen points in the East, and shall continue to do so as long as necessary." Swift in turn shipped live cattle east to supply their trade in Boston, Springfield, and Holyoke in Massachusetts, and to Albany and Troy in New York. The Packers' Association had amassed a fund of between $65,000 and $70,000 ($1.6 million to $1.8 million in 2014) to recall the Pinkertons to Packingtown, and they rallied government support as well. The recently reelected sheriff sent 150 deputies into the stockyards, while Governor Richard J. Oglesby sent two regiments of militia and they set up headquarters at the J. C. Ferguson warehouse. Meanwhile, workers voiced discontent with the way the first strike had ended and declared support for a second walkout.

The second strike began on November 6 as some twenty-five thousand workers left the packing plants, demanding a return to the eight-hour day. The two unnamed companies that Barry believed would break with Armour and the other packers stood firm and the Pinkertons returned to the Union Stock Yard. Barry arrived shortly after the Pinkertons did. Butler and Barry soon openly quarreled as Barry accused his fellow Knight of using the strike to promote himself in Town of Lake politics. On November 8, the packers, meeting at the Board of Trade, decided to fight the union but not the workers, thereby trying to divide the workers from the local Knights leadership. They resolved to hire only men loyal to the companies and not the union. Management demanded any worker they hired to renounce the Knights of Labor in order to drive them from the workforce. Armour was asked if he would reopen his plant; he retorted, "Oh yes, and we will settle this strike this time. We will settle this strike business among our old hands. We have got tired of strikes Monday before breakfast, and we will never have another one of them." Meanwhile, large crowds of strikers and their supporters gathered at the packinghouses and turned away those looking for employment.

On the evening of November 8, several companies of militia had marched to Halsted Street from their garrison in Packingtown as fights broke out along that strip just east of the Union Stock Yard. The militia cleared the street of all "loafers and hangers-on." Law enforcement officers guarded all of the entrances to both the Union Stock Yard and Packingtown, allowing entry to only those with business in the yards. Town of Lake Supervisor John E. Stanford ordered all taverns along Halsted Street closed. The packers signed a resolution on November 8 that all returning men would have to resign from all labor organizations. In response, the Knights of Labor issued a circular calling for order and reminding the strikers that the armed forces gathered in the yards could easily slaughter them in any confrontation. At 3 p.m., a crowd stopped and turned around a wagonload of cabbage intended as food for strikebreakers quartered in Armour's packinghouse. A brawl broke out in front of the Town of Lake police station on Halsted Street and constables arrested six armed men.

That Tuesday, November 9, the market for hogs collapsed as the strike proved effective in continuing to curtail operations. On that day, Barry also suggested an arbitration board be set up. Occasional skirmishes broke out between union men and strikebreakers, and the Executive Committee of Local Assembly 57 called for workers to stay away from the stockyards and to "boycott whiskey" to minimize disorder, which made the cause look bad to the general public. Meanwhile, nearly 1,200 militiamen and deputy sheriffs patrolled the yards as more strikebreakers arrived daily, including a large number of African Americans. At one point, a crowd of strikers got ugly and hurled racial epithets, but a Knight reminded them of a recent accord at the Richmond convention declaring equality between the races.

On November 11 at ten o'clock in the morning, a Grand Trunk train stopped at Forty-Ninth and Racine just to the south of the stockyards and militia escorted seven hundred strikebreakers down Center (Racine) Avenue to the packinghouses. Three hundred of the men went to Fowler's while the rest went to Armour's plant. At the same time, the militia held prisoners arrested on the streets in a stable at Fergusson's packinghouse. Obviously, the modern did not mean the end to barbaric conditions imposed by those with armed power on the weak.

That same day, twenty-three firms—including the USY&T Company—signed an agreement, somewhat tempering their earlier statement refusing to hire union men. Nevertheless, they stated that they had the right to hire whom they pleased. Barry wrote Powderly, "This is the Order's fight and must be won." Powderly, never a proponent of supporting strikes he saw as unwinnable, also saw the stockyard strike as illegitimate. The grand master workman disagreed with the martyrdom approach to labor conflicts, so on November 10 he had issued an order to end the strike. At first, the local Knights leadership denied that Powderly had called off the strike, but finally on Saturday, November 13, Barry called a meeting at the Germania Turner Hall and told the gathering the strike was over. The next day, local Knights' assemblies voted to return to work under protest of Powderly's actions. Many in the ranks of the Knights, especially in Chicago, disagreed with the grand master workman and wanted Powderly to throw his full support behind the strikers. Radicals condemned Powderly and many of the unskilled packinghouse workers believed that packers had bribed him. It took almost a week, but by November 19 Packingtown returned to normal, including the ten-hour day. Management made returning workers sign a contract promising two weeks' notice if they intended to leave their positions and requiring a week's wages to be placed in escrow as a guarantee of the contract. All but some forty men agreed to accept the terms. On November 17, the *Daily Drovers Journal* reported an attempt to poison Armour and his family, but made no connection to the strike.[26]

The conflict between labor and management was not settled, and eight years later in 1894 stockyard railroad workers boycotted the rail-roads in an event now known as the Pullman strike. The conflict grew quickly into a clash between workers, the railroads, and the packers. In early July, reports had Packingtown shut down. Armour, Morris, and Swift killed what livestock they had left. Crowds blocked rail lines going in and out of the stockyards. Troops arrived and fired upon crowds as they fought for control over the rail yards leading into the Square Mile. Thousands of protestors clashed with police, the army, and the state militia, destroying property throughout the Stock Yard District in perhaps the most violent strike in the city's history. Back of the Yards and Canaryville witnessed much of the fighting while federal troops camped out in Dexter Park as the combat escalated. Wrecked railroad cars lay along the tracks leading in and out of Packingtown as crowds gathered at Fortieth and Halsted and attacked police. By July 7, both cavalry and artillery units moved into position near Forty-Seventh and Halsted and that afternoon the militia opened fire on strikers and supporters at Forty-Ninth and Loomis, killing an unknown number of people. Martial law was firmly established, and the strike ended in defeat as trains loaded with chilled beef left the yards on July 10. The next day, regular livestock shipments resumed at the Union Stock Yard. Butchers later struck the packinghouses, but overall the strike was fin-ished. One result of the butchers strike was the introduction of women to more departments, and for the first time the company allowed them to use the knife, the butchers' most symbolic tool.

The 1894 strike recalled the 1877 conflict rather than the 1886 Knights of Labor–led shutdown. Hardly well organized, it resembled mob action as the frustration of working-class citizens spontaneously erupted across the stockyard neighborhoods. They had demonstrated in sympathy with the Pullman workers, but had little formal leadership and much less institutional support. The crowds of men and women workers of Canaryville and Back of the Yards grew into an angry mob, which raised the specter of anarchy to the general public. Such conflict and fears were part of the birth of the modern.[27]

By the 1890s, the neighborhood to the south and west of Packing-town sometimes referred to as New City, but more commonly called Back of the Yards, had begun to fill up with working-class housing. In 1883, Samuel E. Gross began building affordable housing between Forty-Fifth and Forty-Seventh Streets and Loomis and Ashland in the Square Mile. These wooden one-story cottages stood above grade and on twenty-foot lots. After 1885, multifamily dwellings appeared in the neighborhood. Soon much of Back of the Yards became a neighborhood of small tenements rather than cottages. By the 1890s, the neighborhood resembled a western frontier settlement rather than a city neighborhood with dirt streets, ramshackle wooden structures, and wooden sidewalks.[28]

Mary Eliza McDowell came to Back of the Yards to head the University of Chicago Settlement House in 1894. She arrived on September 17 in the midst of the stockyard strike in support of the Pullman workers. Blood had already been shed in the neighborhood as McDowell settled in as head resident. In 1896, the University Settlement rented four small flats at 4638 South Ashland Avenue above a feed store. McDowell faced a neighborhood that seemed to be in constant flux as immigration and technology changed the neighborhood. Her goal of being a good neighbor pitted her against the worst of the modern as it transformed the area. McDowell struggled to deal with the various challenges faced by the neighborhood. As environmental historian Sylvia Hood Washington has pointed out, Mary McDowell eventually took on the sobriquet of "Garbage Lady," as she emerged as the neighborhood's great environmental activist and struggled to remove the huge dumps that the city located in Back of the Yards along Robey Street (Damen Avenue).[29]

The late nineteenth century saw the emergence of the modern in many ways. The structural shifts that appeared in the twentieth century were born in places like the Union Stock Yards and Packingtown in the last quarter of the nineteenth century. As cattlemen opened the West and took advantage of the nation's natural resources, molding a new capitalist dynamic on the vast ranges, so too did entrepreneurs change the basic way that Americans, and others, understood food. An enormous ecological and economic change took place, centered first on hogs and then on cattle and sheep. The creation of the disassembly lines and the development of technology on the kill floors, as well as throughout the meatpacking plants; vast transportation changes, such as the development of refrigerated cars—all of this together created large-scale national corporations. In turn, the labor movement evolved as a response to an America fundamentally changed by the capitalist and technological revolutions of the last half of the nineteenth century.

The 1886 strike was, in many ways, the first modern labor clash in the Union Stock Yard and Packingtown. It was led by an organization that attempted to unite workers beyond ethnic, racial, gender, and skill boundaries, something not seen in previous conflicts. The 1886 strike involved both the skilled and unskilled men, although once again in its aftermath labor fragmented along those lines, as well as ethnic, racial, and gender divisions. Furthermore, the Knights attempted to control labor violence and conflicts with both management and the state. These methods would prove crucial to future unionization efforts. Every strike situation included three active players: workers—organized or not; management; and the state. In most cases in the post–Civil War era, the state supported management. The 1894 conflict was a throwback to earlier confrontations between unorganized and violent workers and management, with its ally, the state. As historian Louise Wade has pointed out, there was no feasible way to rebuild a packinghouse workers' organization once it was broken. The Haymarket affair and the stockyard conflict of 1886 brought Chicago firmly into the modern. The strike presented a modern organizational form even if not fully developed in the Knights of Labor. It also presented the power of the modern combinations of corporations to fight the union. Armour's leadership achieved unity among the packers in their opposition to the union. Those companies that wavered were soon brought into the fold. Modern industrial America emerged out of the clashes of the late nineteenth century as did the workers' response of organizing and demanding their rights.[30]

4

"SUCCESS COMES TO THOSE WHO HUSTLE WISELY"

The Emergence of the Greatest Livestock Market in the World

The enormous increase in the capacity and performance of the stockyards and its dependent and tributary plants is not measurable in its growth of area nor even in the extraordinary quantity of live stock daily uploaded within its limits. The application of every swift and ingenious device of modern machinery is one of the best explanations of its astounding performance. Millions of meat creatures are literally shot from the stock cars into the soldered, labeled cans of the packing establishments. Today you can buy buttons on Halsted Street that yesterday were galloping over the chutes of the stockyards.

JONAS HOWARD, *Chicago Tribune*, October 10, 1904

Hog Butcher for the World,
Tool Maker, Stacker of Wheat,
Player with Railroads and the Nation's Freight Handler;
Stormy, husky, brawling,
City of the Big Shoulders

CARL SANDBURG, "Chicago" (1914)

*

After the 1886 strike, the packers felt free to develop their industrial power without resistance from organized labor. The thirty-five years from 1890 to 1925, while not without industrial and labor conflict (1894, 1904, and 1921–22 would see major strikes) was a period of almost unlimited growth for the industry. During that time, Chicago secured its position as both the nation's most important livestock market and its leading packing center. These heady years witnessed the expansion of the city's reach across the country as railroads expanded and solidified the national systems to move both raw materials and finished goods. The packers continued to oppose organized labor, and the public came to perceive them as robber barons. Earlier trends in immigration streams persisted, although their sources shifted, as the packinghouses required more unskilled labor. While some labeled this era as the "golden years" of the industry, others saw it in the darkest terms. The publication of Upton Sinclair's muckraking novel *The Jungle* (1906) and subsequent government investigations represented the peak of criticism and controversy. Despite these challenges, the industry sustained its growth, and livestock receipts at the Union Stock Yard reached their height in the early 1920s.

Expansion and Growth

Building on its earlier advances, the USY&T Company continued to expand. Within sixteen years of its opening, the capital stock of the corporation increased from $1 million to $13.2 million ($14.5 million to $307 million in 2014) and the trading in livestock which had initially taken part primarily on the north side of Exchange Avenue gradually spread south. By 1896, the Union Stock Yard had grown from 120 acres of pens, railroad docks, and buildings to 340 acres, which included five thousand pens, stables, as well as the other structures required for the market. The combined territory of Packingtown and the stockyards increased to some 560 acres, even as 80 acres in the southwest corner of the Square Mile developed as housing and as a cabbage field.

One writer claimed that nearly 40,000 men, women, and children worked in the square mile that made up the Union Stock Yard proper and the adjacent Packingtown. Most Chicagoans commonly referred to the entire area as simply "the yards." W. Joseph Grand asserted that one-fourth of Chicago's population of nearly 2 million people received support directly or indirectly from the industry. The stockyard company itself employed over 1,000 men and women. In addition, over 200 commission firms employed some 3,500 salesmen, stenographers, typists, bookkeepers, accountants, messengers, brokers, and others. More than 30,000 labored in the packinghouses. This legion of workers and their families in turn encouraged local businesses such as saloons, grocery stores, retail stores, and the like in the surrounding

Dexter Park Pavilion (Dexter Park International Amphitheater) fronted on Halsted Street south of the Transit House. Horse barns and the market stood behind the massive structure. (Postcard, Author's Collection.)

neighborhoods, all dependent on the meatpacking industry for their livelihood.[1]

Adding to its regular market business, the USY&T Company built a new pavilion on Halsted Street for the horse market, which had grown from a rather modest beginning in the early 1870s. By the 1890s, some 1,500 horses moved through the stockyards every market day. It drew visitors from around the world, and more horses were sold there than in any other market. Horses purchased on the Chicago market provided much of the muscle for transportation and deliveries across urban areas in the nineteenth century as well as for farmwork, breeding, and racing. Buyers gathered to view the animals in the stables behind the Transit House. The USY&T Company erected the Dexter Park Horse Exchange and Pavilion at a cost of over $100,000 ($2.6 million in 2014). It contained a display track thirty-six feet wide and over five hundred feet long covered by an iron dome and skylight, and included an amphitheater, which could seat 3,000 people. Arc and incandescent electric lights lit the building, which housed an elegant lunch counter, and all facilities needed by a first-rate horse market.[2]

The Dexter Park Pavilion, like its predecessor the Dexter Park racetrack, drew people to the stockyards, but it too proved too small for the needs of the horse market, and later for the International Livestock Show established in 1900. In 1905, the USY&T Company built a new structure, at times also referred to as the Dexter Park Pavilion, and at other times as the Dexter Park or International Amphitheater. The massive structure was 660 by 310 feet, with an auditorium that ran 310 feet by 200 feet with a 260 by 100 foot arena with a capacity of 10,000 people. The USY&T Company built the 243,000-square-foot, supposedly fireproof building at a cost of $326,000 ($8.8 million) out of brick, steel, and glass.

Being fireproof was an important feature since several times fire had destroyed the Dexter Park Horse Exchange and Pavilion. At 2:45 p.m. on October 6, 1897, just two days before the annual commemoration of the Great Chicago Fire of 1871, a fire broke out in the horse market, destroyed some $71,000 ($2 million) in property, and killed several people. The huge barn, which extended from Forty-Third Street to Forty-Fifth Street, contained some two thousand horses at the time. Miraculously, only six or seven horses died in the fire, as about one hundred stockyard workers on horseback brought the animals to safety in the cattle pens to the west. The fire threatened to jump over Forty-Third Street and ignite the Horse Pavilion. A strong gale carried burning embers across Halsted Street and into Canaryville; numerous buildings, all two-story wooden-frame structures, soon burst into flames. Winds carried flaming embers as far as Wallace Street, while smoke filled the neighborhood making it hard to see or breathe. The conflagration destroyed six stables and a small auction amphitheater as well as several hundred tons of hay and feed.

Two years later in September 1899, another fire produced about $300,000 ($8.5 million in 2014) in damages. The fire flattened twelve acres of property of the Union Stock Yard; even causing roughly $30,000 ($857,143) in loses to the Transit House. This conflagration also destroyed the stockyard company's hospital and several residential structures. The USY&T Company rebuilt the horse market, which by the turn of the century dealt with one hundred thousand horses annually. The large number of wooden stockyard structures often filled with hay and other combustible material presented a constant danger to animals and humans alike.[3]

Despite the fires, the Union Stock Yard continued to grow. The *Thirty-Fifth Annual Livestock Report of the Union Stock Yard and Transit Company* detailed the growth of the stockyards by 1900. The account of the physical plant gave the capacity of the nearly 500 acres of the market as 75,000 cattle, 80,000 sheep, 300,000 hogs, and 6,000 horses. Of those 500 acres, 420 were planked or bricked and contained

13,000 uncovered pens and 8,500 double-decked or covered pens with 25,000 gates. Two hundred and fifty miles of railway lie within the yards itself. More than 400 million head of livestock had been received since that Christmas Day in 1865 at a total value of $5.5 billion ($157.1 billion). Six years later, the number of livestock handled would increase to more than 16 million annually, and the total value would jump by roughly $2 million.

By that time, the entire stockyard had been bricked; the wooden planked pens a thing of the past. A water system served the stockyards with ninety miles of pipelines and fifty miles of sewer lines. The water tower had a capacity of 30,000 gallons, and the pumps a daily capacity of 8 million gallons. If all the water troughs for animals were laid end to end, they would run for twenty-five miles. On a hot day, the market consumed about 7 million gallons of water. Some 450 arc lamps and 10,000 incandescent lamps lit the stockyards at night. Four banks were necessary to serve the Union Stock Yard. In addition, near the main entrance, the Record Building housed the chronicles of most of the livestock associations of the United States as well as the home of the prestigious Saddle and Sirloin Club, a private club to which the principal packers, commission men, bankers, and officers of the USY&T Company belonged. The Square Mile truly was a city, if not a world unto itself.[4]

Institutional Growth

The number of financial transactions at the Union Stock Yard and the need for some assurance of honesty necessitated an overseer of operations beyond the USY&T Company. That company's main job remained to furnish the facilities, take care of the animals placed in its trust, and organize the operations of the market itself. The pioneer organization known as the Chicago Livestock Exchange emerged out of a need to defend the livestock trade in various disputes against dishonest or disreputable buyers and sellers, or unjust discrimination in railroad rates. The exchange also regularized the commissions for selling livestock. Organized in 1885, the exchange encouraged the production, sale, and distribution of livestock and meat products. It also acted to ensure the uniformity of business procedures on the market, adequate inspection of animals and meat, and to promote legislation to protect the industry against what it considered unnecessary outside regulation. The exchange enforced a rigorous code of conduct and made sure that the market worked honestly and profitably. It could ban dishonest men from buying and selling on the market and worked hard to gain the trust of livestock shippers to the Union Stock Yard. Modern capitalism demanded such regulation, if not from the government, then from the industry itself. This of course fit well with Sherman's earlier move to guarantee transparency in the dealings between producer, commission men, and buyers.[5]

In another sign of the rise of the modern, concerned outsiders promoted the careful handling of livestock in the yards and to guarantee their adequate watering and feeding both during transportation and in the stockyards. Edwin Lee Brown of Englewood and John C. Dore founded the Illinois Humane Society in 1870 with the help of Dore's college friend George T. Angell, the president of the Massachusetts Society for the Prevention of Cruelty to Animals. Angell arrived in Chicago on October 1, 1870, and visited the stockyards, where he witnessed various cruelties to animals. He went about, with Dore's help, contacting various Chicago newspapers and laid the groundwork for the society. The new organization closely resembled those established in other states. Dore, however, focused on the transportation of animals by the railroads to market; in 1869, he had helped obtain a state law requiring that all livestock be unloaded, fed, and watered every twenty-eight hours as they made their way across Illinois by rail. But the reformers needed more than the Illinois regulation as most animals sent to the Chicago market crossed state lines. In 1872, Angell published *Cattle Transportation in the United States*. The pamphlet shocked the American public, with the depiction of the treatment of cattle shipped by rail across the country, and alarmed livestock shippers, who feared a public reaction to the prevailing conditions and possible government regulation. In 1873, Congress responded with a federal law based on the Illinois statue.

In September 1871, the Illinois Humane Society brought Patrick Ryder and Thomas Hanlon, proprietors of a so-called second-class slaughterhouse near the Union Stock Yards, before the courts on the charge of cruelty to animals. Patrick Clark testified that he worked for Ryder and Hanlon, who purchased hogs at the Union Stock Yards and treated them with unnecessary brutality. Livestock handlers drove healthy hogs up to a pen some seven or eight feet high, workers hoisted sick ones by steam, and brought those who could not walk in a wagon and inserted a hook into their lower jaw and lifted them to the pen for slaughter. One eyewitness said that gangs elevated between ten and twenty hogs a day in this manner. Various witnesses testified that they thought this method not torture, but a necessity. Nevertheless, the court fined Ryder and Hanlon $30 ($577 in 2014) each.

The Humane Society kept an agent at the Union Stock Yards to keep an eye on conditions in the market and the packinghouses. In 1874, the society reported that it had admonished nearly two thousand persons for unnecessary cruelty to animals. The society's report focused especially on brutality at the Union Stock Yards, and sent an appeal to local clergy urging them to preach at least once a year upon the duty of kindness to animals. The report pointed out that the Stockyard general superintendent, John B. Sherman, aided the society's agent in his investigations and served as a member of the board of directors. Both the USY&T Company and the meatpackers feared that public opinion would rise up against them and result in further regulation or a lack of trust in the quality of their product. For this reason, both the Union Stock Yard and the larger companies allowed the Illinois Humane Society to inspect their facilities.

Over a six-month period in 1879, Zadok Street, an Illinois Humane Society investigator, traveled for more than eighteen thousand miles on the railroads that carried livestock to Chicago. Street told of abominable conditions along the railroad lines, of mud-filled pens crowded with livestock that were neither fed nor watered after being driven to the railheads. Many shippers drove the animals and shipped them to markets where they were then given great amounts of water so that they weighed in heavy. Street praised the Chicago Stockyards, but warned that animals shipped from there hardly had time to be adequately fed or watered before being put on trains to the East Coast, and he complained of the way workers treated crippled animals.

The Humane Society also reported on the tremendous financial loss shouldered as a result of poor conditions and pointed out that shrinkage and sick animals presented a problem for the commission men who worked the yards. It argued that Chicago should lead the way toward humane treatment, which was both good in itself and potentially more profitable for all concerned. That year the society, with Sherman's permission, printed notices to be posted in the cattle pens concerning the proper handling of animals. Sherman gave the Humane Society offices in the Stone Gate and allowed them to inspect conditions throughout the Union Stock Yards. The society continued to frequently make charges against individuals who did not feed or water livestock in the Union Stock Yards. In 1882, Humane Society officers charged Adolf Hess, a buyer for the Nelson Morris Company, with not feeding or watering three hundred cattle for several days. They also saw to the arrest of John Halpin, a drover, charged with allowing a cow to go without food for two days.[6]

The International Livestock Exposition

Another institution also appeared that built upon the showmanship that was already evident in the early days of the Union Stock Yard and increased the sense of spectacle in the Square Mile while encouraging developments in the livestock industry. The Union Stock Yard and Transit Company and John B. Sherman in particular encouraged a series of livestock exhibitions in the nineteenth century. As early as 1871, livestock dealers convinced the USY&T Company to sponsor a swine exhibition at Dexter Park. Seven years later, the Illinois State Board of Agriculture established a Chicago Fat Stock Show. At first, it displayed fancy Christmas cattle only: no breeding stock, no draft horses, just big finished bullocks. The Fat Stock Show drew breeders from across the country as well as Canada and England. John D. Gillett's shorthorn bullock, nicknamed "Sherman," won the top award for the best animal in all categories. John B. Sherman purchased the animal for $1,000 and used it for Christmas beef at the Transit House. The shorthorn attained immortality in 1879 as his likeness adorned the new Stone Gate entryway to the Union Stock Yard. It remains there today, looking down Exchange Avenue.[7]

The 1882 Fat Stock Show claimed to be the finest assemblage of cattle ever put on display in the United States. Stockmen put a total of 482 animals on exhibit at the Exposition Building located on the downtown lakefront, a 59 percent increase over the previous year. The *Daily Drovers Journal* complained that few Chicagoans had shown interest in the exposition over the years, but a record number of people now flocked to see the exhibits. The reported attendance, in addition to those given free tickets, numbered over 3,200. The 1882 show was the first to cover its cost and make a profit. In 1885, the Fat Stock Show included an American Dairy Show and the following year added the American Horse Show.[8]

The display briefly became nationally popular, but ceased in the 1890s because of the demolition of the lakefront building, for the construction of the Chicago Art Institute at the time of the 1893 Columbian Exposition. Both breeders and the public showed a great degree of disappointment in the abandonment of the stock show, and the stockyard company decided to pursue the possibility of another larger livestock exposition to improve relations with livestock producers and maintain their lead among the various terminal markets in the Midwest.[9] The USY&T Company constantly worked to promote itself to both the rural and urban public.

William E. Skinner, an employee of the USY&T Company, who had a wide contact with stockmen across the United States and Canada, played an important role in bringing the various constituencies together to create the new livestock show. After much talk concerning the how and why of the exposition, interested parties met in the Exchange Building in 1899. The stockyard company asked each to put up $100 as a show of support. The Board of Directors invited a foreign judge to participate in the contest to make sure that no prejudice existed in favor of one or another producer. Not only did this gesture increase the likelihood of a fair contest, but it also gave the show an international profile.

The International Livestock Exposition first took place in 1900 and immediately became the primary showcase for livestock in the United States. Held in the stockyard's Dexter Park amphitheater and twenty adjoining buildings, the show brought up to an unheard of 10,000 animals to compete for roughly 2,600 prizes which amounted to more than $75,000 ($2.1 million in 2014). Producers were awarded special prizes trophies, and badges of honor for their livestock. Nearly four hundred thousand people attended the exhibition during its first year.

As early as 1904, commentators saw the benefits of the exposition for the livestock industry. The International Livestock Exposition, often simply called the International, stressed the importance of modern scientific feeding and breeding practices. It encouraged the thoroughbred rather than the "scrub" animal. By improving the standards of "blood and handling," American meat could dominate the world market. The fair also promoted the idea that the "best bred, fattest, and sleekest cattle produced the most profit." It encouraged importers and breeders of fancy stock, and emphasized the importance of the federal government in the development of scientific forage farming and economic breeding. The exposition prizes attracted ambitious breeders from across the country and also lured the headquarters of the major breeders' associations to Chicago. The stockyard company built the Pure Bred Livestock Building at a cost of $100,000 ($2.7 million in 2014) to house these organizations.

Changes in the livestock industry itself brought about the International Livestock Exposition; the exhibit then encouraged more changes. A more structured type of life spread across the West in the late nineteenth and early twentieth centuries. By 1900, the days of the large cattle drives freely feeding on open ranges owned by the federal government had begun to pass. The old herds that roamed the open ranges produced a lesser quality of beef, more stringy and not as good tasting as meat from more carefully raised animals. Landowners fenced in their property, and smaller producers replaced the large cattle barons. The cost of raising cattle rose as these livestock men bred smaller but higher-quality meat herds. They invested in covered barns to protect cattle from the elements and grew their own crops to feed them. The International helped to bring the idea of the modern to rural areas. Cattle should be raised in an economical, efficient way, and the federal government could play an important role in bringing this about. While a romantic idea about pastoral farm life might persist in the popular mind, farmers had long before entered the capitalist market system embracing not only machinery, but also modern methods concerning livestock breeding. The Chicago exposition simply expanded on these and acted as an educational tool across the Midwest and West.[10] Another sign of the influence of the modern was the inclusion in the show early on of educational exhibits from the U.S. Department of Agriculture, various agricultural colleges and experiment stations, and from other educational institutions.

Beyond its influence on the industry, the International captured both the rural and urban public's imagination, and some of its glory accrued to the Union Stock Yard. In 1941, Alvin H. Sanders, one of the founders and vice president of the International Livestock Exposition Association, wrote that the show "offers an added attraction to all visitors that vast spectacle, the greatest livestock market place in either hemisphere, the Union Stock Yards." In 1900, it proved to be one of the chief topics of conversation at the National Live Stock Association meeting in Fort Worth, Texas. The Chicago delegation handed out a much sought after souvenir emblazoned with the words, "Success

This medal handed out by the USY&T Company at the 1923 International Live-
stock Exposition is inscribed with the term "Success Comes to Those Who Hustle
Wisely," which had been a motto of the show since its earliest days. (Artifact,
Author's Collection.)

Comes to Those Who Hustle Wisely." The USY&T Company certainly
knew how to hustle wisely as it promoted itself as "the" livestock market in the country.[11]

The International proved to be an immediate success. In 1902, organizers and railroad managers estimated that thousands of people from
outside of Chicago would visit the third annual exposition. Eighteen
state governors announced plans to attend, and eleven agricultural
colleges sent students and faculty to Chicago. Even Germany sent a
delegation of faculty and students. While few farmers arrived until
after the formal opening, thousands of city dwellers attended the first
days of the 1902 exhibition. The number of Chicagoans going down to
the stockyard to see a bit of rural life clogged the elevated rail lines and
streetcars, and filled the exposition hall. On the evening of the formal
opening, Secretary of Agriculture James Wilson delivered the principal address at the dedication of the Pure Bread Live Stock Record
Building. Those who hoped to move the International Livestock Exposition from under the financial sponsorship of the Union Stock Yard
to some other venue and perhaps even to have it moved annually to
different cities argued with those who thought that such a decision
would be folly. Critics called the livestock show the "exposition of the
union stockyards."[12]

Year after year, the annual presentation grew in popularity with
not only producers, but with Chicagoans and others who visited the

Red ribbon for canning budget competition, 1938 International Livestock Exposition. (Artifact, Author's Collection.)

city. On November 30, 1904, a record crowd of over seventy thousand people surged through the doors of the Dexter Park Pavilion and Amphitheater to witness the grand opening. General von Loewenfeld, the personal representative of the German kaiser, attended the extravaganza. John H. Spoor, the president of the exposition, entertained the general and his party at the Saddle and Sirloin Club.[13] The following year, 2,805 horses, cattle, swine, and sheep made their way into the new exposition hall built for the International. The modern structure made an even larger International possible, the largest aggregation of prize animals ever collected under one roof. The show ring for the Horse Fair, the evening feature of the International, was forty feet broader and ten feet longer than the Chicago Coliseum ring on South Wabash Avenue. High advance sales proved that Chicagoans wanted to visit the new structure and the larger improved livestock exposition. On the night of the grand opening, stockyard workers put on a show and competed in livestock driving contests.[14]

The show's popularity continued to grow. In 1909, the International Livestock Exposition featured the annual meeting of twenty-six breeders' associations. Railroads agreed to charge the lowest passenger rates ever granted from twenty-two states to Chicago during the fair. Organizers expected 250,000 out-of-town visitors to attend the exhibition. They invited William Heap, the president of the British Meat Dealers United Association of London, to judge the grade and crossbred cattle as well as to select the blue-ribbon grand champion steers. Heap stated, "This show passes anything I have ever seen for magnitude, nowhere on earth except in Chicago can be seen the four great breeds of horses, Shire, Clydesdale, Belgian and Percheron."[15]

Despite its rousing successes, a breakout out of hoof-and-mouth disease cancelled the International Livestock Exposition in 1914 and 1915. Producers enthusiastically greeted its return in 1916, and the directors kept expanding the show and adding other features to attract farmers to Chicago. In 1918, they added a seed corn show to the attractions. Planners felt that more attractions than cattle, sheep, and hog contests had to be presented. The first such showcase included a horse show. Later performances included a collie dog sheepherding demonstration. The International Grain and Hay Show joined the livestock exposition in 1919. In the 1920s, the National Live Stock and Meat Board presented an exhibit on meat that became a regular feature of the annual exposition. Directors introduced a wool show in 1928. All of these various displays added to the spectacle of the Union Stock Yard and made it a destination for hundreds of thousands of spectators and visitors annually.[16] In 1924, WLS Radio, owned and operated by Sears, Roebuck and Company, announced that it would broadcast the winners from the livestock exposition. Sears also planned to publish a daily newspaper with news from the International. WLS Radio broadcast the National Boys and Girls Club banquet in 1927, from the Sherman House in the Loop held in connection with the livestock show. The International showed how the modern had even transformed rural America. Indeed, the counsel that "Success Comes to Those Who Hustle Wisely" proved to be true for the Union Stock Yard as well as for the city of Chicago.[17]

The Big Six

Changes not only on the farm, but also in the meatpacking industry altered the nature of the livestock industry. Concentration continued at a fast pace, and by 1905 six western packers dominated meatpacking: Armour, Swift, Morris, National Packing, Schwarzschild and Sulzberger (S&S), and Cudahy. All except Cudahy had major plants in Chicago. The public often referred to these meatpacking companies as the "Big Six." The growth of these firms depended on the development of the refrigerated railcar, which allowed them to expand their reach across the country and beyond its borders. They maintained large branch houses to distribute their products in cities and towns through which they marketed as wholesalers; the greatest proportion of their products were dressed beef. All of these establishments, however, slaughtered enormous numbers of cattle, hogs, sheep, and calves. Most also did an extensive business in the purchase, storage, and sale of dairy products, eggs, and poultry as well, while some engaged in other related industries.

These packers retained private car lines to move their goods to markets: the six companies owned about twenty-five thousand refrigerated railroad cars in 1900. The average distance beef traveled did not exceed eight hundred miles. An average car of dressed beef weighed at least twenty-thousand pounds. Refrigerated cars needed to be re-iced every day or two of their journey. The major packers maintained icing stations along the railway lines for the four or five days required to ship chilled beef between Chicago and New York. They paid the ordinary freight rates on their products, but in turn the railroad paid a rental fee for the use of each car. This gave the large companies a great advantage in supplying meat to eastern markets. In addition, two of the Chicago packers transported enormous quantities of poultry, dairy products, vegetables, and fruits in their cars and so became extensive dealers in these products. Armour and Company operated the largest fleet of refrigerated cars, totaling nearly fourteen thousand. At an average valuation of $800 ($22,857 in 2014) the total investment in the Armour Car Lines stood at approximately $10 million ($285.7 million). The addition of Armour's Continental Fruit Express added another $1.3 million ($37.1 million) to this sum. Swift and Company maintained over five thousand cars. Capitalism and technology spurred each other on in the creation of the modern.[18]

The first era of refrigeration should more properly be referred to as the period of natural-ice refrigeration, since the packers used ice gathered from the streams and glacial lakes of the Midwest. In the 1890s, the development of mechanical refrigeration created a new era in the history of Chicago's packinghouses. Now not as dependent on Mother Nature's ice, the packers once again transformed the industry. Not only did refrigeration first open a national market for the large packers, but also the innovation of mechanical refrigeration brought about a larger role for scientists and engineers in the industry. The large packers had to employ engineers, bacteriologists, and other experts to work to maintain equipment as well as meet quality and safety standards.

Technological improvements constantly altered the industry. Originally, Chicago workers moved carcasses by hand on overhead rails. The speed of the process was irregular and production was slipshod. The packers devoted much time to innovate labor-saving equipment that would make everything as regular and predictable as possible. Management first installed an endless chain to move the bodies by power around the killing floor, probably the first time any industry attempted to control by a power source the flow of raw product during any manufacturing process. With the endless chain and refrigeration, the plant necessary to power these innovations became one of the most important features of any packinghouse.[19]

The numbers of animals sold to packers at Chicago and the number shipped from that terminal market to off-market slaughterhouses show that refrigeration had a tremendous impact on the livestock business. In 1866, the first full year of the market's operation, the Union Stock Yard received 393,007 head of cattle and shipped 263,693 (or 67 percent) to off-market packers. In 1867, the Chicago Stockyard shipped 61.8 percent; in 1868, it conveyed 66.5 percent of cattle sold on the market to off-market slaughterhouses. The shipment of cattle from Chicago to eastern markets remained relatively steady: as late as 1881, 62.6 percent of the cattle received in Chicago left for the East.

Three years later, the percentage had dropped to 43.5 percent as the Chicago packers used technology to dominate the chilled beef trade. Throughout the 1880s, the percentage shipped to off-market packers continued to decline until it stabilized at just below 30 percent.[20]

The numbers for hogs and sheep followed a similar pattern. In 1866, 961,746 hogs and 207,987 sheep arrived at the Union Stock Yard, and 50.2 percent of the hogs and 36.2 percent of the sheep moved east. Hog receipts grew at a very fast pace and in 1871 for the first time passed 2 million. Nearly 49 percent of these hogs continued on to packers outside of Chicago. The following year, the number of hogs counted more than 3 million, and over 56 percent went on to other destinations. In 1873, the market continued to grow, and hog receipts numbered 4.4 million with 49.5 percent shipped elsewhere. It seemed as if the number of hogs available at the Chicago Stockyards was unlimited: in 1880, 7 million hogs arrived in Chicago, but by then only 19.7 percent were shipped. The market remained steady reaching a peak number of hog receipts in 1923 with 10.4 million hogs arriving at the Chicago market and 22.6 percent moving on to other markets and packers. On December 15, 1924, a one-day record for hog receipts was set at 122,749 head, and a record number 3 million or 28.6 percent of hogs went to off-market packers that year. Actual arrivals in 1924, including hogs sent directly to Chicago packers and not to be sold on the market, topped the previous year with 11 million hogs unloaded at the stockyard train docks. After 1924, the number of hog receipts declined. Sheep runs followed comparable statistics peaking in 1910 with almost as many sheep as hogs showing up for sale at Chicago. Nearly 29 percent of those sheep left the yards for off-market packers. Two years later, a record 6 million sheep arrived at market, and 28.8 percent were shipped elsewhere. Most livestock reached the Union Stock Yard by train throughout the thirty-five-year period 1885 to 1920. In 1890, the greatest number of carloads arrived at the stockyards as livestock handlers unloaded 311,557 livestock railcars and loaded another 185,439 to other markets or packers.[21]

While refrigeration allowed the Chicago packers to dominate the nation's meat markets, other advances in the development of by-products also transformed the industry. Before the Civil War, packers simply discarded most of what they considered waste. They dumped grease and blood as well as offal in the Chicago River or in nearby fields, causing noxious smells and health problems. Increasingly, these by-products came to be seen as moneymaking parts of the industry, providing the larger meatpackers with yet another economic scale advantage. The often-told story of August Swift walking along Bubbly Creek to see how much waste flowed from his plant into the Chicago River's West Fork may be a Back of the Yards myth, but like all myths, it shows something important. Supposedly, Swift rushed back to the slaughterhouse to discover the source of the waste and made sure that his employees stopped the practice and used grease and offal for profit. Certainly, early on Swift understood the role that by-products could play his bottom line. His invitation to his colleague Lucius Bowles Darling to establish a rendering plant in Chicago in 1882, with Swift as one of the partners, and then his attempt to purchase the company speaks to his awareness. The Darling family held on to control of the company until 1903 when Lucius Bowles Darling Jr. sold his interests to Edward Morris, the son of Nelson Morris. Edward Morris had wed Gus Swift's daughter, Helen, so in a way a branch of the Swifts again became partners in that rendering company.[22]

Generally speaking, by-products consisted of a wide variety of goods ranging from hides to horns to the pineal glands taken from the brains of a steer; they comprised basically anything produced on the killing floor other than dressed meat. Chicago's major packers differed as to what by-products they produced. In 1905, Armour and Company produced sandpaper—a means of utilizing some of the glue manufactured—and numerous chemical preparations, such as pepsin. By-products from cattle included hides, glue from sinews, blood meal lubricating oil, soap, inedible tallow, inedible gelatin, candles, stearin, sausage casings, pituitary tablets, calf drumheads, buttons, neat's-foot oil, bonemeal, granulated bone, combs, pipes, and hair clips, among others. Hogs produced glue, oil, bone lime, benzoinated lard, hair for mattresses, gloves, pig's foot oil, sausage casings, and a host of other products. In turn, sheep also provided glue, meat meal, mutton tallow, tennis strings, soap, cello and violin strings, and more.[23]

But the early efforts to produce by-products were not the most efficient. Rendering companies often located near packinghouses and began to process their waste. Large refineries took the nonuniform, steam-rendered lard from packers, refined and bleached it, and sold it on the open market. Butterine (a butter substitute) manufacturers used neutral lard and oleo oil from packing plants for the manufacture of oleomargarine, a cheap butter substitute for urban consumers.

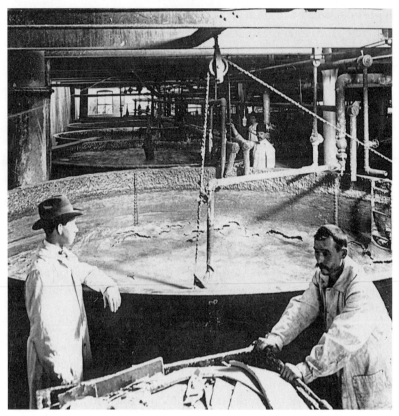

Men preparing soap kettles in a Chicago packinghouse. Soap became an important by-product of the meatpacking industry in the years after the Civil War. (Stereopticon, Author's Collection.)

In turn, soap manufactories bought various grades of tallow from the plants, while fertilizer plants carted off the pressed tankage and raw or pressed blood, dried and sold it, or manufactured mixed fertilizer from it. Glue works made their products from bones, sinews, and other animal parts. As these firms became more and more profitable, the larger packers either acquired or competed against them. While major meat products fueled the terrific growth of the packing industry in the 1890s, by-products increasingly played a larger role in the Square Mile.[24]

Hides and skins had afforded the first, and most obvious and important, by-product of the packing industry. Values differed according to species and type of livestock, but experts generally figured that at the time of World War One they provided 10 to 12 percent of the gross value of packinghouse products. Observers estimated that hides made up roughly one-third of all profits from by-products in the 1920s.

In the packing industry, hides and skins fell into three classes, according to sizes: hides, kips, and skins. Hides comprised the pelts from large mature animals such as cattle. They provided thick and heavy leather that could be used for shoe soles, machinery belting, harnesses, and other products where stiffness, strength, and wearing qualities were needed. Split hides also produced shoe uppers, and bag, case, strap, automobile, carriage, furniture, and upholstery leathers. Kips came from immature or undersized cattle, and small animals such as calves, sheep, and goat provided the skins. These both yielded a lighter type of leather used for a variety of products such as pocketbooks, bookbinding, shoe uppers, and gloves.[25]

Hides provided the most valuable by-product derived from cattle. Skins fell under various complicated classifications, but were still part of the rationalization of the modern industry. Workers removed packer hides uniformly, and made them available in great numbers so that buyers could purchase several thousand of a particular grade at one time. Cattle hide categories included those from steers, cows, bulls, and kips. The industry further subdivided these into native, Colorado, and Texas hides. Packinghouses discounted kosher hides because of the deep cut in the throat necessitated by the religious ritual demanded for the slaughtering of cattle for the Jewish trade. Various other discounts depended on whether or not hides had been infected by grubs, carried a considerable amount of tare in the form of manure or dirt, or had been accidently damaged. Shoe, belting, pocketbook, glove, coat, and vest makers, among others, purchased sheepskins. Pigskins provided only a small part of the trade in hides and skins.[26]

Inedible animal parts made up most by-products, but some provided saleable food at a substantial financial return to the packers. The U.S. Department of Agriculture defined these as clean, sound, and properly dressed edible parts other than meat from one or more carcasses of cattle, swine, sheep, or goats. The edible by-products from hogs included brains, cheek and head meat, cutlets, ears, faces, giblet meats, hearts, kidneys, leaf lard, lips, livers, snouts, stomachs, tongues, sweetbreads, sausage trimmings, chitterlings, and tails. All pork trimmings could be used for sausage, and fat went into lard. Workers divided hog viscera into various products both edible and inedible. Hog stomachs provided pepsin, while the pancreas or hog sweetbreads provided a source for insulin. Similar products could also be gleaned from cattle and sheep. The packers even used the delicate hairs on the inside of cows' ears to make artist's brushes. Hog hairs filled the cushions of sofas, davenports, mattresses, and automobile seats as well as providing insulation. They really did use every part of the hog but the squeal.[27]

The big packinghouses ventured into other "unrelated lines" including the production of peanut butter, cheese, poultry butter, and eggs. It seemed inevitable that the meat companies would become important agents in the distribution of dairy and poultry products as a result of their development of refrigerator cars and branch houses. The big packers had a natural advantage over potential competitors because of their plant locations, technical skills, research facilities, and branch outlets. Since they already maintained a large distribution system for meat, it was only natural—and good business—to use that system to distribute a wider range of products. The same retailers to which the packinghouses sold meat bought dairy products, and salesmen could sell both. Advertising of these "unrelated lines" could also be done economically considering the organization already in place to promote meat products. Chicago's packers managed this nationwide, and in some cases worldwide, system from their offices in Chicago. By the 1920s, the development of by-products and unrelated lines seemed to guarantee almost unlimited future profits for the Chicago packers. The packers' extensive investment in the distribution of their finished products provided an important goad to continued expansion as they used canning facilities built for meat to pack salmon, sardines, tuna, evaporated milk, and even vegetables.[28]

The Organizational Revolution

Chicago's packinghouses innovated not only in the creation of products, but also in the configuration of their business. They participated in an organizational revolution that transformed American capitalism in the late nineteenth century and brought the modern to the entire business process. These huge profit-making industrial companies could not be run in the same manner as the small packing companies of the Civil War era. Armour, Swift, and Morris needed more control, more information to process in order to maintain and expand profits. They required a new effective organizational structure. Modern capitalism of course emerged in various industries, but the alteration of

Swift and Company's General Office in the Union Stock Yard. Notice the construction of an elevator tower connected to the main office by a ramp. The doorway was decorated with a steer head much like the Stone Gate at the main entrance to the Union Stock Yard. The offices were located on the top floors, while the rest of the building was dedicated to a packing house market. Notice the refrigerated cars on the rail line alongside the plant. This structure burned down in 1906. (Author's Collection.)

the age-old business of butchering provided one of the most innovative stages for management to develop. A growing class of white-collar management workers emerged to run the multifaceted business.

Since chilled beef had to be consumed within three to four weeks after slaughter, it led to an immense investment in capital equipment and to the creation of a bureaucracy to manage the business, now national in scope. Swift's and Armour's embrace of the refrigerated railroad car and a network of branch houses altered the industry. Chicago's packers sold from 60 to 90 percent of the dressed meat in the large eastern cities, and sent 95 percent of American beef exports overseas.

Consideration of stockyard and packinghouse workers usually calls to mind industrial laborers, but the Union Stock Yard and Packingtown also employed a legion of new white-collar workers. The great packers kept large clerical staffs in their Chicago offices: Swift and Armour each employed about one thousand male and female clerks. From at least the mid-1890s on, these companies created a modern, complex, sophisticated hierarchy to operate their vast enterprises. The creation of a bureaucracy and the delegation of authority to qualified and goal-oriented employees was certainly part of the modern. In turn, it affected the entire business model. The high volume generated by their national sales and distribution networks led to the specialized subdivision of labor in the process of slaughtering and dressing livestock, but only after a carefully designed administrative arrangement permitted the movement of large numbers of animals through the packing plants. A network of livestock buyers plied not only the Chicago Stockyards, but also rival stockyards and the countryside in order to fuel the great packing machine. The packers maintained a purchasing division that bought the large amount of supplies necessary to maintain the trade. From clerks to buyers, and salesmen, this was a modern business.

Armour and Company divided its sales organization into two large subunits and a small one. The large units dealt in beef and hog products. The smaller unit dealt in laboratory by-products. All three marketed products in 1900 through Armour's 200 nationwide branch houses. Armour and Swift organized their carlines and branch houses to report to twenty-five district superintendents. The branch houses took orders, arranged for local advertising, handled billing and the transfer of funds back to Chicago. Swift had 193 such branch houses in 1900, while Morris maintained 77, and S&S had 44.

The Chicago headquarters then assigned a packing plant to supply each of the branch and car lines. If the supplying plant fell short because of a lack of livestock, a strike, or some other problem, Chicago supplied the car lines and branch houses from another plant. They handled surpluses in the same centralized way. In this manner, the Chicago offices could control the entire market for their products and make logical—and profitable—choices as to supply and demand. The head offices maintained constant telegraphic communication with their agents, and as early as 1889 Armour had established a division of its accounting department devoted exclusively to the branch houses.[29]

The massive organizational model that developed as a consequence

General Office
Swift & Company
Chicago

Swift and Company's new office building replaced the older structure and was the first air-conditioned office building in Chicago in 1907. This stand-alone structure held the company's national offices. It remained the General Office of the company until it left the Union Stock Yard in 1961 (Postcard, Author's Collection.)

of these changes in the meat industry not only altered it, but also provided a model for other manufacturers. The story told of Henry Ford getting the idea for his automobile assembly lines from the packers is just one example of the impact these "new" businesses had on industrial development. The packers became, what is now called, "vertically integrated," at least exercising some control over the livestock markets, the advertising and supply chains, as well as distribution. They attempted to control the entire industry from the farmyard to the dinner table, creating a vast meat monopoly. While the big packers would be less successful in these ventures, they took part in a pattern first set by Standard Oil and U.S. Steel in their monopolistic stages.

The Packer Threat

In 1890, a group of largely British and eastern investors headed by the Vanderbilt interests and Frederick H. Prince of Boston took control of the Union Stock Yard and created the Chicago Junction Railways and Chicago Stockyard Company, with a New Jersey charter. Chi-

Sales department, General Office, Swift and Company. Swift employed over one thousand men and women at the company's Chicago headquarters. (Postcard, Author's Collection.)

cago lawyer Levy Mayer had helped the British investment group buy grain elevators and breweries, and he contacted Stockyard President Nathaniel Thayer about the investor interest in the USY&T Company. The reorganization of the USY&T Company as a subsidiary of the New Jersey company left John Sherman as vice president and general manager of the stockyards. While the British investment group held 95 percent of the New Jersey company's shares, Frederick H. Winston, a longtime director of the USY&T Company and the only Chicagoan on the Board of Directors, became president. After the 1890 deal, the packers and the heads of the new stockyard company began to argue. The packers wanted more of say in stockyard operations, and without it they threatened to destroy the new corporation.

Prior to the purchase of the company, the problem of who would haul and switch the vast number of railroad cars in the stockyards and Packingtown presented a problem for the packers, railroads, and the Union Stock Yard alike. Labor issues had come to a head in the 1880s as the various players made attempts to deal with the problem. At first, the railroads employed switchmen. This arrangement changed in 1887, and all of the interests agreed that Sherman and the Union Stock Yard should manage all switching in Packingtown, thus creating the Railway Switching Association. After a brief period of peace, labor issues again arose, and the association voted itself out of existence; and the factions organized the Chicago Railway Transfer Association to replace it. Sherman and the packers again insisted that the Union Stock Yard should do the switching. During the prolonged negotiations over switching fees and who should do the switching, the packers began to resent the fact that they had given up their place on the USY&T Company's board. They now had a large stake in the operation of the Union Stock Yard, but no voice in its practical day-to-day operations upon which their profits depended.[30]

As early as 1887, a proposal for a competing stockyard in the Town of Lyons (Stickney, Illinois) about five miles southwest of the Square Mile was floated as an alternative to the Union Stock Yard. Several years later, another effort took place, fueled by Armour, Swift, and Morris. They proposed a new 3,700-acre site in Tolleston, Indiana, in the area eventually developed by U.S. Steel as the town of Gary— in part because the USY&T Company charged for the movement of dead freight (chilled beef and other products) on the tracks that ran through Packingtown that they controlled. Armour, Swift, and Morris threatened to move their operations to Tolleston and open a competing stockyard; their scheme called for attracting other packers and manufacturers to the site. The Union Stock Yard responded that if the packers left for Indiana, the USY&T Company would go into the packing business itself. British investors would fund a firm that would build on land owned by the Union Stock Yard and might prove to be a mighty competitor to the packers who were threatening to leave the city. Winston admitted to the possibility, pointing out that Chicago remained an excellent location for the packing business. Meanwhile, fourteen of Chicago's twenty-three railroads seemed pledged to the Stickney location. These roads felt they had the upper hand and could force the packers to come to their new proposed stockyard. In turn, the packers planned to build an independent railroad connecting Tolleston to the Stickney site if necessary. Meanwhile, the *Daily Sun* reported that despite threats to close their Chicago operations, Armour and Company had decided to transfer their downtown headquarters to the Union

Stock Yard. The company originally occupied three floors of the Home Insurance Building in the heart of Chicago's financial district, but decided to move closer to their packing operations like their rivals.

The entire complicated matter resulted from the packers' attempt to control their costs and to integrate vertically. To understand the situation it must be remembered that the railroads originally had a major voice in the operation of the Union Stock Yard, but they had given up a controlling interest in the USY&T Company in the 1870s. They maintained a presence of four members of the eleven-man Board of Directors until 1894 when they resigned their position due to a disagreement over livestock trackage fees.[31]

The Chicago Junction Railway and Chicago Stockyard Company (New Jersey Company) signed an agreement on July 27, 1891, with the three packers who had planned the proposed Tolleston stockyard. The Armour, Swift, and Morris companies agreed to remain at the Union Stock Yard for at least fifteen years. They also consented that all of their business concerning packing, canning, and the handling of livestock conducted within two hundred miles of Chicago would profit the Chicago Union Stock Yards, thus basically killing any prospects for the Stickney site. Armour, Swift, and Morris also guaranteed $2 million ($52.6 million in 2014) profits to the USY&T Company over six years regarding the usual yardage fees and vowed not to build a competing stockyard. The three packers transferred one thousand acres of the Tolleston property of their Central Stock-Yards Company to the Union Stock Yards—and discontinued plans for the remaining three thousand acres. The big packers also dropped any further lawsuits against the Chicago Stockyards. In turn, the USY&T Company transferred to Armour, Swift, and Morris $3 million ($78.9 million) in fifteen-year 5 percent bonds that could be exchanged at any time for an equivalent amount of stock in the company. The only negative votes of shareholders at the Jersey City meeting of the holding company that owned the stockyards were those held by a group of smaller packers who feared they would be discriminated against under the new arrangement.[32]

The signers of the agreement denied that they were in any way creating a monopoly at the Chicago Stockyards, and that the later lawsuit by the smaller packers was intended to aid the newly established Chicago National Stock Yards Company in Stickney. This company had been promoted by several of the "nonassociated packers," most of who operated hog slaughterhouses and were indeed behind the lawsuit. In 1892, the Union Stock Yard came to an agreement with the smaller packers and one of their leaders, Henry Botsford, joined the Board of Directors of the New Jersey Company. Shortly thereafter, rumors concerning the stockyards and the meatpackers abounded. One had the stockyard company buying land in the Calumet region for a stockyard annex. Another had the consolidation of various packers into one large firm. The packers had originally given up their seats on the USY&T Company's Board of Directors in 1866, but with the new agreement they began to have a voice in the new company and they moved against the railroads.[33]

The new owners modernized the Union Stock Yard and many of its old employees found themselves without a job once they decided to reorganize operations at the livestock market. Other stockyards had opened farther west, particularly in Kansas City, Omaha, and South St. Paul, and they now threatened Chicago's position in the marketplace. The Vanderbilt interests felt that Sherman was a relic who could no longer lead the Union Stock Yard and that new blood was needed to manage and modernize the vast enterprise. The Board of Directors installed a new leadership team to revitalize operations and maintain Chicago's position as the leading livestock market. The company invested millions of dollars in improvements. By November 1899, Sherman announced that he would step down as president of the Union Stock Yard and Transit Company, and at the beginning of 1900 John A. Spoor, a Vanderbilt man previously vice president of the USY&T Company, took the position. The reorganizers separated the combined office of vice president and general manager and named A. G. Leonard as general manager. Sherman died two years later at the age of seventy-seven. Spoor and Leonard oversaw the pavement of alleys and pens with brick and the installation of a new sewage system and modern equipment throughout the yards. Whoever was in charge, expansion and modernization continued its relentless pace.[34]

The Beef Trust

For years, various groups accused Chicago's large meatpacking firms of forming a Beef Trust, an illegal monopoly to profiteer over control of its market. The industry had grown quickly and a general concentration took place with Chicago's Big Three: Armour, Swift, and Morris.

Industrial output had increased phenomenally during this period, as refrigeration and mechanization had allowed the creation of larger and more efficient plants. These factors in turn put smaller firms out of business, as the four dominant meatpackers (including Cudahy) at the turn of the century did control 50 percent of the market, and took advantage of various economies and the by-products industry. While these packers did not have total control over the Union Stock Yard, they had tremendous influence over it. Their ownership of smaller packing firms and stockyards outside of Chicago again provided them with advantages not available to smaller firms, as did their proprietorship of refrigerated railroad cars and branch houses throughout the nation. Furthermore, their owners' presence on various boards of directors, especially of banks, railroads, and other corporations, gave them enormous financial power.

The packers did aim at creating a monopoly. In 1888, Swift, Armour, Morris, and Hammond formed the Allerton Pool, to set prices and dominate the industry. A committee of the U.S. Senate charged the pool as an attempt to eliminate competition as well as fix meat prices, control livestock costs, and share sales territories. The Allerton Pool and other such arrangements resulted in the passage of the Sherman Anti-Trust Act (1890), which forbade any such combination to restrict trade. Three years later, Armour, Cudahy, Swift, Hammond, and Morris formed the Veeder Pool to circumvent the law and accomplish similar goals. Lawyers Henry Veeder Sr. and his son Henry Veeder Jr., both employed by the Chicago packers, later testified to various behind-the-scenes agreements between the firms. Their representatives met weekly at Veeder's office and used a code to refer to themselves in all correspondence as they set prices on beef, mutton, and veal. The emergence of Schwarzschild and Sulzberger (S&S) as a competitor with the Chicago packers broke up the old pool temporarily, but the companies brought S&S into their arrangements in 1898. The federal government continued to look into the so-called Beef Trust, and in 1902 filed suit against the "pool" packers. The following year, the court enjoined the packers from operating under the 1898 pool agreement as a violation of the Sherman Anti-Trust Act. In 1905, the Supreme Court sustained the injunction. The packers eventually decided that the pool agreements were not only illegal, but also inefficient. Other possibilities soon presented themselves.[35]

With the emergence of U.S. Steel in 1901 and its purchase of land in the area around Tolleston for the creation in 1906 of Gary, a new phase of monopolistic capitalism appeared. Gary annexed the town of Tolleston itself in 1910. The Chicago packers moved to mimic U.S. Steel and create a meat monopoly. In 1902, Armour, Swift, and Morris agreed to purchase several independent firms and combine them into a new company with both Cudahy and S&S joining the plan, but investment bankers balked at granting a $60 million ($1.7 billion in 2014) loan to guarantee the deal. Nonetheless, the following year the National Packing Company, a $15 million ($405 million) corporation, was formed under New Jersey laws with the Hammond and Fowler packing companies at its core (Armour and Company had absorbed the Hammond Company the previous year). The new corporation consisted of smaller companies already bought or contracted to be purchased by Armour, Swift, and Morris, and combined them under the new name. At first, it seemed as if this was the beginning of one large corporation to bring together all or most of the assets of the major meatpackers, but it never fully developed in that manner. But given the previous actions of the big Chicago packers, it is obvious that the major packers saw this as a natural outcome of National Packing's creation.

The company did create a strong community of interest among the large packers as can be seen by the membership of the Board of Directors in 1905:

J. Ogden Armour, president of Armour & Co.
P. A. Valentine, treasurer of Armour & Co.
Arthur Meeker, director in Armour & Co.
Thomas J. Connors, director in Armour & Co.
Louis F. Swift, president of Swift & Co.
Edward F. Swift, vice president of Swift & Co.
Lawrence A. Carton, treasurer of Swift & Co.
Edward Tilden, president of Libby, McNeill & Libby.
Edward Morris, of Nelson Morris & Co.
Ira N. Morris, of Nelson Morris & Co.
Thomas E. Wilson, with Nelson Morris & Co.[36]

The National Packing Company became the sixth of the now Big Six packers.

The new corporation immediately drew the attention of both the public and the federal government. In March 1905, a federal grand jury assembled to look again into the matter of the Beef Trust. Many of the expected witnesses reportedly left for Europe the week before the grand jury met. Phone calls to their offices and homes garnered the answer that no one knew their whereabouts. The grand jury still summoned eight witnesses to appear on March 21. John S. Miler, the packers' lawyer, made the novel argument that the companies could not be held responsible for any violation of the Sherman Anti-Trust Act or the earlier injunction if individuals working for the firms disregarded the explicit instructions of the directors. The packers were trying to use the very complexity they had created to evade the law. He also assured the court that there had been no violation of the Interstate Commerce Act.

In early April, government prosecutors focused on the lucrative by-products industry, especially cattle casings or intestines. Many of those the court called to testify in this matter had also disappeared. Unnamed government informants said that the casings alone paid for the slaughtering and dressing of cattle. Witnesses claimed that the 1905 *Report of the Commissioner of Corporations on the Beef Industry* did not have proper information as to the costs of slaughtering and to the benefits of the casing industry, which it basically ignored. The Amalgamated Meat Cutters and Butcher Workmen Union called the report of the commissioner of corporations, James R. Garfield, "the most cold-blooded proposition to deceive the public" and referred to the commissioner either a "fool or a knave."[37] Casings were used to manufacture sausage, as well as strings for violins, guitars, and other instruments. The government claimed a mysterious corporation, the Etna Trading Company, manipulated the market in conjunction with Chicago's packers. Etna's records disappeared from its offices in the Fischer Building located on Dearborn Street in the Loop, and then reappeared in six brass bound trunks in a bank after a short but mysterious stay on the South Side. The officers of the firm also vanished. The federal government claimed that the packers and the Etna Company controlled casing prices and maintained them at a price 50 percent higher than warranted by the market. The grand jury called James P. Lyman, the former head of the National Packing Company, to testify about the Etna Company. Meanwhile, several other industrialists of interest could not be found, including Carl Levi, head of the Berthold Levi and Company sausage casing company, and August Reiser, head of the casing department at Morris and Company. So the grand jury summoned the wives of the missing witnesses.

More trouble for the packers appeared on the horizon, as the Interstate Commerce Commission decided to investigate the private refrigerated car lines in May. In June, the grand jury called Samuel A. Maclean Jr., head of the National Packing Company, to testify. On July 1, 1905, after three months inquiry into the Beef Trust, the government delivered indictments of twenty-one men for conspiracy to control the beef trade, including six millionaires who led companies found to be involved in the affair. They stood accused of conspiring to restrain trade and commerce in violation of the Sherman Anti-Trust Act. The other four were representatives of the S&S Company, whom the prosecutors accused of scheming to secure rebates from various railroads regarding meat shipments. The charges included destroying competition in the purchase of cattle, fixing excessive prices for dressed cattle, and organizing restraint of trade in the foreign and domestic markets for both fresh beef and by-products. Finally, the federal government accused the packers of illegally combining smaller packing companies into the National Packing Company in order to stifle competition and the growth of trade.[38]

The packers invoked the Fifth Amendment, claiming they originally provided evidence under compulsion to the commissioner of the U.S. Bureau of Corporations and that this evidence became part of the prosecution's arguments. Judge Otis Humphrey, presiding over the U.S. District Court at Chicago, ruled in their favor and granted immunity. President Theodore Roosevelt angrily commented, "Such interpretation of the law comes measurably near making the law a farce." The decision ended the case, but did not legalize the status of the National Packing Company. That battle continued into the next decade.[39]

In 1908, the federal government began another investigation of the National Packing Company. The government suspected it of controlling Hammond Packing, Cudahy Packing, and Libby, McNeil and Libby along with several smaller concerns. These companies came under the dominance of this holding company when the big packers formed it in 1903. Edward Tilden, the former head of Libby, McNeil and Libby, served at this time as president of National Packing. Again the federal government suspected the big Chicago packers of attempting to create a monopoly.[40] Over the next four years, the federal government continued to examine the packing industry looking for evidence of restraint of trade. Finally, in December 1911 the government brought another action against the packers, and the following year it forced the dissolution of the National Packing Company. While the packers continued to deny their guilt, they agreed to put an end to the company and divide its components among themselves.

Five years later, the Federal Trade Commission led yet another inquiry into the big packers. The packers maintained that the investigation was biased and unfair, but they agreed to a consent degree in which the government said that the packers were not guilty of unlawful acts and that the agreement of the packers did not constitute an admission of guilt. The decree further prohibited certain practices already against the law, transgressions of which the packers claimed innocence. It banned the five large packers from handling canned fruits, vegetables, and other grocery products, and also from owning retail stores. The consent degree required the packers to sell their interests in any stockyards. This last provision negated much of the 1891 Tolleston agreement. In 1912, the Frederick H. Prince interests had organized a new corporation, the Chicago Stock Yards Company of Maine, which replaced the New Jersey Company. Armour and Company maintained some 19 percent control in the new concern until 1920, when it passed to the Prince interests outright.[41] In the first decades of the twentieth century, the packers found themselves under assault from all sides, but perhaps the most devastating blow came from the muckraking press, which appeared first in the 1890s and hounded monopolies during the so-called Gilded Age and into the twentieth century.

The Jungle and the Investigation

As the federal government moved against the packers' control of the meat supply, a young socialist, Upton Sinclair, published *The Jungle* (1906), a novel that shook the nation's trust in the industry. While the author intended to expose working conditions in American industry in general, he triggered instead a crusade for better sanitary conditions within the meatpacking industry. Sinclair famously said, "I aimed at the public's heart, and by accident hit it in the stomach." The novel was originally serially published in the socialist magazine *Appeal to Reason*. It portrayed a Lithuanian immigrant, Jurgis Rudkus, and his family's struggles to make a life in Back of the Yards. The book painted a portrait of incredible hardship. *The Jungle* moreover depicted unsanitary conditions in Chicago's packinghouses, and it was this that caught the public's attention. Sinclair's novel brought to the fore many of the rumors that had persisted about the industry over the previous quarter of a century. It also fueled fears about the modern.[42]

As they considered whether to publish *The Jungle*, publisher Frank Doubleday and his partner, Walter H. Page, consulted with journalist Isaac Marcosson, who had experience promoting books. Marcosson told Page, "If the revelations in this book are true we should have guardians appointed for us if we do not publish it. It will be either a sensational success or a magnificent failure. In either case it is well worth trying." Both Doubleday and Page agreed.

Marcosson traveled to Chicago to verify Sinclair's descriptions of conditions in the packinghouses to avoid possible lawsuits. There he met Dr. W. K. Jaques, formerly bacteriologist for the city of Chicago. Marcosson asked Dr. Jaques to write an article, "A Picture of Meat Inspection," which substantiated *The Jungle*. He also secured an article by Dr. Caroline Hedger, a local physician, on the conditions in Packingtown and the neighborhoods surrounding it. The publicist said that much of what Sinclair wrote he gathered secondhand from employees and settlement house workers, but once Marcosson acquired a meat inspector's badge he maintained he saw more than even the "muckraker." Sinclair, in a 1906 interview, admitted that he had only visited the slaughterhouses three times and that his knowledge of the fertilizer plant came from a man he met in a saloon. Many of the stories that appeared in *The Jungle* had been told over and over again in Back of the Yards, the neighborhood to the west and south of Packingtown. The story of a man falling into a vat, for instance, had occurred years prior to Sinclair's visit to Chicago, but his body had been taken out quickly and not rendered into lard.

Marcosson devised the first fully modern promotional campaign in publishing history, with a campaign based on his experiences in the newspaper business. At this time, most publishers simply sent out rather formal "Literary Notes" hoping that a book might catch on with the reading public. Afterward, if the book was selling, they might launch a fairly costly campaign. Marcosson felt that the introduction of a book should be treated as news. With two earlier publications, Thomas Dixon's *The Clansman* and the *Recollections and Letters of*

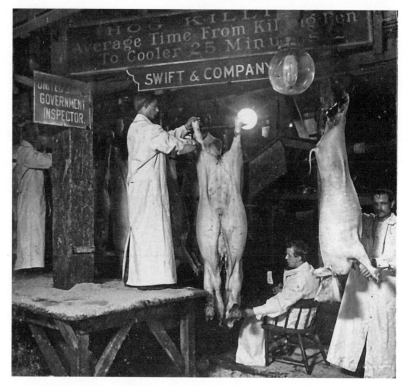

Meat inspectors examine hog carcasses at Swift and Company, circa 1900. Notice the sign that proudly proclaims that the average time spent to get the hog from the kill floor to the cooler was twenty-five minutes. (Stereopticon, Authors Collection.)

General Robert E. Lee, he had sent dispatches to the Associated Press and soon found the books written and talked about throughout the nation. He jumped at the chance to try his methods on the Sinclair book, which he knew would make news, especially given the ascendency of Progressive politics at the time. Marcosson planned to send advance notices of the book prior to release, with an agreement not to publish the news until the book came out. He also sent page proofs to major newspapers and to both the United Press and Associated Press services. On Monday, January 25, 1906, *The Jungle* became front-page news across the country. The following day Sinclair woke up a famous author. Even Mr. Dooley, journalist Finley Peter Dunne's fictional character, spoke about the book and said in his native brogue, "If ye want to rajooce ye'er butcher's bills buy *The Jungle*."

Marcosson considered President Theodore Roosevelt to be his ultimate press agent and sent the president an advance copy with a letter calling for drastic action. The first of three "Progressive" presidents, Roosevelt had the reputation of not only a "Trust Buster," but also a reformer bent on protecting the public from rapacious industrialists. After reading the book, Roosevelt telegraphed Sinclair with an invitation to lunch at the White House.[43]

Roosevelt sent Dr. John R. Mohler, chief of the Division of Pathology of the Bureau of Animal Industry; Dr. Rice P. Steddom, chief of the Inspection Division of the Bureau; and George R. McCabe, solicitor of the Department of Agriculture to the Union Stock Yard, to verify Sinclair's claims regarding dishonest federal meat inspectors. They began their inspection on March 12 and ended it ten days later, and while they admitted some need for improvement as to sanitary conditions, these had little to do with the quality of meat products and they called Sinclair's charges false. The committee inspected all the buildings, departments, and rooms of the abattoirs in Chicago subject to federal inspection, and two abattoirs that were not. (Federal inspectors only examined those packing plants that sent meat overseas.) The commission pointed out that sanitary conditions at slaughterhouses where the bureau maintained inspection, while not always satisfactory, seemed much superior to those at the average establishment without such inspection. They also commented on the conditions in the Union Stock Yard, stating that "the drainage is good, and the pens are kept as clean as the character of their use would permit."[44]

The controversy raged on as Sinclair's charges struck the industry at many levels. In April 1906, the same month the Committee on Meat Inspection made its report in Washington, DC, Dr. Jaques presented a paper before the Chicago Medical Society, accusing the U.S. government of contributing to conditions in the stockyards. He chastised the public and the medical profession for ignorance of the actual circumstances. At the same time, Dr. S. E. Bennett, head of the Chicago Branch of the Bureau of the Animal Industry, defended the meat inspectors, denying any bribery or corruption. While head of the bureau only since the beginning of 1906, he dismissed any possibility of corruption under his predecessor. He further claimed to have put even more checks on inspectors, moving them not only from plant to plant, but from department to department to avoid favoritism. One hundred government inspectors worked in the stockyards, and at busy times another seventy-five joined them. The head inspector articulated that every inspector was a check on every other inspector and that only some grand "graft society" could pull off the kinds of corruption portrayed by Sinclair. Bennett dismissed *The Jungle* saying, "There is absolutely nothing in the charges of corruption and bribery made about government inspectors and the packers." The head of the Chicago Branch of the Bureau of Animal Husbandry obviously chose to disregard the very ethos of Chicago and its rampant capitalism, which tended to encourage a culture of graft, corruption, and cronyism.

Meanwhile, another source of criticism of Sinclair came from the University of Chicago Settlement House. A spokesperson for the settlement, Miss Laura B. Bass, declared, "Upton Sinclair is a bright young man, but he has stated a great many exaggerations concerning conditions in the stockyards. Miss McDowell has never endorsed the book on that account. We know that conditions in the yards are not all they could be, but they are not so bad as the book would have us believe."[45]

Sinclair had turned a spotlight on Chicago's meatpackers, and they took up the challenge. The packers attempted to discredit the story in every conceivable way. Marcosson considered it part of his task to combat them. He claimed that the investigators had fallen under the spell of the packinghouse owners and were only shown a cleaned-up version of the slaughtering process. He asserted, "The members were honest and well-meaning but they fell into the hands of the Beef Trust and were only shown the specially prepared sections of the packing houses usually open to the public. They returned fully prepared to 'whitewash' the packers and denounce 'The Jungle' as the product of a disordered and sensation-seeking mind."

The publicist realized that he had to quickly counteract the impact of the committee. He appealed to Roosevelt to send another delegation, and the president sent Labor Commissioner Charles P. Neill and social worker James B. Reynolds as special investigators. Marcosson asked Dr. Jaques to show the commissioners around Packingtown. They came away with a different picture, but still one hardly as condemning as Sinclair's portrayal. Sinclair gave interview after interview repeating his accusations to a public eager to hear about the evils of embalmed meat and worse coming from the huge packinghouses. These stories that had circulated for a long time, and the writings of Algie Simmons, Ernest Poole, Adolphe Smith, and others had already prepared the way for Sinclair's success.[46]

Roosevelt had been on the packers' trail for sometime and wanted to increase regulation. Both he and Senator Albert J. Beveridge of Indiana supported the passage of the Federal Meat Inspection Act of 1906, authorizing the secretary of agriculture to inspect and condemn meat products found unfit for human consumption. It widened the scope of meat inspection and, along with the Pure Food and Drug Act, proved to be one of the landmarks of Progressive reform. Roosevelt thanked Senator Beveridge for his help in passing the legislation, but never mentioned Sinclair. Roosevelt told William Allen White that Sinclair had been of service to him and the Progressives, but that he was basically untruthful and that three-fourths of the things he said were falsehoods.

As for the packers, J. Ogden Armour spoke out against the accusations in June of 1906, asserting it was impossible to sell diseased meat. He called upon the American tradition of fair play, stating the packers had been unjustly accused and that the entire export trade in meat products had been damaged. According to Armour, "The public has been ignorantly or maliciously misinformed on the two most important phases of the whole question—namely the character of the meat inspection as it is and has been, and the attitude of the large packers toward the proposed legislation." The leader of the packers stated that he and the others supported inspection legislation. He quoted the National Association of Manufacturers as saying that the goal of the reformers seemed to be to kill the industry and then reform it. Armour promised that socialist agitators would not destroy the American meat industry.[47]

Publication of *The Jungle* caused a national uproar. It also made history as one of the first books to be publicized before publication and made into an instant best seller. Jack London praised the book calling it the "Uncle Tom's Cabin of wage slavery," but in the end the federal government and the large meatpackers used it to tighten regulations at the expense of smaller independent packers who could not meet the stricter standards that resulted from the public's agitation. The first quarter of the twentieth century, while days of greatest expansion for the Union Stock Yards, also provided a test of wills and a public relations fiasco for the industry. In many ways, Sinclair had stirred the pot, but did not bring about his hoped for socialist victory.

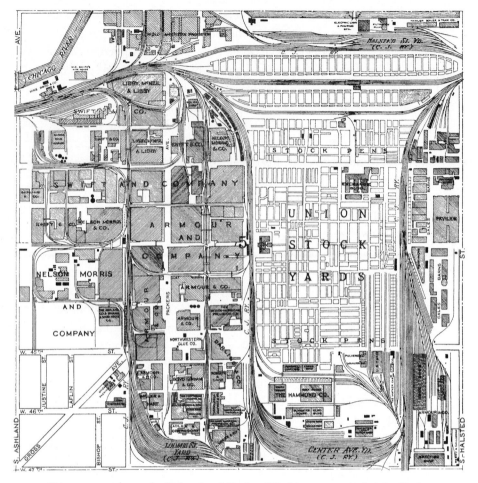

This 1915 map shows the Union Stock Yard and Packingtown at its height. Notice the large amount of land occupied by the Big Three packers. (Reproduced from Chicago Association of Commerce, *Smoke Abatement and Electrification of Railway Terminals in Chicago*, 1915.)

The Institute of American Meat Packers

As the industry came under attack, the public relations aspect of the Chicago Stockyards and Packingtown became more and more important from the nineteenth century into the early twentieth century. In 1905, Swift and Company's general superintendent, Fred W. Wilder, published *The Modern Packinghouse* to explain the methods, machinery, pay scales, and so on, of the plants. The industry used this book in part as an answer to the various charges percolating against it.[48]

The following year, after the publication of Upton Sinclair's condemnation of the industry, the meatpackers created the American Meat Packers Association to aid the three hundred member firms in dealing with the bad publicity created by the muckrakers and the federal reports, as well as federal regulation of the industry. In 1919, the association changed its name to the Institute of American Meat Packers, and tried to counter what the industry considered attacks regarding the fluctuation of meat prices and calls for the further investigation of livestock marketing. Put simply, the industry tried to clean up its public image.

In February of 1922, Thomas E. Wilson, head of Wilson and Company and president of the Institute of American Meat Packers, proposed the creation of a packers "college" to train men interested in entering the industry. Embracing the Progressive era's promotion of "experts," this program was another step in to the idea of the modern. The industry embraced education, expertise, and a more advanced notion of public relations. This was a far cry from the days when Gus Swift could learn his trade in a small town meat market or Nelson Morris could enter the business as a young boy working for John Sherman. Wilson's ambitious program, known as the Institute Plan, hoped to transform the Institute of American Meat Packers into a "combined educational institution, research institute, and industrial museum." In April, the institute's Executive Committee directed that the plan be transmitted to the entire membership and that a commission and committees be appointed. These began work in June of that year, and in October the general session of the institute unanimously endorsed the project. Thomas E. Wilson, by then chairman of the Institute Plan Commission, stated the various objectives of the scheme: to provide a collegiate education for young men interested in the packing industry, to furnish and train prospective department heads already engaged in the industry, to offer continuing education for plant employees and junior office help, and to develop a body of scientific knowledge and practical data for the industry. The recommendations called for the institute to raise $150,000 ($2.1 million in 2014) for educational and research activities.

The representatives of the institute explored the idea that the University of Chicago might cooperate in working out its educational plans. A highly successful series of eight lectures in 1923 held in Mandel Hall on the university's campus provided a survey of the meat industry under the joint auspices of the School of Commerce and Administration and the American Meat Packers Institute. On July 9, after discussions between the two institutions, University of Chicago President Ernest DeWitt Burton recommended the novel relationship and the Board of Trustees approved it. That September, the American Meat Packers Institute ratified the negotiations at their annual convention in Atlantic City. In October, both parties appointed a joint administrative committee and agreed upon activities.

Evening classes began in October 1923, with correspondence courses beginning in January 1924 and a four-year curriculum of day courses planned to start in October 1924. Arthur Lowenstein, chairman of the institute's Committee on Scientific Research and a vice president of Wilson and Company, presented a gift of $2,500 ($34,722) per year for the purpose of creating a research fellowship to be carried on under the guidance of Professor Edwin O. Jordan, chairman of the Department of Hygiene and Bacteriology. The relationship between the Institute of American Meat Packers and the University of Chicago proved beneficial to both organizations. For the packing industry, it provided an elite setting to promote their industry, as well as an opportunity to employ university personnel to do research and to train future management employees, another important symbol of the modern. For the university, the new connection diversified its student body and connected to the business community.

Publications flowed from the alliance. Among the first was the original eight lectures given in Mandel Hall. The association and the university soon took on other aspects of promoting the industry including the printing of various books, pamphlets, and articles lauding the industry as a great example of American entrepreneurship. In 1939, the speech given by the legendary meatpacker Oscar Meyer to the Thirty-Fourth Annual Convention of the Meat Institute in Chicago appeared in pamphlet form. Meyer mentioned the 1923 lectures at Mandel Hall and claimed that there had been a dearth of information about the industry at the time. What the president of the Institute of American Meat Packers did not say was that the institute was not only a disseminator of news, but also a defender of the industry from the attacks of Upton Sinclair and the federal government earlier in the century. The research emanating from the American Meat Institute thus represented an early example of industry-controlled research and promotion.[49]

The Workers

Despite Sinclair's failure to bring about a revolution in the social conscience of America regarding the living and working conditions of industrial laborers, the men and women who worked in the Union Stock Yard and Packingtown remained quite aware of their circumstances. Wage rates varied in the years before World War One, but differences in wages between skilled and unskilled workers did not. Skilled workers always made more, but there were always fewer of them, because the introduction of mechanization and the disassembly line method further increased the need for unskilled labor. Management simplified — or rather deskilled — the process in each department whenever possible. During this period, work remained unsteady for many, if not most, packinghouse workers. Before World War One, even the start of the workday was uncertain. All the employees had to report to the plant at 7:00 a.m. even though there might be no work. At times, they had to wait for hours before the stream of livestock flowed over the ramps. They were not paid for their time, but they had to be there. The companies did not pay until the actual killing began, which at times could be as late as noon. The men in the sheep kill suffered the most from this situation because they had to wait to hear which of twelve different styles of dressing mutton the packers required that day. These men, therefore, waited at times until two o'clock in the afternoon to begin, and then worked late into the night.

Generally, livestock arrived in the Union Stock Yard in larger numbers in the early part of the week. The packers wanted these slaughtered, dressed, and shipped east for sale by the weekend. Thus the workday might last twelve or more hours on Monday and Tuesday. The Union Stock Yard and Transit Company charged fifty cents a head for any animals left in their pens overnight, and the packers did not want to pay the extra yardage. Later in the week, there could be much less work for the men and women in the packinghouses.[50]

The fluctuations in livestock runs affected not only the daily work schedule but also the yearly cycle of employment. Cattle runs peaked at two times in the year: the fall-winter cycle, which ran from October through January, and in the spring with the high point in May. These cycles resulted from the way producers fed cattle. The processing of hogs brought them to the yards in greatest numbers in January; sheep, in September—with the same net effect on the labor force on those kill floors. Day to day, week to week, work varied throughout the year.[51]

Obviously, these fluctuations in hours, whether daily or seasonal, determined family income, especially for the unskilled. The impact of low wages, uncertain schedules, and unhealthy working conditions deeply affected the families of packinghouse workers. Laborers turned time and time again to organized labor to improve their working conditions. The disastrous consequences of strikes in 1877, 1886, and during the 1890s also influenced workers' attitudes, as did the constant flow of new immigrants, often unfamiliar with the industrial world and organized labor in the plants. Despite past failures, labor organizations reappeared at the end of the nineteenth century with the arrival in Chicago of Michael Donnelly, president of the Amalgamated Meat Cutters and Butcher Workmen. In January 1901, he moved his headquarters from Omaha to Chicago. Donnelly encouraged workers to join the union and membership expanded quickly; by July, the union established seven locals in Chicago. Donnelly hoped his organization would present a strong opposition to the meatpackers.[52]

A second generation of packers had come into their own in the industry and seemed more willing to cooperate with the union in order to avoid the costly strikes that hurt production and profits. By September of 1902, the Amalgamated Meat Cutters and Butcher Workmen made progress in dealing with the larger firms. Donnelly also recognized the importance of unskilled workers, as well as women and immigrants. Mary McDowell of the University of Chicago Settlement House threw her support behind the union, especially in relation to the nascent women's labor movement. In February 1900—even before Donnelly arrived in Chicago—a group of largely Irish women working in the canning department spontaneously struck the Libby, McNeil and Libby plant. These women, fired and blacklisted by the packers, began the Maud Gonne Club and continued to organize. Led by Hannah O'Day and Maggie Condon, they formed Local 183 of the Amalgamated in March 1902. This was the first women's local in the stockyards, and despite its Irish nationalist name, it stretched across departmental and ethnic lines, echoing the old Knights of Labor approach. Mollie Daly became Local 183's president as it continued to attract a small but militant membership in the summer of that year. In 1904, the Amalgamated went on strike and lost after a bitter battle with the packers. However, Local 183's legacy can be found in the Chicago

Women's Trade Union League (1904), of which Mary McDowell became the first president and Local 183's business agent, Maud Sutter, its first vice president.

Donnelley's union disappeared from the stockyards until World War One, when another attempt at organization emerged. This time, under the pretext of wartime socialism and national unity, the federal government intervened on the workers' behalf; but once the war ended, the packers again moved against the union. African Americans provided a source of strikebreakers to the packers and so many in the union hoped to drive blacks out of the stockyards. The terrible race riot of 1919 could be blamed in part on competition between white and black workers over packinghouse jobs, yet the Great Migration of the wartime years certainly made African Americans a permanent force in Chicago and in the packing industry. In the winter of 1921–22, the packers defeated the Amalgamated Meat Cutters in a violent strike that decimated the union.[53]

The period from 1886 to the early 1920s witnessed the dramatic growth of Chicago's meatpacking industry, and its spread throughout the nation. As World War One came to an end, it seemed as if Chicago would never relinquish its hold on the industry and the nation's meat supply. Organized labor lay defeated by strong opposition from the packers, its own internal conflicts, and lack of government support. In its place, a type of corporate welfare was established with the hope of keeping unions out permanently, what one author called the "Humanizing of the Packing Industry." During this time, the packers established better working conditions, medical services, some pensions, lunchrooms, and other improvements—all in the name of industrial peace and, of course, corporate profits. The Square Mile continued to generate millions of dollars for investors and to lead the industry's foray into the modern.[54]

5

SLAUGHTERHOUSE BLUES

The Decline and Fall of the
Union Stock Yard

A trend in the direction of private trading has been under way since at least 1920. Such direct trading has been sponsored by both producers and packers, and has been aided by the decentralization of the packing industry and the increased use of motor-truck transportation.

EDWARD A. DUDDY AND DAVID A. REVZAN,
The Distribution of Livestock from the Chicago Market, 1924–29 (1932)

*

On the morning of December 23, 1910, as the city prepared for Christmas, a fire broke out in Building Number 7 of the Morris and Company plant in the stockyards. The meatpacker had been warned various times about the quality of electrical wiring in the structure, but Chicago's building codes were neither strict nor enforced. At about 4 o'clock in the morning, Paul Leska, a night watchman at Morris and Company, noticed smoke coming up out of the hide cellar. He opened the cellar door, and smoke and flames almost overwhelmed him. Leska struggled up the stairs leaving the fire door open. He sounded the alarm and went to search for a fire hose while the flames reached the rest of the warehouse basement and then up the stairs. Grease-soaked wooden floors fed the flames, and the inferno spread. The Chicago Fire Department responded quickly, as they often had—and needed to—to blazes in Packingtown and the Union Stock Yards.

The perpetual challenge of low-water pressure in the stockyards was exacerbated because Morris and Company's workers had shut down the standpipes in fear of them freezing. A Morris employee had to be found to turn the water back on, causing a ten-minute delay before a stream flowed through the hydrants. More firemen raced to the site. The warehouse abutted railroad tracks on Loomis Street, filled with refrigerated cars set up to be filled during the coming morning shift. Firemen found themselves working furiously between the tracks and the warehouse dock covered by a large canopy.

Fire Chief James Horan arrived at roughly 5:00 a.m. to take command of the firefighters. Standing under the canopy, he assessed the situation and quickly gave commands to his men. Pressure from the heat inside the building continued to mount. Horan and his men found themselves in a precarious position between the railroad cars and the building. Suddenly, they heard an "awful grinding sound," and the wall separated from the building, burying Horan and the others in rubble. In the greatest single loss of life in Chicago Fire Department history, twenty-one firemen and three other men died. Ten Chicago Fire Department officers, including Horan and Assistant Fire Marshall William Burroughs perished. Thirty-four other firefighters were injured.[1]

Edward Morris, president of Morris and Company, his wife, and two sons, Edward Jr. and Nelson, arrived on the scene. Morris exclaimed his sorrow for the deaths and injuries. That afternoon he issued a statement, "I regret more than words can tell the loss of Chiefs Horan and Burroughs and all the brave firemen. Chief Horan has been a good friend of mine for years and I mourn the loss of an efficient officer and fireman." Chief Horan had written a letter to the meatpackers on December 16, just days before, recommending a high-pressure water system be built in the stockyards, a safety issue the city had ignored for years. Just twelve hours earlier, he had addressed the city council on the matter. The answer was always no, because of a lack of funds. The packers had offered to build their own system, but the aldermen refused, not wanting to lose the income the city made from supplying water to the industry. Rarely has the human cost of such fiscal politics been made so tragically clear.[2] In addition, Morris estimated the financial loss to his company at $1 million ($25 million in 2014).

The Union Stock Yard had always been a dangerous place for firefighters. The pens, docks, and chutes were wooden, and for much of its first forty years, so were the streets. Disaster struck periodically. Many of the packinghouses had brick walls, but wooden interiors. Grease and blood soaked wood floors, and the many industrial processes used combustible materials, all of which created a tremendous fire hazard.

The ruins of the Morris Company building that collapsed and killed twenty-four men. Notice the railroad tracks that abutted the structure and made it difficult to fight the blaze. (Author's Collection.)

The inferno at the Morris warehouse would not be the last that the Square Mile would know. A few months later on February 18, 1911, a fire struck an Armour and Company building just east of the 1910 Morris fire site. One month later, some five hundred cattle perished when roughly forty cattle pens caught fire in the Union Stock Yard: firemen could not free the animals from the padlocked pens. In mid-May, yet another fire broke out in the Back of the Yards neighborhood just to the southwest of Packingtown. The meat industry monopolized water, and so yet again insufficient water pressure resulted in the destruction of fourteen wooden homes, mostly two-flats, displacing more than two hundred people. Over the next five years, serious fire hit the stockyards at least eleven times. Four of these blazes occurred at the Nelson Morris plant. One of these destroyed the Transit House on January 9, 1912; the USY&T Company replaced the historic structure with another, dubbed the Stockyard Inn.[3]

Adequate insurance and vast profits meant that the burned buildings would quickly be rebuilt, and nothing seemed to faze the management of the huge meatpacking machine. While firemen complained of
the poorly planned buildings and wooden pens, managers kept building and rebuilding, as the stockyard seemed as if it would last forever,
making money to burn—or spend on structures that had burned. In
1922, meatpacking was the largest industry by volume in the United
States, ranking above both the steel and the automobile industries, and
Chicago remained the center of this vast business.[4]

Change

Nelson Morris had died three years before the disastrous 1910 fire; his
son Edward died in 1913, three years after the conflagration. At that
point, their trusted employee Thomas Wilson became president of the
company only to leave three years later to create Wilson and Company
as the successor to the financially troubled Schwarzschild and Sulzberger Company. Wilson returned that company to prosperity, and it
remained one of the Big Four for years. A powerful New York syndi-
cate made an offer to buy the Morris Company, but Edward Morris's
widow, August Swift's daughter Helen, chose not to sell, hoping that
her sons would eventually run the company. In 1923, the Morris name
disappeared as the firm merged with Armour and Company. Some
complained that this acquisition was another move by the Chicago
packers to monopolize the industry, but Armour successfully fought
off the complaints and the purchase went through. What might seem as
business as usual was actually one of the signs of the decline to come.[5]

Even as the Union Stock Yard reached its peak during World War
One and the years directly afterward, the industry began to change,
with a direct impact on the livestock market and Packingtown. During
the war, some fifty thousand employees labored in Chicago's leading
industry. The Square Mile bustled with energy. Forty years earlier,
the *Texas Livestock Journal*, as reported in the *Daily Drovers Journal*,
predicted that refrigeration in general and the refrigerated railcar in
particular would cause the decline of Chicago as a meatpacking center. The huge amount of capital required to take advantage of the new
technology meant further concentration of meatpacking and the end
to smaller independent slaughterhouses. They foresaw that, along with
small independent packers, the hundreds of men engaged in the mar-

keting and shipping of live cattle would be pushed out of the business. Anything—such as the large Chicago conglomerations—that meant less competition between buyers would have a negative impact on producers, and would bring lower prices for livestock.

The *New Mexico News and Press* further forecast that animals would not be slaughtered in large urban centers, but on the range, to be shipped east in refrigerated railcars. Producers could then sell their livestock on contract directly to a local packinghouse. Shippers would simply drive their livestock to the local abattoir and save on shipping charges, yardage fees, feed bills, and payments made to commission agents. Furthermore, the expensive practice of producers accompanying animals to market would also disappear. Livestock men would not lose money on shrinkage or see their profits reduced by crippled or dead animals on arrival after the long trip by rail to Chicago. For the packer, the proposed new system would eliminate yardage and transfer fees at the stockyards and refrigeration would allow them to hold meat until it could bring the highest possible price on eastern markets. Several packers told the *Lake Vindicator* in 1883 that the Union Stock Yards would soon slip into decline, that the record number of hogs arriving at Chicago that year would never be equaled. They asserted that the center of livestock production had moved west and that Chicago would go the way of Cincinnati as a packing center. Other changes magnified the process put in place in the 1880s. Many of these transformations would occur, as the farsighted western journalists had predicted, although not for many decades.[6]

In 1924, the Union Stock Yard received the greatest number of livestock in its history with 18.6 million head of livestock unloaded at its docks. That year on December 14, a record 122,749 hogs arrived at the market. This was the second year in a row that the number of livestock in the yards exceeded 18 million head. These numbers counted only the cattle, hogs, sheep, and horses that arrived for sale in the pens. Even more arrived at the stockyards' rail docks as direct sales to the packers.[7]

Statistics like these can help to explain the industry's endurance, dominance, and decline. In 1927, Chicago had the highest concentration of cold-storage space devoted exclusively to meatpacking. The city boasted 53.8 million cubic feet of cold storage space. Chicago's meat industry could absorb any number of livestock, and so in the 1920s there seemed to be no question as to the Chicago market's continued dominance. Between 1923 and 1929, of the total livestock re-

Cattle buyer and commission salesman in cattle pens in the early 1920s. The vast sea of pens covered an area of over three hundred acres at its peak. Notice the new Exchange Building in the background. (Stereopticon, Author's Collection.)

ceived at the seventeen most important markets, Chicago received 17.8 percent. Kansas City stood as its closest competitor with 13.55 percent. The Omaha Union Stock Yards came in third with 9.66 percent, and these numbers held up when looking at individual species.

By 1920, cattle arrived in Chicago from forty-two of the forty-eight states with fourteen states being significant suppliers. The largest numbers arrived from producers in Illinois, Indiana, and Iowa who sent 70 percent of receipts on the market. Wisconsin sent large numbers of dairy cows to Chicago. Hogs came to the Union Stock Yard largely from the Midwest especially from Illinois (30.20 percent) and Iowa (51.59 percent). Sheep arrived from most of the West and Midwest especially Colorado (16.04 percent), Iowa (14.88 percent), and Illinois

(12.69 percent). The Union Stock Yard set the price for livestock across the country.

Despite Chicago's continued dominance, a significant transformation began in the early 1920s. As a result of the increase in the slaughtering of cattle in packinghouses in Iowa and Wisconsin, cattle receipts from 1923 to 1929 posted an 18 percent decline. This indicated the predicted trend of farmers selling at a market close to them, and to the increased use of trucks. While livestock trucks proved convenient to farmers, the relatively high rates charged for trucking cattle favored the marketing of animals in stockyards or as direct sales closer to producers. Truck deliveries of cattle rose for sixteen markets from 2.9 percent in 1923 to 13.47 percent in 1929. This trend would prove important for all of the large terminal markets. Over the same period, the slaughter of cattle declined in Illinois, Nebraska, and Kansas. Meanwhile, the most significant increases occurred west of the Mississippi. Interior packers, including plants owned by the large Chicago packing companies, cut down the supply of cattle at Chicago.

Swine receipts also declined by just over 19 percent from 1923 to 1924, just a little less than a national decline in hog receipts at sixty-seven public markets. Chicago sold hogs from thirty-five states, while eight Corn Belt states—Illinois, Indiana, Iowa, Minnesota, Missouri, Nebraska, South Dakota, and Wisconsin—provided more than 98 percent of the hogs at the Chicago Stockyards. As rural, and later interstate, highways improved, the trucking of hogs increased by over 16 percent, and direct sales cut directly into the Chicago market. The Union Stock Yard had always been a prime hog market and remained so at the end of the 1920s, but here especially could be seen the shift in transportation and location of packinghouses that directly affected it.[8]

Variations also appeared in the receipts of those animals shipped from Chicago to eastern markets. Shipments of cattle declined absolutely, because of the waning of receipts at the Union Stock Yard, but remained about one-third of total receipts. Slaughter cattle shipments averaged about 25 percent of receipts, while feeders made up the rest. Sheep and lamb shipments for slaughter varied between 14.0 and 17.8 percent of the total number received. Generally speaking, as producers sent more sheep to market, more left for eastern slaughterhouses. In the period 1924 to 1929, the shipment of hogs from Chicago declined absolutely and relatively to the number received. This decline proved greater in Chicago than it did in East St. Louis. Things were changing, slowly, but surely.[9]

Put simply, the increased use of livestock trucks in turn decreased Chicago's advantage as a transportation nexus. Trucks were more flexible, and once reliable refrigerated trucks appeared on the nation's highway system, the railroads that crisscrossed the country and ran through Chicago lost their predominance in the meatpacking industry. Both direct buying of livestock by meatpackers and the use of the truck affected the Union Stock Yard. This would be a trend that increased after the Great Depression and World War Two, but had already made its mark on the industry by 1930.[10]

Disaster Again

The leadership of the big packers continued to change over time. By the late 1920s, another generational transformation was taking place, and outside investors became more and more important. In late 1933 and early 1934, Frederick H. Prince found himself embroiled in a takeover of Armour and Company. Prince, now the largest stockholder in the company, moved to claim the chairmanship vacated since the death of J. Ogden Armour in 1927. Banking interests had been in control of Armour and Company for some time, and Prince moved to restructure the company's finances. He remained the principal owner of the Union Stock Yard. The seventy-four-year-old Prince also was a director of both the First National Bank and the Livestock National Bank of Chicago. His battle for control of the giant packer with the banks and other stockholders, including the Armours, continued into the spring when Prince emerged as chairman of the company's finance committee. In late May, Armour and Company's directors finally agreed on a reorganization and recapitalization proposal, and Prince emerged as a major force in the packing company.[11]

Prince, although still embroiled in the Armour affair, took leave to France. While he vacationed in Europe, a fire again struck the Union Stock Yard on Saturday, May 19, 1934. The city and the Midwest had experienced an extended drought; the U.S. Weather Bureau had predicted an unseasonably warm and uncomfortable day with temperatures in the low nineties. Precipitation was running about a third below normal, and the last rainfall to reach one-tenth of an inch had occurred five weeks earlier. Winds that afternoon averaged fifteen miles per hour out of the southwest, gusting to twenty-two. These conditions echoed those of October 8, 1871, when the Great Chicago Fire broke out.

Sometime around 4:15 p.m., a car traveled over a wooden overpass that ran above the cattle pens and allowed access to Packingtown along Forty-Third Street from Halsted. The car's occupant may have thrown out a lit cigarette that fell on a pile of loose hay; or one of the workers may have been careless with smoking materials or an open flame. Investigators never determined the exact cause, but soon flames engulfed the livestock market, feeding on the dry hay and wooden pens, viaducts, and chutes.[12]

Isaac Means, a sixty-year-old watchman with the USY&T Company, spotted the fire and shouted to his fellow guard, James Fuller, to pull the alarm. Fuller and L. W. Preble later testified that the fire had started on the ground in one of the cattle pens. They both said that they fled for their lives after turning on the alarm. A longtime stockyard veteran, Means knew what to do and attempted to fight the fire and rescue livestock caught in the covered pens. He had worked most of his life in the stockyards and had held several jobs with the company over the years. His father had been a commission man. The watchman freed hundreds of animals before he was killed, the only human loss in the great disaster. Firemen found his charred body the next day.

The fire quickly spread destroying not only much of the cattle division, but both the new and old Exchange Buildings, the Dexter Park International Amphitheater, the Stockyard Inn, the Saddle and Sirloin Club, the Daily Drovers Journal Building, the U.S. Department of Agriculture Offices, the 4-H Boys' and Girls' Club Building, the Pure Bred Record Building, the Livestock National Bank, and a host of other structures. It leaped across Halsted Street and threatened Canaryville to the east. On Halsted Street, the flames consumed the Drovers National Bank as well as Big Jim O'Leary's Saloon. O'Leary— the son of Mrs. O'Leary of Chicago fire fame—had run the two-story gambling emporium at 4183 South Halsted for years.

East of Halsted, the fire destroyed some fifty residences leaving about 150 people homeless. One of the Halsted Street tavern owners, John Russell, gave away five barrels of draught beer and a dozen cases of bottled beer to thirsty firemen fighting the flames. Shortly thereafter, his generosity was rewarded as the firefighters stopped the blaze

Many Union Stock Yard landmarks were destroyed in the 1934 fire. From left to right are the remains of the Pure Bred Livestock Record Building, the 4-H Boys and Girls Club, and the Stock Yard Inn. (Author's Collection.)

and saved his establishment at 4127 South Halsted. The stockyards were in ruins, but because the wind came out of the southwest, the major packers suffered little damage.[13]

An area bounded roughly by Exchange Avenue to the north and Forty-Sixth Street on the south and from Racine on the west and Emerald Avenue to the east suffered the bulk of the tremendous damage. The USY&T Company alone accounted for about three-quarters of the estimated $8 million ($140.4 million in 2014) in losses. The blaze injured 132 firemen; 54 required hospitalization. On Sunday morning, workmen outnumbered firemen who continued to douse hot spots as the Union Stock Yard reopened for business. While 75 percent of the cattle division had been destroyed, the fire had not obliterated the entire stockyard. Since Sunday was not a market day relatively few cattle had been in the pens that Saturday: the cattle stocker and feeder divisions suffered the greatest losses as between 250 and 300 head perished in the covered sheds. The fire spared more than seven hundred unloading chutes, and neither the massive two-story hog house nor the sheep house burned. The rail lines leading into the yards remained for the most part intact.[14]

Immediately after the fire, the USY&T Company, the railroads, and the Chicago Livestock Exchange advised producers to maintain normal livestock shipments to the market. Some railroads that had been refusing to accept consignments to the Union Stock Yard due to the fire rescinded those orders, and livestock began to be loaded for Chicago late Sunday night. The fire had left enough scales unharmed to handle a reasonable day's receipts. Even before nightfall on May 19, ten cattle scales and all of the hog and sheep scales were in working condition. Temporary buildings sprung up from truckloads of lumber and material delivered to the scene. Workmen toiled all night long clearing debris and putting up temporary pens and other structures. Although the Exchange Building had burned, the six-inch concrete floors held, and safes containing commission company records went unharmed. The Chicago Livestock Exchange quickly erected a temporary Exchange Building just north of the shell of the burned out nine-story structure. Both the Livestock National Bank and the Drovers Bank announced that they would conduct operations as usual. Vaults of both banks, including vital records and securities in safety deposit boxes, came through the fire intact. The Drovers Journal Publishing Company, whose plant had been totally destroyed, also vowed to continue operations. A fire would not stop the modern!

On Monday, the first market day after the inferno, both the USY&T Company and the Chicago Livestock Exchange were pleased with operations and stated that they could handle a normal supply of all classes of livestock. The packinghouses, most of which had not been touched by the blaze, bought freely on the market to avert a possible glut should facilities prove inadequate. The packers immediately repaired all docks that had burned in their vicinity, while the stockyard company built a temporary viaduct to move livestock over the burned area to the waiting kill floors. The *Drovers Journal* commented that despite the disaster the market "worked with remarkable smoothness." Receipts for the first market day after the fire stood at 13,741 cattle, 1,316 calves, 26,376 hogs, 4,889 sheep, and 52 horses. The media reported the disaster and the spectacular rebound, and Chicagoans arrived in numbers to witness the aftermath and the rebuilding effort. The fire had provided another sense of spectacle in the Square Mile.

Frederick H. Prince returned to the United States from France on May 22, and announced that new and better structures would replace the burned out buildings and pens. He emphasized the rebuilding of the Exchange Building and the International Amphitheater. Prince arrived in Chicago to witness the damage and the rebuilding process on May 24. After taking a tour, he announced a new building for the Drovers Journal Publishing Company, the remodeling of the burned out Stock Yard Inn, along with the Live Stock Record Building. Prince revealed the plans to encourage producers and commission men to remain in the Chicago market. The next day, the stockyard company announced that the amphitheater would be rebuilt in time for the International Livestock Exposition in December. All of these moves were intended to not only reassure shippers, but to counter the decline of receipts at the Union Stock Yard. While most people could not envision the end of the livestock market, the USY&T Company saw that changes were already affecting their business even before the Great Depression.

As some publicly called to relocate the stockyards and packinghouses away from highly populated areas, the USY&T Company led the way back from the fire. On November 19, six months after the disaster, workmen put the finishing touches on the rebuilt stockyard. Stockyard president Arthur G. Leonard promised that the task of restoring the burned area would be completed by December 1 and the opening of the International Livestock Exposition. The stockyard looked much the same as it had before May 19, but concrete cattle runways, bridges, and wider streets and alleys, along with the provision of more open spaces, distinguished the newly rebuilt marketplace. Abraham Epstein, the structural engineer in charge of construction, spoke about eventually making the stockyards fireproof, but the rebuilt pens remained made of wood.

The new International Amphitheater was the largest edifice to be built. It extended 534 feet along Halsted and cost $1.3 million ($22.8 million in 2014) with $250,000 worth of lighting, heating, and cooling equipment. The building included a ten-thousand-seat arena, which replaced the old four-thousand-seat structure wrecked in the fire, and two new two-story exhibit wings. The USY&T Company also rebuilt the Exchange Building, Stockyard Inn, Pure Bred Livestock Record Building, and Livestock National Bank. Altogether the new and rebuilt structures, pens, cattle runways, bridges, street widening, and other improvements cost approximately $4 million ($70.2 million) and employed 2,500 men, the largest construction project in Chicago since 1929, outside of the Century of Progress Exposition on the lakefront.[15]

The ruins of the Drovers Bank building and other businesses on Halsted Street as the 1934 fire leaped across the major thoroughfare and burned down parts of Canaryville to the east. (Author's Collection.)

In addition, the Saddle and Sirloin Club with its extensive portrait gallery of leaders and innovators of the livestock and meatpacking industry was to be restored. The complex and expensive problem of replacing long-cherished paintings, as well as other valuable furnishings, presented itself to club directors. Insurance claims for over $50,000 ($877,193) were made on the Frederick H. Prince Room furnishings alone. Most of the portraits were replaced by January 1936. Artists painted several of these from photographs of the original or of the subjects themselves. The reconstruction of the collection insured a sense of continuity and identification with the industry, especially in its most important meeting place, the Saddle and Sirloin Club. It also symbolized the determination of the Union Stock Yard to remain the most important livestock market in the world, despite the fire, the decline in livestock receipts, and the Great Depression.[16]

UPWA-CIO

As the Great Depression began and then deepened the urge to organize again swept through Chicago's packinghouses. Defeated in the 1921–22 strike, the Amalgamated Meat Cutters and Butcher Workmen had largely withdrawn from the packing industry and concentrated on organizing retail butchering. The large packers, led by Swift and Company, instituted a welfare capitalism program, which included employee representation plans that were essentially company-run unions. These moves by management were meant to avoid any resurrection of the union movement and to insure stability in the workforce, which suffered from constant turnover. The packers joined a national movement by big corporations, most famously the Ford Motor Company, to provide their employees with various services including regular hours, the eight-hour day, cafeterias, and recreational facilities. The programs were intended to insure employee loyalty and with the employee representation plans to give some limited worker voice in the running of the plants.[17]

While some benefits had been established, the great majority of workers did not feel adequately represented. Once the Great Depression hit the industry, many of the benefits of welfare capitalism disappeared. The general urge to organize that swept across industrial America in the 1930s could not help but affect meat industry workers. A large portion of African American workers also joined the emerging union movement. They had mistrusted the Amalgamated, especially after the 1919 race riot, but now they began to be assimilated into a working-class culture that saw unionism as a positive force in their lives. As blacks overcame their distrust of white unionists and also of the Democratic Party, they began to be active in the labor movement and became New Deal supporters. Polish workers, who had been among the most vigorous advocates of unionism, now saw a much more radicalized element emerge among African American workers.[18]

Conditions in the packinghouses were bad. At the beginning of the Great Depression, Swift and the other meat companies cut wages for the employees they did not lay off. Sophie Kosciowlowski, a longtime union organizer and official, recalled her wages being cut from 31.5 cents per hour to 28.5 cents. Men's wages listed at about a dime higher. By the late 1930s, workers at Armour's began to organize in secret. Kosciowlowski described conditions as terrible, close to slavery. She

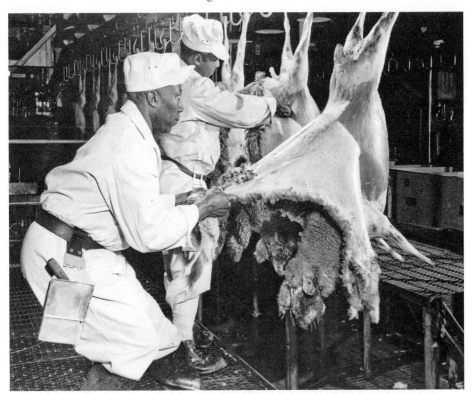

These African American workers are pulling sheep hides at Swift and Company. They represent the growing number of black men and women entering the packinghouses after 1915. By the 1930s and 1940s, blacks took up many of the skilled and semiskilled positions in the plant. They proved crucial to the organizing efforts of the CIO in Packingtown. (iCHi-21358, Courtesy of Chicago History Museum.)

complained of cockroaches, especially the flying roaches called "bombers" in the stockyards. These could be as big as one and a half inches, and they "buzzed" around inside the packinghouses. Union men and women went about the Armour plants and pasted or wrote CIO (Congress of Industrial Organizations) on the clocks. Union adherents wore Packinghouse Workers Organizing Committee (PWOC) buttons in secret. They noted that, as far as conditions went, not much had changed since Sinclair wrote *The Jungle*.[19]

While the Amalgamated Meat Cutters had shown little interest in organizing packinghouse workers, they did regard the efforts of the CIO a matter of dual unionism and thus opposed its efforts. The PWOC represented the new industrial unionism of the CIO led by the United

Mine Workers' John L. Lewis in opposition to the old AFL approach of craft unionism. This industrial union approach was actually used by the Amalgamated during its earlier attempts to organize the stockyards and Packingtown. In October 1938, despite opposition not only from management, but the Amalgamated Meat Cutters, PWOC won a resounding victory at Armour's Chicago plant. By mid-1940, all of Armour's three major plants had been organized by PWOC. In addition, PWOC Local 28 made gains at Swift and Company. The packer followed the departmental seniority policy demanded by Local 28 during the spring seasonal layoffs. A decision by the National Labor Relations Board (NLRB) in Sioux City that found Swift guilty of unfair labor practices mandated the dissolution of the company employee representation plan, encouraging the growth of Local 28. Two gangs in the Chicago plant's dry cure department joined PWOC. Dues payments also jumped after the NLRB decision. By mid-May, nearly one hundred union stewards worked to organize the Swift plant. PWOC felt that soon all the major Chicago packing plants would have contracts. The union demanded all packers agree to a nondiscrimination clause, to put an end to ethnic and racial discrimination in hiring practices. By the fall of 1940, the Swift organizational drive had made big strides, and the union expected a federal conciliator to break the deadlock at Wilson and Company, which still refused to negotiate with PWOC.[20]

In February 1941, Armour and Company's workers demanded a national contract with the CIO union. Negotiations began on April 1 in Omaha. Armour's workers appealed for national unity, but workers from some plants boycotted the conference. Meanwhile, the Chicago Swift PWOC organized more workers. On April 29, the NLRB declared Wilson's Employee Representation Plan illegal. The company in turn openly defied the order and allowed its company union to conduct an election on May 6, 1941. In many departments, pro-CIO activists drove out the Wilson representatives and refused to participate in the balloting. It took until 1943, but PWOC-CIO won a NLRB election at Wilson's. In December 1943, the Back of the Yards Neighborhood Council, a local neighborhood organization, lent its support to the CIO's wage demands in the stockyards.[21]

During World War Two, union certification and national contracts reduced management's arbitrary authority, but work conditions did not change for the better. The National War Labor Board (NWLB), with its goal of production in support of the war effort, hindered the union's attempt to improve conditions. The NWLB had a great deal of power and did not hesitate to use it. Its main goal was to keep the supply of meat flowing to the armed forces. Indeed, during the conflict Chicago's meat industry performed admirably. Armour and Company won the prestigious Army-Navy "E" Pennant for outstanding production in support of the war effort in both its Chicago packinghouse and at the Armour laboratory. The company pointed out that it struggled to maintain its labor force as nationwide it lost more than fifteen thousand men and women to the armed forces with female workers growing in proportion to male Armour employees.[22]

The series of victories by organized labor in the late 1930s and early 1940s resulted to some extent from New Deal reforms that established the NLRB. It also benefited from a group of dedicated leftist organizers not only from the CIO, but also from the neighborhoods surrounding the Union Stock Yard. Herb March, who was shot during an organizing campaign and later forced out of the United Packinghouse Workers because of his ties to the Communist Party, was among the most active. Other left-leaning organizers, and some avowed communists, served as a base for the union locals in the stockyards. The union headquarters was initially located in Sikora's Hall in Back of the Yards on Forty-Eighth and Marshfield Street, but after an organization affiliated with the Communist Party ran into financial difficulties, the United Packinghouse Workers took over its building on Wabash Avenue in Bronzeville to the east of the stockyards. The union moved its head office to Bronzeville, Chicago's segregated African American neighborhood to the east of Canaryville and Bridgeport, not only to bail out the left-wing group, but also to acknowledge the growing importance of African American workers among its ranks.

World War Two had sped up the turnover of packinghouse jobs from white to black. Until 1939, perhaps 80 percent of the mostly white-ethnic families in Back of the Yards, depended directly on the packing industry for their livelihoods. After the war, much of the younger American-born generation abandoned the plants and moved on to what they considered "clean" industries to the south and west of the neighborhood. Saul Alinsky, one of the founders of the Back of the Yards Neighborhood Council, said, "You can't get the younger fellows to take those jobs at all. Most of them have better paying jobs in new

Women workers from Armour and Company's canning department, circa 1940. These women joined the United Packinghouse Workers early in their campaign to organize Armour and Company in Chicago (Author's Collection.)

factories that have sprung up west of the neighborhood where they live." By 1958, nearly 80 percent of the packinghouse workforce was black, with a growing Mexican minority.

The organizational structure of the industry and especially of the newly formed UPWA-CIO left a good deal of power in the hands of the union locals, often without the national leadership exerting much control. The relationship resembled that between the Knights of Labor and their local packinghouse assemblies in the 1886 strike. Locals dominated the structure, and rank and file pressure often determined relationships with management. Management in turn remained generally opposed to the union, and often refused to work with union leadership.

Militancy often marked the Chicago labor movement. Workers disobeyed or ignored the national leadership, a long tradition in Packingtown, and a coalition of African Americans, left-wing radicals, and white unionists came together to form PWOC. While these three groups worked together to oppose the national CIO leadership's attempt to enforce discipline, tensions existed among them. The formation of the United Packinghouse Workers (UPWA) from the PWOC in October 1943 created a formidable union in meatpacking, although clashes between the new union and management frequently erupted in the form of wildcat strikes. The union claimed that supervisors often provoked these actions by harassing workers and violating established seniority procedures. When the union and management reached an agreement, it sometimes took weeks to enforce a decision.[23]

As the war came to an end, both packers and the union each saw the other as adversaries. The UPWA allowed black workers to take a greater leadership role, and many saw the struggle for the union as part of a larger struggle for civil rights. As the war ended, the UPWA began to feel it could improve wages and conditions. Workers obviously favored a strike. In September and October 1945, five brief work stoppages occurred at the Chicago Armour plant alone. Management refused to meet union demands and offered only a 7.5-cent increase. The locals voted by a 20 to 1 ratio to call a national meatpacking strike.[24]

On January 16, 1946, the UPWA along with the Amalgamated Meat Cutters announced a strike. Local support proved invaluable as the Back of the Yards Neighborhood Council (BYNC) spent $7,500 ($91,463 in 2014) to feed union pickets and Chicago police alike. In addition, the organization gave food, clothing, and medical care to strikers' families. The BYNC president, Father Ambrose Ondrak of St. Michael's Slovak Catholic Church on Damen Avenue, walked the picket line along with Joe Meegan, director of the BYNC, and Father Edward Plewinski of St. John of God, one of three Polish parishes in Back of the Yards. Ten days later, President Harry Truman nationalized the packing companies under the still in force War Labor Disputes Act. The UPWA threatened to continue the strike unless the federal government could give it assurances, and a federal commission awarded the packinghouse workers a 16-cent per-hour raise, the largest in the history of the industry. But because the union had wanted a 25-cent raise, many considered the 1946 strike a failure.[25]

Among the packers, Wilson and Company emerged as the most antiunion. Vice president James D. Cooney stated that during the war the federal government made the packers give the unions more than

An interracial group of white, African American, and Hispanic UPWA-CIO members rally in front of Swift Local 28's office on Ashland Avenue's Whiskey Row in 1946. (Photo by Acme Newspictures, Author's Collection.)

they wanted or could give, because they had to deliver meat to the armed forces. But he stated that "now there is not a friendly administration begging for them, who can make us give them more than is warranted from the merits of the situation." Cooney bitterly resented the UPWA and the militancy of its membership. He promised that now with the help of more friendly federal, state, and local governments the packers would tame the UPWA or destroy it. Chicago's Mayor Ed Kelly sat on Wilson and Company's Board of Directors, and the political reaction against the New Deal and the labor movement had set in.[26]

Union leadership hoped that the postwar era would see stabilization in the industry and the acknowledgment of the union as a major partner in the industry. Elected union president in 1946, Ralph Helstein represented a growing center-left faction in the UPWA that hoped to reduce shop floor disorders by reaching a stable accord with the dominant firms in the meatpacking industry. The following year, the Labor

Management Relations Act of 1947, better know as the Taft-Hartley Act, curtailed union activities. It passed over President Truman's veto and empowered management. The bill restricted the unions; power and effectively demobilized labor by putting limits on organized labor's ability to strike; it was part of a reaction against the national wave of strikes that took place in 1946.[27] The packers supported such antiunion legislation and were prepared for a showdown.

In January 1948, as the UPWA jockeyed for a 29-cent per-hour pay increase, the American Federation of Labor's Amalgamated Meat Cutters settled for a 9-cent raise. Dual unionism presented a problem, as this ensured that those plants with an Amalgamated contract could not walk out in support of a UPWA strike. Also, members of the Swift independent union, the National Brotherhood of Packinghouse Workers (NBPW), probably would not strike. It seemed that the UPWA would be unable to pull off a successful national stoppage. Nevertheless, the union maintained its demands, and in February local unions authorized a national walk out, union leaders gave the companies a March 16 deadline, and refused to take a call from President Harry Truman to delay the confrontation. Taft-Hartley rules hindered the union and made it possible for the packers to prepare for the clash. The strike dragged on for thirteen weeks and was marred by violence. Chicago unionist Santo Cicardo died when a truck driven by a strikebreaker barreled through a picket line at Armour and Company. This time, federal, state, and local authorities proved hostile to the packinghouse workers, both nationally and locally. The changed political atmosphere encouraged the packers to hold their ground, and more violence between police and strikers broke out as management attempted to import strikebreakers.

Although nationally the atmosphere remained hostile to strike actions, locally the UPWA again garnered much support from the Back of the Yards Neighborhood Council, Catholic parishes in Back of the Yards, and African American Protestant churches in Bronzeville. Soup kitchens at the University of Chicago Settlement House in Back of the Yards and the union headquarters in Bronzeville fed 3,000 workers each day. UPWA strike funds ran low still. The UPWA dominated the Big Five packers, but the Amalgamated had about 11,000 members in the Big Five plants and the NBPW probably had between 10,000 and 12,000 members in Swift plants nationally. The union lost the 1948 strike and reaction against leftist leadership emerged, with Herb

March forced out after Swift employees complained about his influence, raising the question of whether the union could survive. The
Packinghouse Workers eventually recovered, but the strike's impact
on Chicago as a meatpacking center would soon be apparent.[28]

In the early 1950s, the Jesuit sociologist Theodore V. Purcell interviewed workers at the Chicago Swift plant. Despite the Cold War
purges and the 1948 defeat, the union remained popular with the
men and women in the plant. But Purcell's study also found that Swift
workers' allegiance to the union was not as pronounced as to the company. Swift had been among the first to promote welfare capitalism in
the stockyards, and such practices made it a very popular employer.
Still nearly 80 percent of Swift workers also felt an allegiance to the
UPWA. Those opposed to the union tended to be older long-term employees, both white and black, who saw the company as providing a
sense of security. In addition, some of the white workers had become
alienated from the union after the headquarters moved to Bronzeville and the union stressed racial justice issues. The UPWA became
very involved in the civil rights movement of the 1950s and 1960s, and
Chicago's mixture of race and neighborhood politics could not but influence the local union movement. That a division remained between
traditional bread-and-butter union issues and larger societal ones
was not surprising. Many workers felt that job protection, increased
wages, and benefits should be the main goal of the labor movement,
and so they sometime chafed under the larger societal goals of radical
unionism.[29]

More Innovation and the End of Spectacle:
The Big Packers Leave

The journalist Alan Ehrenhalt, in his book *Lost City*, claims that before
the 1960s, Chicago's industries remained loyal to their city and their
employees. This vision of the past is not accurate, however attractive
it might be. In actuality, the packers constantly threatened to move out
of Chicago beginning as early as 1886. Chicago's packinghouse workers
knew all too well that ownership remained loyal only to the bottom
line. After 1933, as livestock receipts decreased at the Union Stock
Yard, the packinghouses continued to develop off-market plants and
the threat of plant closings hung over the workforce. The emergence of
the UPWA-CIO in the late 1930s and 1940s further complicated mat-

ters for the meatpackers, who began to see their Chicago location with its increasingly pro-union political culture as a less valuable asset.[30]

Once the Great Depression and World War Two ended, management looked—as it always had—toward modernization and new technologies. The increased use of trucks to move livestock and the refrigerated truck to move meat products provided a greater geographical flexibility for the industry. Once again, Chicago's packers were at the forefront of change as they worked to maintain their market position. In the immediate postwar era decentralization, the truck, single-story plants, interstate highways, and the suburbs created a new sense of the modern.

In October 1952, Swift and Company closed down its hog slaughtering operations in Chicago claiming that hog receipts were too small and the buildings too expensive to maintain. What the *Chicago Tribune* called one of the stockyards "best-known spectacles" came to an end. Swift and Company maintained that it intended to continue purchasing hogs on the Chicago market for shipment to its plants in other cities and towns, but nonetheless the Swift decision portended the complete decline of the industry in Chicago.[31]

That same year, Wilson opened a modern packinghouse in Kansas City. The new structure proved to be more efficient than the old, giant, nine-story packinghouse it replaced. The old Kansas City plant had consisted of several buildings over thirteen acres and occupied more than a million square feet. Wilson replaced it with a two-story building that covered only one acre. The hog butchering functions, which had processed 150 hogs per hour, had taken up two stories in the older structures; now, the hog kill floor was contained in a single eighty-by-fifty-foot room. The new slaughterhouse took advantage of modern manufacturing techniques, especially an engineered line layout in the pork cutting and trimming department. It proved to be a pacesetting plant for Wilson and Company as well as for the industry, symbolic of the way that earlier innovations had set the pace on the Chicago kill floors.[32]

Three years later, in 1955, Wilson and Company shuttered its massive slaughtering operations in Chicago. On September 17, Wilson ceased all cattle operations in the city. A week later, the company closed down its hog kill. The shutdown took its toll on some three thousand workers, of which over two thousand were African Americans, and shocked Packingtown employees. The company said that

Charles Tormoehlen on the far left and three other hog salesmen in the old two-story hog house, circa 1956. (Courtesy of Rob Berekery.)

the plant was old, outmoded, and expensive and that it planned to move operations to Cedar Rapids, Iowa, Albert Lea, Minnesota, and Omaha, Nebraska, while relocating its national headquarters to the Loop. Ralph Helstein and Charles Hayes, officials of the United Packinghouse Workers, charged that Wilson would move most operations to its nonunion plant in Oklahoma City. It seemed obvious to many that Wilson had decided to leave the UPWA behind in Chicago as it expanded operations in states with antiunion laws.[33]

Swift and Armour maintained their Chicago shops for a while longer, but in April 1957 Swift stopped processing fresh pork in Packingtown. The next year, it announced that it had consolidated some operations and hoped to improve efficiency across all of its locations. The company had spent $300 million on new facilities nationwide since World War Two, and that year construction began on a new fifty-nine-acre plant in Wilson, North Carolina. The new slaughterhouse would slaughter cattle, calves, and hogs, and the company planned to purchase as great a portion of its requirements as possible directly from the local producers, avoiding livestock markets altogether.

In January 1959, the company stopped slaughtering lambs and calves in Chicago, again with the excuse of low livestock receipts. Then in April, Swift closed down its domestic sausage and canned meat production. Finally in May, it announced that it would discontinue the cattle kill at Chicago on June 13. Walter Schuette, the Chicago plant manager, said that studies had shown that continuation of the beef operations was no longer profitable. A fire on May 2, which had damaged beef cutting and boning operations, simply accelerated the inevitable. Swift vowed to continue purchasing livestock on the Chicago market and to employ about three thousand workers in the stockyards. Several nonslaughtering operations continued, but the complete closure of the Swift plant was only a matter of time. The number of workers employed at Swift had fallen by roughly three thousand since 1952.

In October 1959, Swift announced it would build a slaughterhouse eighty miles west of Chicago on the southeast outskirts of Rochelle, Illinois, proclaiming that the new plant would be the most modern in the company's history. Swift President Porter Jarvis stated, "Rochelle is in the heart of an important live stock producing area, where there has been a definite and continuing increase in cattle feeding and hog production." The plant would be ideally situated to take advantage of highway and railroad connections to enable livestock producers to bring animals directly to the plant. Obviously, livestock brought to the Rochelle plant would be purchased direct from such producers, circumventing the terminal livestock market middlemen. The new full-line facility would basically replace the Chicago plant and slaughter all types of livestock. Construction began in the spring of 1960, and Swift officials pledged that it would provide better service to consumers in northern Illinois and the Chicago area. Jarvis explained to reporters, "The day of the big packinghouse is gone. It was built to handle the maximum amount of livestock at any given time. Now with changes in feeding and production, there is no need for such plants." Jarvis emphasized thrift and the elimination of waste in operations while making the best possible products for the consumer as long-standing Swift traditions. The new plant began operations in March 1962, and on June 23 more than thirty thousand people toured the facility. Meatpacking was again, a public spectacle, showcasing the modern.[34]

In 1960, Swift and Company celebrated its seventy-fifth anniversary as an Illinois corporation. During that time A. H. Fritschel, the company's secretary, noted that Swift had grown from one plant with annual sales of $5 million to a corporate giant with more than five hundred units and sales of over $2.5 billion ($20 billion in 2014). Swift began the year on an upswing, with a prediction of even greater profits. Jarvis explained to stockholders in January that earnings were off to a good start for 1960. While not mentioned at the meeting, Swift workers in Chicago faced a bleak future. The next year Libby, McNeil and Libby, a Swift subsidiary, left Packingtown after seventy-three years. Once a major slaughterer, the company now produced other sorts of canned goods, and they built a new, smaller plant in suburban Blue Island that had virtually doubled the output of the old plant. Again, streamlined and mechanized handling operations increased worker output and efficiencies. In August 1961, Swift closed its head-quarters in the Union Stock Yard and moved to the Loop at 115 West Jackson Boulevard.[35]

In 1954, Armour and Company announced a vast modernization program of its plant in Chicago, part of a promise that the company had made to stockholders when the war ended nine years earlier. The $10 million scheme ($87.7 million) called for the elimination of some 50 buildings as the company planned to reduce its footprint from 121 buildings on twenty-three blocks to about 70 structures on eleven city blocks. Company president F. W. Specht had outlined the proposal at the annual stockholders meeting in Chicago. He told of large losses in the hog operation, and said it would be about a year and a half be-fore a new hog operation was in place. Specht predicted that once the modernization program was complete, the Chicago plant would be as efficient as any in the company. In 1957, the former president of the Union Stock Yard and Transit Company, William Wood Prince, be-came president of Armour and Company. He had served as a director of the company since 1950 and as vice chairman since February 1957. Many thought that Prince's elevation to the presidency and the fact that he, like his stepfather Frederick H. Prince, still retained control-ling interest in the USY&T Company guaranteed the packer's pres-ence in Chicago.

Armour and Company, however, announced in 1958 that it planned to move its general offices out of the Union Stock Yard to a downtown location at 401 North Wabash. The company had occupied its office building at Forty-Third and Racine Avenue since the early 1900s, and about 1,100 personnel worked in the structure next to the market's cattle pens. The original move from the downtown to the Union Stock Yard symbolized the close relationship between Armour and the stockyards. Now Armour and Company's headquarters abandoned the livestock market and moved back to the Loop, Chicago's vibrant business center. In addition, Armour would only occupy one floor in the new location. The company explained that the functions of the administrative staff had been reduced as responsibilities had been realigned in the corporation.

Nineteen months later, on July 11, 1959, despite the fact that Armour and Company had recently modernized its Chicago operations, the firm ceased all slaughtering operations at the Union Stock Yard, letting go some two thousand employees. The Chicago closing marked the beginning of the shutdown of other Armour plants across the country as William Wood Prince led the drive to modernize and decentralize the packer's plants. By this time, Chicago's packinghouse workers had become accustomed to the realities of a dying and, perhaps more importantly, de-unionizing and decentralizing industry: in six years, the number of workers in Packingtown had fallen from twenty-two thousand to six thousand. Armour initially held out the hope that it might return slaughtering operations to Chicago. Like Swift, the company also promised to continue to purchase livestock on the market for its East Coast plants. In October 1960, despite these promises, Armour cut its last ties with the Union Stock Yard and sold its property. In realigning its production, Armour purchased four plants and construction of a new plant in Houston had already begun with another plant soon to be built in Oklahoma City, two non-union-friendly states. The last of the Big Three packers was gone.[36]

As the packers it supplied left town, the Union Stock Yard and Transit Company attempted to adjust to the times. It had been first established as a shipping market, and it looked to that past. In 1957, Chicago remained the largest livestock market in the country with 4.9 million head of livestock, but this was a mere fraction of the numbers that arrived at the market before 1933. St. Paul, East St. Louis, and Omaha ranked close behind with over 4 million receipts each. Charles S. Potter, Prince's friend who had replaced him as president of the Union Stock Yard, optimistically pointed to 1958 as a better year for the market. An advertisement in the *Chicago Daily Drovers Journal* boasted that over three hundred off-market packers purchased livestock at the stockyards and that high-speed rail service and truck service connected Chicago to important eastern packers.[37] In January 1958, the USY&T Company announced a vast modernization plan. Potter declared, "Chicago will not be only the largest livestock market in the world, but also the most up to date in facilities for both buyer and seller." The announcement outlined an ambitious plan that would free up land north of Exchange Avenue for other industrial development. The stockyard company also made known plans for a new hog house, a rail shipping division, new cattle pens, aluminum shelter houses throughout the pen area, a comfortable waiting area in the Exchange Building for visiting farm families, and a covered overhead walkway so that guests could walk above the pens and see market operations.

Management emphasized the fact that off-market buyers played an increasingly important role. Since 1949, off-market firms had greatly increased their presence at the Union Stock Yard. That year, these companies shipped 37.8 percent of salable cattle receipts, while in the first six months of 1959 they purchased 59.3 percent. The same trend could be seen in the hog and sheep markets as well. Potter asserted that while the yards would be cutting back on acreage, it simply concentrated its operations to become more efficient. In 1961, the company opened a new rail shipping division along Racine Avenue.

Small, local, independent packers served an important function on the Chicago market, expanding operations and taking up some of the slack left by the Big Three. Millard Cook, vice president of the USY&T Company, drew a contrast between operations decades previously when most livestock were slaughtered in Chicago. Cook claimed that despite the closing of the Wilson plant, competition on the market had increased. So-called Hot Shot rail service, which commenced four months previous to Wilson's closing, allowed the market to continue without even feeling Wilson's absence. He noted that more than 1,000 rail cars left the Union Stock Yard each week. Faster rail service to the East Coast meant that animals did not have to be watered and fed en route. New fifty-foot all-steel rail cars introduced in 1959 increased the load capacity of the old forty-foot cars allowing for 33 head of cattle per car as compared with 22 in the older units. Cook also pointed out that some 1,600 trucks unloaded livestock at the stockyards every Sunday night. Double-deck and triple-deck trucks now connected the yards with eastern packing plants, carrying from 135 to 160 hogs per load. The triple-deckers could carry 160 to 211 head and reach their destinations in time for the next morning's slaughter.[38]

Charles Potter's reaction to the closing of Armour and Company again showed that in the previous ten years purchases by meatpackers outside of Chicago had grown and had just about balanced any loses in local meatpacking operations. During that period, the total salable receipts averaged 5 million head annually. Potter exclaimed that "other major packers—Swift and Wilson—have previously stopped slaughtering operations in Chicago, but the market each time has attracted new buyers." A good example of this was Harold Shannon and Company, the largest livestock-order-buying firm on the Indianapolis market, which started buying in Chicago on June 1, 1959. Potter also pointed out that local independent packers had increased their kills. In 1959, American Meat Packing, run by Edward Ochylski, moved its operations from Detroit to Chicago. F. R. (Lee) Miller, president of the Chicago Livestock Exchange, optimistically alleged that in previous years Chicago's small packers could not compete with Armour, Swift, and Wilson for livestock on the market, and therefore had not operated at full capacity. He claimed that independent packing firms operating at points farther west would make more purchases at Chicago. Indeed, the city's small, union-organized packers did increase their purchase of cattle on the market by 68 percent over a ten-year period beginning in 1949.[39]

Despite continued business and new efficiencies in the Union Stock Yard, Packingtown took on the appearance of an industrial ghost town, with its abandoned buildings, docks, and railroad tracks. Row after row of eight- and ten-story buildings stood vacant. Rubble-strewn fields replaced demolished buildings. A few remained in use, but they provided only a small fraction of the number of jobs once offered in the district. Packingtown, and its workers' neighborhoods, which had benefited before from technological change, now suffered from it, portending the postindustrial future.[40]

Longtime trends, and receipt numbers, could not be denied. In 1933 during the Great Depression, 7.8 million hogs arrived for sale at Chicago. Twenty years later, 2.3 million hogs came to the market, a decline of more than 70 percent. In 1936, 2.6 million sheep went on sale as compared to 834,993 in 1953, a 67 percent drop. Cattle receipts did stay consistent throughout the period. Chicago, with its proximity to

The Stockyard Kilty Band marches through the Stone Gate during commemorations marking the one hundredth anniversary of the opening of the Union Stock Yard in 1965. (Courtesy of the Stockyard Kilty Band.)

midwestern farms, remained a strong fine-cattle market despite the fact that other species had dropped off considerably. During the crises of World War Two, livestock receipts topped 10 million three times in 1942, 1943, and 1944, never to reach that number again. In 1950, 6.2 million head arrived at the stockyards. Seven years later, the numbers slipped below 6 million, and in 1962 only 3.7 million head of livestock arrived at the Union Stock Yard. Of these, 2.3 million sold to off-market packers. These downward trends continued throughout the 1960s. As unanticipated as it was, the end of the Union Stock Yard was clear to anyone who looked.[41]

The Stockyards Close

The decline of the meatpacking industry in Chicago continued after the Big Three abandoned the stockyards. In August 1963, the Agar

Packing and Provision Corporation announced it was shutting its plant just east of the stockyards at 4057 South Union Avenue. John Bradley, Agar's managing director, said that henceforth all slaughtering would be done at the company's new plant in Momence, Illinois. Their processing of canned hams and bacon had previously been transferred to Hately Brothers on Thirty-Seventh Street. Both Agar and Hately were subsidiaries of the Commercial Credit Corporation of Baltimore. The Momence plant began operation on November 19, 1962, and slaughtered 2,700 hogs a day, delivering the carcasses to the Chicago plant for processing. It employed roughly three hundred workers and covered about five acres of the ten-acre site. Agar, with a daily capacity of 4,000 hogs, had been the biggest hog slaughterer in the stockyards once the Big Three departed. Tougher federal inspection laws led to the closing of even more Chicago slaughtering and meatpacking operations.[42]

In the 1960s, the city put more and more pressure on the Union Stock Yard and nearby plants to curtail odors. The legendary stockyard "stench" still seemed to prevail, as Darling and Company maintained a major fertilizer and rendering plant in Packingtown. Neighborhood complaints against that company forced them to modernize and cut back on much of the smell. The Union Stock Yard, on the other hand, maintained its large manure dump. The new hog house also emitted odors, as it could hold upward to six thousand hogs on a given day. Employing tens of thousands fewer workers, the industry no longer seemed so important to Chicago, and now was more of a nuisance than a benefit to residents. Despite the fact that Mayor Richard J. Daley had worked in the offices of the Dolan, Ludeman and Company Livestock Commission firm in the Union Stock Yard and his wife's father had made a living in the packinghouses, he showed little enthusiasm for keeping either the packing industry or the livestock market itself in operation. It hardly fit into Daley's vision of a modern city that included skyscrapers, clean industries, and global trade. For him the stockyards and the stench of the packinghouses and fertilizer plants were an old-fashioned reminder of the city's past. He envisioned a city of the future that no longer relied on "dirty" industries such as meatpacking.[43]

On March 10, 1970, the Union Stock Yard and Transit Company announced it planned to close the hog market within thirty to ninety days—but said the cattle market would remain. The company attrib-

Long after the big packers left Chicago many of their buildings still dotted the land-scape of Packingtown. This view east from the Damen Avenue overpass in 1985 shows many of the old packinghouses still standing and abandoned. (Photo by Joseph Ficner.)

uted its decision to the steady decline of hog receipts over the previous five years dropping from 1.7 million hogs to fewer than 1 million. In 1970, hog receipts had slipped 26 percent from the previous year. Observers pointed to direct selling as one of the prime reasons for the decline in hog trading, and employment statistics also bore out this claim. In 1970, fewer than fifty hog buyers and commission men worked in the hog house as compared to the several hundred who had worked the old hog house on the north end. The last hog speculator had retired the year before.

With the announcement of the closing of the hog market, reports emerged that the stockyard would soon close and be turned into a hundred-acre industrial park. A spokesman for the USY&T Company denied the report and said that the company planned to continue the cattle market on the remaining eighty acres of pens. The Central Manufacturing District (CMD), a holding company of the Prince estate, had already developed the ninety-acre Morgan Industrial District on what had been the north end of the Union Stock Yards before 1958. That district, which represented an investment of $20 million ($163.9 million in 2014), was fully occupied.[44]

On April 30, 1970, the stockyard company finally announced the closing date of the hog market, May 15. Again spokesmen for the Union Stock Yard claimed that cattle operations would continue. Some commission men attempted to save the hog market, but their efforts failed. Various commission firms planned to leave for the Peoria Stockyards and other markets.[45]

The *Drovers Journal* editorialized on May 29 that "none who saw that bustling market during its day of glory would have believed they would ever see the day when hog trading was not carried on there." The writer, while lamenting the closing of the hog market, looked beyond the Square Mile to interpret what it might mean for farmers. The closing marked the trend in livestock marketing that had been in progress since the 1920s when direct hog marketing first began to cut into the monopoly enjoyed by the big central markets. Improved highways and trucks had reduced farmer reliance on the railroads. Better communications had put buyers and sellers in almost instant touch with any market anywhere. Farms had become larger and more specialized. The gradual decentralization of the industry meant that packers once again located close to producers. In 1970, at least half of the buying and selling of livestock occurred on a direct basis. The *Drovers Journal* advocated for competitive markets, but the future did not portend well for the concept upon which the entire Union Stock Yard/Packingtown world had been built.[46]

Indeed, the raising of livestock had gone through a vast transformation since World War Two. The factory system, which had so transformed the packing industry in the nineteenth century, now provided a model for livestock producers. As early as the 1920s, farm advocates touted the factory-like farm as a way of ensuring farmers' profits and maintaining low food prices. Shortages during World War Two, especially of animal feed, had forced farmers to look beyond traditional sources such as corn to feed cattle and hogs. Also the use of antibiotics transformed the industry. The war and its aftermath increased the rural labor shortage and farmers again began to look at technology to replace hired hands. In addition, the growth of chain stores such as A&P, National Tea, and Kroger also influenced the market for meat animals.

One result was the emergence of factory farms that produced great quantities of livestock. These new farms provided a quality product at a reasonable cost to a quickly expanding American consumer society. By 1966, Colorado's Monfort feedlots resembled a modern high-tech plant. Computers regulated the daily diets of animals, and fewer workers were needed to manage the huge herds. Trucks and a network of paved roads now connected these feedlots with urban centers. Meatpackers no longer had to rely on stockyards and commission men for the bulk of the livestock needed for their plants.

The removal of millions of acres of western range for grazing also affected livestock producers who were now confined to smaller and smaller spaces. Federal land policies therefore also contributed to animal confinement and the use of feedlots. In addition, packers began to open their own feedlots. The quest for efficiency and for cheap meat created a new era for meatpacking, which would eventually see the emergence of new companies such as Iowa Beef Packing that would cater to the convenience store and institutional food market.

Swift, in its attempt to purchase enough hogs for its North Carolina plant, leased sows to farmers who agreed to take at least fifty of them and to guarantee their sale to Swift. As one reporter wrote, "The businessman at one end of the line ships out standardized pigs to farmers who will feed them according to a set pattern." The result was a revolution in hog raising that swept across the country and hit midwestern farms hard as they began to lose their control over the industry to other parts of the country. In response to these changes, meatpackers left cities and opened plants in rural areas. Efficiency became a key word, and the new plants hardly resembled the old structures that had dominated Chicago's Packingtown. Now instead of symbolizing modern techniques, Packingtown looked old and backward. The modern, which had transformed the Square Mile, now began to leave it behind.[47]

Despite the Union Stock Yard's management's claims that the cattle market would continue, rumors continued that plans were afoot to turn the entire area into an industrial park for other businesses to develop. The hog house came down, and repairs in the cattle yard were not made, which reduced the usable pen area. The closing of the hog market had an immediate impact. Rather than dividing their livestock, producers who usually sent both cattle and hogs now shipped to Peoria, shipped to one of the other markets, or sold direct to packers. As a result, cattle numbers in the Union Stock Yard decreased.

In October 1970, less than five months after the closing of the hog market, the USY&T Company announced that the cattle market would also close on February 1, 1971. Charles Potter said that lower cattle receipts did not justify keeping the stockyard open, as only an estimated 860,000 head of cattle would arrive for sale in 1970. Seven small meatpackers who still operated in or near the stockyards faced a future without a market in which to purchase livestock. A stockyard company spokesman said that they could buy direct and continue operations. He also claimed that there would be no impact on the International Livestock Exposition, and that the show would continue to run as usual into the foreseeable future. Directors of the International, however, had already cut the exhibition to six days from the usual nine days and eliminated the dairy show.

In response to the announcement of the closing, the city zoned the stockyard area for light industry, and the USY&T Company said that negotiations had begun with several companies to develop the land. Charles Potter noted that the stockyard area had become an important industrial site as well as an exposition complex based at the International Amphitheater. The closing meant that it could be further developed under the auspices of the Central Manufacturing District.[48]

John "Happy" Durant, the general livestock supervisor of the Union Stock Yard, was fifty-seven years old and had worked in the stockyards for thirty-nine years. He remarked, "All the yards are going downhill. The whole trend started in World War II. The government tried to get farmers to ship closer, to save on gas and tires. The packing companies started moving closer to the farmers." Employees interviewed by reporters found many to blame. Some blamed the unions, whose demands drove the meatpacking plants out of town. Others said the farmers did not support the market, and sold direct to packers. Still others claimed that the Department of Agriculture, the various cattlemen's organizations, as well as industry leaders had simply turned their backs on the stockyard. Wally Manders, the president of the Lincoln Meat Company, exclaimed, "Now what will we do?" In reality, the decline of both the Union Stock Yard and Packingtown resulted neither from the unions, although antiunion attitudes predominated among the packers, nor from the cattlemen's organizations, the Department of Agriculture, or the attitude of the packers toward Chicago. It was a result of changes in transportation, manufacturing, and in the raising and purchasing of livestock.[49]

The livestock commission men, hoping to keep their businesses alive and in the Chicago area, did not leave the Union Stock Yard without a battle. On January 21, 1971, the Chicago Livestock Exchange filed a suit to keep the yards open until a new market could be built in Joliet. Eight days later, just before the yards were to close, Judge Hubert L. Will of the Federal District Court delayed the closing for at least ten days. He did this to allow negotiations to proceed, and to keep the Union Stock Yard open until other facilities could be provided for cattle trading. Judge Will said that if an agreement was not reached by February 8, he would contemplate extending the court order for another ten days, and on February 1 he ordered the Chicago Union Stock Yards to continue operation until August. The ruling called for the Chicago Livestock Exchange to pay the USY&T Company $1,000 for each day the market stayed open. The total amount would be $124,000 ($725,146 in 2014). Will ruled that the company could remove unused facilities as preparation for the eventual closing as long as it did not hamper current cattle operations.[50]

On August 1, 1971, the National Wrecking Company began the demolition of the Union Stock Yard. The company paid for the clearing of the 102-acre site bounded by Exchange Avenue to the north, Racine Avenue to the west, Forty-Fifth Street to the south, and the International Amphitheater to the east. The USY&T Company expected new construction for the proposed Donovan Industrial Park of the Central Manufacturing District to begin later in the year, and already new sewer construction had taken place on Forty-Third Street between Racine Avenue and Morgan Street.[51]

The next day, a temporary livestock market opened on a site off of highway I-55 on the Arsenal Road turnoff, eight miles southwest of Joliet. Investors predicted a huge cattle market and the return of hog trading. The new market would have a daily capacity of 8,000 cattle and 6,500 hogs. By the mid-1970s, the new stockyard handled about 500,000 cattle and 300,000 hogs annually, never reaching the optimistic predictions of 2 million cattle per year. The Chicago-Joliet Livestock Market faced the same realities that the Union Stock Yard and the other central markets did, and it too finally closed in 1987.[52]

The End of Spectacle

Stockyard management certainly understood the importance of spectacle and good public relations, especially celebrations of industrial and agricultural accomplishments as well as Chicago history. The International Livestock Exposition continued through the Great Depression, and during its depths in 1933 some 13,500 animals went on display in the International Amphitheater. That year as Chicago celebrated its one hundredth birthday, six horses brought a huge cake standing fifteen feet high and weighing three hundred pounds into the amphitheater before presenting it to Mayor Ed Kelly at City Hall. Three years later, the International included a great deal of advertising not only in the press, but also on the radio. The USY&T Company received over five hundred newspaper clippings from clippings services on January 4, 1937 alone. Various radio presentations concerning the exposition appeared on networks across the country. Newsreel coverage brought the spectacle to moviegoers across America.[53]

The spectacle, like any show, had to go on despite disasters. In 1934, the livestock show opened despite the fire the previous May. The USY&T Company erected a new International Amphitheater in just five months, and Britain's Prince of Wales exhibited at the International for the first time in ten years, sending a Clydesdale draft horse and five shorthorn cattle from his farm in Canada. While the International survived the economic downturn of the 1930s and the fire of 1934, World War Two cancelled the 1942 exposition. Federal transportation officials opposed all large-scale exhibitions because of the pressure they put on the nation's rail system. The International promised to reopen in 1943, but on a much smaller scale, and permitting only animals ready for market at Chicago so that no added burden would be placed on the railroads. The much smaller Chicago Fat Stock and Carlot Exhibition Market substituted for the International in both 1943 and 1944. Managers held the 1944 exhibition in tents and in the Union Stock Yard sheep house, as the International Amphitheater now served as an army storehouse. The lack of spectator accommodations and wartime transportation restrictions forced the cancellation of many other events.[54]

Finally with the war's end, the International Livestock Exposition reemerged in 1946 promising to be the biggest ever. The horse show and the grain and hay show reappeared. Organizers revived the traditional draft horse display after five years. Meadow Brook Farms from Rochester, Michigan, won the title of champion six-horse hitch. More than ten thousand animals went on display showing the might of American agriculture. More than 450,000 postwar visitors freely spent their money at the "Victory" edition of the International. Clearly, the return of the livestock show boosted the economy of the stockyards and also the producers from thirty-five states and Canada who brought their livestock to the fair. The Firestone Tire and Rubber Company purchased Royal Jupiter, the 1,380-pound grand champion steer, for $14,490 ($176,707 in 2014), the highest price ever paid for a steer up to that time at the International. The total sales receipts for animals at the exposition in the purebred and fat divisions brought their owners $1.8 million ($22 million). All auctions featured record-breaking prices. Television provided another hallmark of the 1946 show. For the first time, any Chicagoans who owned a television set could watch sheep being skillfully herded by dogs in the amphitheater. Meanwhile, the press and radio provided more coverage of the show than ever before as Chicago and America's agricultural community celebrated the return of peace and the International Livestock Show.[55]

The International outlived the Union Stock Yard that had given it birth: the last stock show took place in 1975. While few mourned the passing of the livestock market, the show remained popular with the public. The International was born on the same principle that had influenced John B. Sherman to open the Dexter Park racetrack, to have his menagerie put on exhibit, and to support various livestock expositions. The same principle influenced the Union Stock Yard and Transit Company to build the monumental Stone Gate entrance and an observer's platform on the water tower and a series of amphitheaters. Simply put, it centered fascination on the Chicago Stockyards as a premier actor in the city's economy and a major public attraction.

The International Amphitheater became a profit maker on its own. It operated the largest public venue for exhibitions, shows, and conventions until the opening of McCormick Place. The amphitheater hosted the Chicago Auto Show, the Sportsmen Show, the Chicago Boat Show, the International Kennel Club of Chicago Show, among others. Both the Democratic and Republican Parties held their conventions here in 1952, and the Democrats returned four years later. In 1960, the Republicans nominated Richard M. Nixon for the presidency there. Eight years later, the Democratic Party again occupied the amphitheater for a violent and fateful convention. Various musical acts played the amphitheater from Frank Sinatra to Elvis Presley, the Beatles, the Jackson Five, and Johnny Cash. It hosted the circus and the roller derby, as well as boxing and wrestling matches.

Pictured here is Mike Chiappetti who purchased the 1954 grand champion wether sheep for the Plaza Steak House in Evergreen Park, Illinois. (Courtesy of Chiappetti Packing Company.)

The addition of exhibit space in the 1950s greatly expanded the exposition center, as the nation's largest, making it possible to host even larger shows. Once McCormick Place opened on the lakefront in 1960, and after a new and expanded McCormick Place reopened after the 1967 fire destroyed the first hall, the amphitheater's days as a major exposition venue were numbered. The closing of the stockyards and the downsizing of the International Livestock Exposition also reduced the exhibition hall's viability. In 1984, nine years after the

International left Chicago, an investor who hoped to revive the International Amphitheater purchased the building for $250,000 from the USY&T Company. The sale did not include the two additions to the south, which now served as warehouses. Developer Sam Frontera reopened the amphitheater in 1987 as the home of the Loyola Ramblers basketball team. Finally in 1999, the city of Chicago acquired the site, knocked it down, and sold it for industrial purposes. Only the Stone Gate and the shuttered building that once held the Livestock National Bank remained of the Union Stock Yard. An era of spectacle and innovation had come to an end.[56]

6

INNOVATE FOR EFFICIENCY— THOUGH WITH LESS STENCH

The Square Mile after the Union Stock Yard

It is all about using what you have in an innovative way and not wishing you had something else. The greenest building is one that you don't do anything to except make it more efficient.

JOHN EDEL, founder of The Plant

We only have one earth and if we don't take care of it now, future generations will pay the price. It's the right thing to do, and it has to start with us.

ANGELA BRADER, marketing coordinator,
Testa Produce Company

*

After the Union Stock Yard closed and demolition began in August 1971, it seemed as if the Square Mile might fade into obscurity as just another bland industrial park. Certainly, the plans of the Central Manufacturing District (CMD) to create the new Donovan Industrial Park, a development by the CMD Midwest Incorporated, on the land formerly occupied by the Union Stock Yard portended such a future.

The original CMD had been the first planned industrial park in the United States and was developed by Frederick H. Prince, who also controlled the Chicago Junction Railroad and the Union Stock Yard. In 1902, the Prince interests began to accumulate land to the north of the stockyards. Within three years, Prince and his investors announced their plans and created the Central Manufacturing District, bordered by Thirty-Fifth Street on the north, Ashland Avenue on the west, Thirty-Ninth Street (Pershing Road) on the south, and Morgan Street on the east, which built its own infrastructure of rail and street access, water, steam, lighting, and power. The CMD was an innovation, as it served as a large-scale incubator for small businesses that might not have the resources to build their own plants. It constructed buildings for these concerns and leased them while thereby providing customers for Prince's Chicago Junction Railroad, which served the CMD, Packingtown, and the Union Stock Yard. Others companies could build their own plants on land bought or leased from the organization. The CMD also created a bank to make loans to small local businesses, and a club where owners and employees could meet to discuss concerns and opportunities. By 1915, the CMD's original east district was filled with various industries, and was a thriving industrial community of over one hundred companies. The CMD then spread west of Ashland Avenue to Western Avenue along Thirty-Ninth Street, creating the CMD's so-called Magnificent Mile years before the name was used to describe the city's North Michigan Avenue. The CMD set an important example of how to develop an industrial incubator and its influence is still felt in the Chicago Stockyards Industrial Park and beyond. It was the original model for countless industrial parks nationwide and around the world.[1]

Prince's CMD also provided a good deal of leadership in the movement to fill in Bubbly Creek and extend Pershing Road west through the Stock Yard District connecting both its original development and the new site. This process included the filling in of the old Stock Yard Slip that brought Bubbly Creek as far as Halsted Street to the east. At one time, part of the South Fork reached almost to Western Avenue, and sections were filled in at various times ending much of the environmental threat to the neighborhoods bordering the Union Stock Yard.

A section of Bubbly Creek north of Pershing Road remains to this day and is still part of the river system making its way through the old CMD and into Bridgeport. The Metropolitan Water Reclamation District (MWRD) of Greater Chicago had made various attempts to clean up the stream, which still suffers from years of abuse as the open sewer for stockyard area businesses. Today, the section of Bubbly Creek that remains also receives sewer overflows when the Racine Avenue Pumping Station is activated to reduce flooding during periods of heavy rainfall. Scientists studied the waterway in 2004 and found up to three feet of fibrous material at the bottom including cattle and hog parts that had been dumped decades earlier. According to Michael Padilla of the Army Corps of Engineers, the sediment at the bottom of the creek is soft "like toothpaste" and thus not conducive to life. Proposals have been made to cap the sediment and allow the creek to recover. The South Fork, however, is still so polluted that the natural breakdown of waste cannot happen, in part because in 1900 when the Chicago River was permanently reversed Bubbly Creek became a stagnant backwater. Over the last decade or so, some progress had been made on cleaning up Bubbly Creek, but the stream still has no current. Despite this, the banks of the creek have seen a good deal of residential development over the last ten years in the area north of Thirty-Fifth Street known as Bridgeport Village. While the stench emanating from the creek has waned, on hot days the river still smells and bubbles present themselves on the surface—a reminder of its notorious history.[2]

After the Union Stock Yard closed, various small packinghouses still operated nearby, but most soon left. Lincoln Meat and Illinois Meat closed, as did Russell Packing, Reliable Packing, and other small slaughterhouses and meat outlets. American Meat Packing first moved close by to Pershing Road from its original stockyard site, and then in 2001 to Iowa. The demise of the International Amphitheater and the development on its former site of the Aramark Uniform Services plant further cemented a bland and quiet future for the location. Gone were the spectacles of the International Amphitheater, the livestock market, the vast packinghouses, the Stock Yard Inn, the Livestock National Bank, the Stockyard Elevated Line, a host of restaurants and bars on Halsted Street, the tens of thousands of men and women who made their living in the meat industry as well as the thousands of tourists who came to see the Square Mile. In their place, stood a blighted postindustrial site with some minor investment in the years after 1971. It seemed as if spectacle and innovation fled the site just as the major packers did in the 1950s.

The labor unions and the various professional organizations also left. The United Packinghouse Workers of America merged with their rivals the Amalgamated Meat Cutters and Butcher Workmen in 1968. The Amalgamated in turn joined with the Retail Clerks International Union in 1979 to form the United Food and Commercial Workers Union (UFCW), then the largest union in the AFL-CIO.[3] The Saddle and Sirloin Club, with its portrait gallery of innovators of the meatpacking industry and important figures in the livestock trade, moved to the Kentucky Exposition Center in Louisville in 1977 where the North American International Livestock Exposition, the successor to the Chicago International Livestock Show, is held.[4]

Yet small echoes of the past endure. A small independent packer, Park Packing, opened in 1967 and remained past the closing of the Union Stock Yard to kill hogs on Ashland Avenue just inside Packingtown. The plant, owned by the Bairaktaris family since 1987, employs about seventy workers and currently slaughters hogs, sheep, and goats. The daily kill depends on suppliers but usually runs between 120 and 230 hogs a day Monday through Thursday. The plant slaughters roughly 100 sheep and goats a week. They also operate a wholesale and retail market on the site of the packinghouse.

Chiappetti Packing also remains. Founded by Italian immigrant Fiore Chiappetti in 1927, the firm began slaughtering during the Great Depression on Halsted Street just north of the Union Stock Yard. Today it slaughters calves in Wisconsin as part of Straus Brands but maintains its sheep and lamb operations on Halsted Street. Headed by the grandson of the founder, Dennis Chiappetti, the firm maintains the traditions of meatpacking in Chicago, and Dennis's son Franco represents the fourth generation of the family to be involved in the business. Barkaat Foods, a Muslim-operated sheep-slaughtering firm, now leases the Chiappetti site and butchers some 3,000 sheep and 100 goats weekly for both firms. They slaughter sheep under halal and kosher rules as well as a standard slaughtering operation. Down the street, the Great Western Beef Company, a portion control meat purveyor founded by James Joseph Ebzery, has been in business since 1907 and has chosen to remain in the Union Stock Yard. The company purchases meat from slaughterhouses in Iowa, Kansas, Nebraska, and South Dakota.[5]

Despite the remaining meatpacking business, change is the real constant in the Square Mile. In 1979, James F. Donovan and the other trustee of F. H. Prince and Company, William N. Wood Prince Sr., decided to pass the reins on to a younger generation, William N. Wood Prince Jr. and Frederick H. Prince. Four years later, the CMD started the Meridian Business Campus, a 617-acre development in Aurora, Illinois, and it soon sold off most of its interests in the old Stock Yard District and original CMD location.

Although the state of Illinois established a tax increment financing

(TIF) law in 1977, the city of Chicago did not participate until 1984 under Mayor Harold Washington. In TIF districts, the amount of tax revenue generated by the area is set as a baseline to be paid to local tax districts during the lifetime of the TIF. As vacant or dilapidated structures and properties are redeveloped, the value and taxes in the district increase, and the city uses this increase to promote further investment in the zone. After the TIF expires, the taxes are then to be shared among the seven city taxing bodies that rely on real estate taxes.[6]

By 1989 when Mayor Richard M. Daley took office, there were twelve TIF districts in the city. Daley expanded the program citywide. By the end of 1997, there were seventy-five TIFs in Chicago, and in 2013 the number grew to 163, not all concerned with industrial development. In order for a location to be eligible under the Illinois TIF program, it had to meet several of the following criteria including age; obsolescence; illegal use of structures that did not meet building codes; excessive vacancies; overcrowding of facilities; lack of ventilation, light, and/or sanitary facilities; inadequate utilities; excessive land coverage; deleterious land use or layout; lack of physical maintenance; lack of community planning; or dilapidation or deterioration. By the 1980s, much of the stockyard and Packingtown area met most if not all of those criteria.[7]

The city of Chicago invested heavily in the old stockyard/Packingtown site, and in 1989 it established part of the site as a public TIF zone intended to foster commercial and industrial expansion in the area. As one of the oldest such projects in the city, it was intended to provide for the district's revitalization through various projects including the demolition of old structures, the construction of new streets, sewers, lighting, and other public works, and job training. The city later designated a Southeast Stockyard Quadrant TIF in 1992. The seventy-acre site needed resources to analyze and remediate soil in the district in preparation for redevelopment. Debris covered a great deal of the area and abandoned railroad tracks that once served the livestock industry occupied much of the land.

Four years later, the city designated a 295-acre annex to the original TIF, extending west through the Square Mile and east through Canaryville and Fuller Park as far as the Dan Ryan Expressway (I-90/94). This $45 million investment by the city was part of Mayor Richard M. Daley's demand for a more aggressive industrial development policy.

This addition to the Chicago's most successful industrial park called for a coordinated mixed-use of land resources. The combined TIF proved to be the second largest in the state, and together the three TIF areas covered 628 acres once almost exclusively dedicated to the meatpacking industry. They proved to be somewhat successful magnets for attracting and maintaining manufacturers in the Stock Yard District, and in 1993 two deals prevented an exodus of some eight hundred jobs to the suburbs.

Stockyard land prices nearly doubled in value as a result of the TIF and the resulting investment in the Stock Yard District during the four-year period from 1989 to 1993. To combat the suburbanization of Chicago's manufacturing base, the city acquired plots of land and combined them into larger parcels in order to attract modern industrial development. Chicago's Deputy Planning Commissioner Ron Johnson said, "It's like a zonal approach to the problem, not a piecemeal approach." Patrick Salmon, then executive director of the Back of the Yards Neighborhood Council (BYNC) explained, "We have really marketed (to manufacturers) that we have got the best and cheapest water in the country, and we have an ongoing labor pool that is (among) the best in the country." In terms of sheer scope and scale, Chicago's industrial TIF program was unprecedented in urban America.[8]

The three TIF districts generated a great deal of money for the improvement of the Chicago Stockyards Industrial Park. That the TIF program has been successful in the Stock Yard District is without question; still, various critics disagree with the way the city spends the money. Tom Tresser, cofounder of Civiclab, an organization that encourages civic responsibility and transparency, stated that the TIF program was the equivalent of a shadow city budget and it should be used to create better neighborhoods citywide. City officials, including Eleventh Ward Alderman James Balcer from Bridgeport, claimed that is exactly what TIFs accomplished by increasing manufacturing jobs in the city.[9]

The city has spent down TIF accounts as they expired. In 2009, the Daley administration went on a spending spree with money accumulated from the Central Loop TIF. As journalist Ben Joravsky has pointed out, "The process for phasing out a TIF is fairly straightforward, at least according to the state. The city can either spend all the money before it's closed or hand over what it didn't spend to the schools, parks, county, and other taxing bodies." Generally speaking,

The Chicago Stockyards Industrial Park looking west across Peoria Street toward Ashland Avenue, circa 2013. The area has seen a good deal of investment since the closing of the Union Stock Yard in 1971. (Courtesy of the Back of the Yards Neighborhood Council.)

the money has been spent before the TIF closes, but in some cases these funds have been seen as a slush fund for City Hall.[10] Despite these issues, it does seem that in the case of the Stockyards Industrial Park, the TIF has generated jobs and put industrial land back on the tax rolls. It seems that the Stock Yard District TIF is an example of how the TIFs were intended to be used, even if that in not the case in much of the rest of the city.

In 2010, roughly seventy firms occupied the old stockyard and Packingtown site. Three years later, these firms employed approximately fifteen thousand workers, about a third of the number employed by the Union Stock Yard and Packingtown at its height. The 1-million-square-foot business park included businesses such as Luster Products, a leading African American–owned personal care products manufacturer; the Rexam Beverage Can Company; Gypsum Supply Company; Clear Channel Communications; Ebro Foods; and Tyson Foods.

While Park Packing was the only slaughterhouse left in Packing-town, the meatpacking industry remains well represented; other meat purveyors continue in the area long defined as the Stock Yard District. These include Evans, the world's largest producer of pork rinds, as well as Kaminski Packing, and Allen Brothers just north of the yards on Halsted Street in Bridgeport. In 2013, Vienna Beef, a longtime Chicago company, also announced they planned to move from the Near North Side of the city to just north of the former stockyard site on Pershing Road. Chicago Gourmet Steaks operates on Exchange Avenue. The Chicago Meat Authority, which employed approximately three hundred laborers, occupies a site just south of the old stockyards on West Forty-Seventh Street.[11]

The results of the TIF and other investments in the Stockyards Industrial Park have been quite dramatic. New industries arrived and redeveloped much of the area. Testa Produce built a state-of-the-art, 91,300-square-foot facility on the site of the old Hammond Packing-house at 4555 South Racine Avenue at a cost of $24 million. Testa spent approximately $1.5 million to buy three parcels of land that covered roughly thirteen acres. Chicago backed the project with $15.2 million in low-interest bonds, authorized by the 2009 federal bailout of the economy. The Epstein engineering firm planned the structure, and its energy efficient mechanical design resulted in a 30 percent reduction in planned energy consumption. Epstein has had a long history in the Union Stock Yard and the Central Manufacturing District, designing the International Amphitheater, the Livestock National Bank, and the rebuilding of the stockyards after the disastrous 1934 fire. Continuity happens in the midst of change.

Testa Produce began operations in 1912. The company is family owned, and currently the fourth generation is involved in its opera-tion. Originally located in the South Water Street Produce Market on the West Side, it moved to Fifteenth and Racine after that market closed, and opened its environmentally advanced stockyard facility on May 10, 2011. A partially vegetated, green, barrel-shaped roof, per-meated pavers, bioswales, and a 756,085-gallon external retention pond make the recycling of water a major end product of the facility. The 140,132-gallon bioswale system encourages rainwater to soak into existing soils and filters water into the retention pond that virtually eliminates the use of public sewers on the property. Rainwater pro-vides all the water needed for the flushing of toilets in the building and for washing the trucks in the company's delivery fleet.

The Testa plant in the Chicago Stockyards Industrial Park. Notice the windmill, solar trees, and retention pond. (Photograph by Johanna A. Pacyga.)

Renewable energy accounts for another 40 percent energy reduction in the facility, which saves the company an estimated $185,000 each year. The site includes 180 photovoltaic solar panels on the rear docks and on pole-mounted solar trees in the parking lots. Roof-mounted solar panels generate 100 percent of the facility's hot water and eliminate the use of natural gas, while a five-thousand-gallon water storage and treatment system recycles rainwater for nonpotable uses throughout the building. The 750-kilowatt, 238-foot-high freestanding wind turbine provides enough energy to power about eighty homes each year and now stands as a modern symbol of the Stockyards Industrial Park for miles around. The turbine provides 30 percent of the energy needed for operations of the plant. During roughly thirty to forty days of the year, the Testa plant is completely off the electrical grid. The entire facility is run on an energy efficient and green basis from its roof to the cooling facilities. A series of green screens are being grown to protect windows from the hot summer sun and thus preserve energy.

Granite pavers from the stockyards were recycled to pave part of the site, as a connection to the past and to fit into the bioswale system. Even concrete found on the location was ground up and used for part of the foundation. The company uses electric and compressed natural gas trucks, and hopes to be completely off diesel fuel in the near future. All company cars are hybrid vehicles, and the company instituted preferred parking for fuel-efficient cars close to the building as well as bicycle racks and electric charging ports powered by the solar trees for electric vehicles. Natural lighting and light-emitting diode (LED) fixtures furnish the interior lighting of the plant and offices. The U.S. Green Building Council awarded Testa's facility its LEED (Leadership in Energy and Environmental Design) Platinum Certification, the first such refrigerated food-service facility in the nation. The *Engineering News-Record* named it the Best Green Building Project of 2011. Just as the packers once used all but the squeal, today's stockyard industrialists innovate for efficiency—though with less stench.

Chicago's commissioner of housing and economic development, Andy Mooney, said at the opening of Testa's building that "not only will this project serve to revitalize a long blighted and vacant parcel, it will serve as a new standard bearer for environmentally sensitive design by incorporating countless sustainable components, not the least of which is the wind turbine, the first of its kind in Chicago." Testa Produce certainly brought a new kind of spectacle and innovation to the stockyards; the company revived a longtime stockyard tradition, as it runs tours of its facilities. Groups of visitors from school children to engineers, environmentalists, consumers, customers, and interested neighborhood residents regularly visit the structure.[12]

Besides the Testa facility, other innovations and even new spectacles have appeared in the stockyards. An organization called The Plant founded by John Edel in the old Peer Food packinghouse on Forty-Sixth Street is a fascinating new kind of organization in an old building that provides a site for sustainable food production and economic development. It is a not-for-profit-business incubator, which hopes to create a green and sustainable future for food manufacturing in Chicago.

The building has a history long connected to the Union Stock Yard. In the 1860s, Christian Buehler entered the meat industry and started a pork packing operation in Peoria, Illinois. Around 1894, three of his children came to Chicago and started the Buehler Brothers Meat

Market. Their business did well, and by 1915 they had numerous markets throughout the central and midwestern states. In 1925, Buehler Brothers, looking for the same market advantages enjoyed by Armour and Swift, built their own packing plant in the Chicago Stockyards. During World War Two, the facility was renamed Peer Food Products in order to differentiate it from the markets and to allow it to enter the wholesale business, and in 2006 Peer Foods closed the site.

In July 2010, John Edel purchased the 93,500-square-foot plant property for $525,000, the estimated salvage value of the metal in the building. While originally pitching it as a recycling operation, Edel soon had bigger plans for the structure, which contained food-grade factory features such as floor drains, aseptic surfaces, and heavy floor loadings. He could now realize his dream of starting a large green-food incubator and a vertical urban farm. Edel explained that "Chicago — and the stockyards in particular — has always been a center for food innovation, going back 150 years, and this is the logical place to take the next step forward in how we produce food."

In 2002 Edel, who has a degree in industrial design from the University of Illinois at Chicago, purchased a twenty-four-thousand-square-foot former paint warehouse about a mile north of The Plant. Located in the old CMD at 1048 West Thirty-Seventh Street, he transformed it into a successful green-business incubator now known as the Chicago Sustainable Manufacturing Center and run by his company Bubbly Dynamics. The building was in deplorable condition when Edel took it over and began remodeling. By 2013, it held more than a dozen businesses, employed fifty-two people, and boasted a green roof. Edel has a lifelong love of and interest in the city's industrial history, and has sought ways to find new productive uses for old structures. He had already confronted some of the problems he would have at the Peer Foods site.

From the beginning, The Plant was to be a food-business incubator, and Edel pioneered the idea of urban and vertical farming there. Generally, the growing of vegetables takes place indoors on the site, although outdoor and roof gardens have also been introduced. On the third floor is a humid hothouse filled with rows of greens and sprouts, which includes a closed aquaponics system. Aquaponics is the combination of aquaculture (growing fish in a farm setting) and hydroponics (growing plants in water without soil). As opposed to routine hydroponics and aquaculture, in aquaponics the fish, bacteria, and plants all rely on each other to thrive. It is a system Edel has called "closing loops." He explained, "Energy loops, material loops, money loops, labor loops—if the loops are closed, that's a sustainable system." The relationship between fish and plants is an example of the complex closed-loop system envisioned by Edel where waste from one activity will fuel another process. Garden greens are fertilized by the waste produced in huge tanks of tilapia, one of the easiest fish to breed indoors. Edel hopes soon to introduce prawns and perch. The process produces virtually no waste.

In September 2012, SkyyGreens Aquaponics, a tenant at The Plant, received an urban farming license from the city of Chicago. Former classmates at the University of Chicago Booth School of Business started the company out of their frustration at not being able to source local produce year round. SkyyGreens simply took the farm indoors, and they naturally hooked up with The Plant. Like Armour and Swift with refrigeration, they attempted to conquer the seasons. In 2011, the mayoral administration of Rahm Emanuel changed zoning laws to encourage urban farming, and SkyyGreens was the first indoor farm to be licensed under the new ordinance. Edel also runs a nonprofit company, Plant Chicago, which, along with Greens and Gills and Urban Canopy, operates one of the four urban farms on the property. Pleasant House Bakery, a Bridgeport restaurant located at Thirty-First and Morgan Street, also does some farming on the site. Plans call for greenhouses to be erected on the roof of the building that will increase the usable space to roughly one hundred thousand square feet. Bees are also raised on the rooftop of the old factory.

Other firms in The Plant include bakeries, a kombucha tea brewery, and a nano-brewery. Edel hopes to attract a craft beer company, which would produce fertilizer for the farms along with beer to close the loops needed to make a fully sustainable small-food-business incubator. Long-range plans call for the building to include a cooperative café that will sell the products produced in the structure itself, as well as a shared industrial kitchen. These spaces will be rented on a sliding scale to help local residents get started in the food business. A demonstration kitchen, operated by the nonprofit to teach healthy eating habits, will also be included in the final build out. Collaborative office space will allow the small businesses in the incubator to share information and ideas with each other, as well as resources.

In 2013, Edel introduced an anaerobic digester to consume waste

Plant Chicago, a nonprofit vertical urban farm, grows produce sold to local restaurants and at farmers markets in Chicago by using the aquaponics closed system. (Photograph by Johanna A. Pacyga.)

from nearby food manufacturers, supermarkets, breweries, and other businesses. The companies that haul the waste will pay a tipping fee to The Plant to dump it at the site instead of trucking it further out of the city to landfills. An anaerobic digester can consume any biomass. In turn, it produces biogas that will be burned in a reciprocating generator, which will create four hundred kilowatt hours of electricity. This is enough to power the entire facility, but it will also create waste heat that will be harvested and run into an absorption chiller that will make cold water to cool the entire facility. Edel plans to sell electric power back to Commonwealth Edison. The new device was paid for with a $1.5 million grant from the Illinois Department of Commerce and Economic Opportunity.[13]

The Plant works with the Back of the Yards Neighborhood Council (BYNC) to educate residents about urban farming and organize volunteers to help out with various events, and classrooms will be built in the structure to further its educational goals. Edel's organization has helped run a local farmers market for the BYNC, and has a good working relationship with its leadership.

The Plant is located in the old Peer Food packinghouse on the left in the photograph. In the distance is the Vantage plant, a rendering firm on the old Darling and Company site and the Testa turbine just beyond it. (Photograph by Johanna A. Pacyga.)

The goal of The Plant is to counter the wastefulness of industrial society. Edel says that Americans waste too much, but much of it can be successfully and profitably reused, from old buildings to energy. Volunteers are helping to renovate the building, and it is to be fully functional in 2016, creating about 140 permanent jobs in the neighborhood and diverting more than ten thousand tons of food waste from landfills each year. As Edel explains, "What is unusual about The Plant is that we're doing a whole lot of things that have been done before, but they've never been done together on one site." Edel welcomes tour groups and has regular times allotted for visits, again maintaining the longtime stockyard tradition. Despite the fact that the stockyards have long ago disappeared from tourist guides to the city, in 2013 some six thousand visitors toured The Plant. Indeed innovation and spectacle remain alive within the square mile that once made up the stockyards and Packingtown.

More innovations are planned for the industrial park. In October 2012, the Chicago City Council approved measures to build a $13 million chemical plant at Forty-First and Packers Avenue in Packing-town. The fifty-nine-thousand-square-foot facility will manufacture lubricants and other ingredients that are used in various personal care and household cleaning products. Cedar Concepts (Chemical Com-positions, LLC), the only African American female–owned chemical manufacturer, began construction of the new building in 2012. The TIF district contributed $2.3 million to support the facility's devel-opment. Additional aid came from the city with the sale of an addi-tional 2.4-acre parcel of city-owned land (once part of the old Swift and Company facility) to the company for one dollar. The land was appraised for $625,000, and the total area covered by the new facility would be 5.5 acres. The plan called for a plant, parking, and a tank farm with overhead pipes feeding chemicals into the building on the site. In addition, owner Linda Boasmond promised to have the project de-signed to obtain LEED certification and create energy saving devices including solar paneling and a wind turbine. The new structure will join the Testa plant in tying into wind and solar power sources as the Chicago Stockyards Industrial Park continues to pave the way toward the use of reusable energy. Mayor Rahm Emanuel stated in support of the plan that "this is a great opportunity to support the expansion goals of an established Chicago manufacturer while reinforcing the diversity of the City's economy." Cedar Concepts planned to move thirty jobs to the new plant and add ten more. Construction would create seventy-five to one hundred temporary jobs. More importantly, it returned an abandoned property to the tax rolls and will hopefully spur further development in this section of the industrial park, which has been largely underutilized. The company ships some 50 million pounds of products, through $10 million in sales annually.[14]

The new plants built in the Stockyards Industrial Park generally speaking follow the single-floor flow model with most production occurring on the ground floor. Natural resources enter on one end of the building and finished products leave at the opposite end. This type of structure and the amount of land needed for it led to the original demise of Packingtown after World War Two, with its mostly multi-story buildings. Much room remains in the Stockyards Industrial Park for manufacturers to locate, especially in the area west of Racine Ave-nue.

Besides TIFs, the city used other methods to spur investment in the Stockyards Industrial Park. In another move to redevelop the stock-

This map shows SSA #13 in relation to the original Union Stock Yard site. The SSA covers much of the area occupied by Packingtown and adjacent meatpacking sites as well as the original CMD. (Chicago CartoGraphics.)

map by: Chicago CartoGraphics

▬▬ boundary of Stockyards Industrial Corridor   ⋯⋯⋯ boundary of Special Service District #13 yards, the city of Chicago established Special Service Area 13 (SSA #13) for the Stockyards Industrial Park on July 24, 1991. Special Service Areas are local tax districts that fund expanded services and programs through a localized property tax levy within contiguous areas. The city contracts with neighborhood nonprofit organizations to manage the SSAs, and the city commissioned the Back of the Yards Neighborhood Council (BYNC), the local neighborhood organization organized in 1939 and headed by Craig Chico since 2008, to manage SSA #13 along with several other SSAs in the district. The city of Chicago funnels roughly 1 percent of the equalized assessed value on the industrial property tax bills in the area to the BYNC as the service provider. The BYNC uses the funds to provide services, which individual businesses could not afford on their own, such as street maintenance and beautification, street banners, marketing, business retention and attraction, special events and promotional activities, facade improvements, and other economic initiatives. These also include various security initiatives as security gates at the primary entrances to the industrial park that limit traffic in the nighttime hours. Also in November 2011, the BYNC hired Securitas Security Services to provide three units to patrol SSA #13 overnight and on weekends The BYNC placed decorative planters at stockyard entrances, and crews work five days a week to keep the SSA clean. They remove litter and weeds in addition to performing routine maintenance tasks, to minimize flooding and decrease the rodent population. In 2013, the BYNC contracted with Business Only Broadline to provide Internet service to the Special Service Area. The BYNC also acts as a mediator between the Stockyards Industrial Park and the city government.[15]

The BYNC supports various other events that promote SSA #13 and the Stockyards Industrial Park. It established the Back of the Yards Quality-of-Life Plan, an initiative that partnered with all major community organizations to identify and address key neighborhood issues. The BYNC held the first Quality of Life Plan Jobs Fair on August 2, 2012. More than five hundred job seekers attended the fair searching for employment opportunities with more than twenty-five firms at Chicago Indoor Sports on Thirty-Ninth and Ashland just outside the Stockyards Industrial Park. Various companies hired several residents on the spot and participants filled out hundreds of applications. The SSA #13 Commission also held the annual "Stamp-Eat!" get-together on September 27, 2012. The yearly event represented an opportunity

The BYNC and SSA #13 installed banners on every other light pole surrounding the Stockyards Industrial Park, branding the area and helping to promote the area to businesses and possible investors. (Photograph by Johanna A. Pacyga.)

for business owners and employees to network with each other, SSA #13 commissioners, BYNC staff members, and meet elected officials. Held on the grounds of the Engineered Glass Products (formerly Marsco Glass Products) next to the Stone Gate, Allen Brothers provided steaks and Evans Brothers pork rinds for the guests as the BYNC and SSA #13 brought together local companies to work for the industrial parks success.[16]

Both the TIF areas and SSA #13 have revived the Square Mile and adjacent industrial areas after the demise of the city's livestock and meatpacking industries. When the Central Manufacturing District left the area in the 1980s, SSA #13 took over many of the services that the CMD provided including landscaping, beautification, and security. The SSA #13 in many ways is not new, but is instead a public body that provides many of the amenities once delivered by a private concern.

In early 2013, Stockyard TIF money was used to create neighborhood signs depicting the boundary between Bridgeport and Canaryville to the east of the Chicago Stockyards Industrial Park. The city erected signs that included stars that light up at night, apparently to recall the Chicago flag. Chicago's Department of Transportation said construction costs for the signs totaled $553,760 as part of a general $2.7 million Halsted Street streetscape program. While the signs remain controversial—many called it a waste of TIF money—they pointed to the general attempt to make the district more attractive to investors and businesses. (Photograph by Johanna A. Pacyga.)

With TIF money and the city council's participation the TIF districts and the SSA work to attract and help build industrial sites in the area, much as the old CMD and the Union Stock Yard and Transit Company did earlier in the nineteenth and first half of the twentieth century. The plan, then privately sponsored by the Frederick H. Prince and his investors, has been revived and continues to transform industrial development in the district now with a combined public-private partnership.[17]

The surrounding neighborhoods have undergone a significant amount of change in the years since the Union Stock Yard and Transit Company altered the swamp and prairie on the edge of the city into its industrial heartland. Bridgeport, Canaryville, Back of the Yards, and

McKinley Park all experienced tremendous transformations over the decades. Originally settled by large groups of immigrants from Ireland, Germany, and Bohemia (Czech Republic), they then became the American home of those from Poland, Lithuania, Slovakia, and Russia before World War One. These immigrant groups today have been largely supplanted by immigrants from Mexico in all four neighborhoods, and by African Americans in the southern half of Back of the Yards. Bridgeport is now also experiencing gentrification. New investment by Chinese and Mexican Americans is an important factor in both Bridgeport and McKinley Park as social class change comes to these neighborhoods situated close to the Loop and well served by public transportation. What these neighborhoods have always offered, and continue to provide to the industries that locate in them, is a pool of willing workers, many of whom are highly skilled and bring their talents to the workshops in the district.

Chicago itself has gone through many changes over the last 150 years, evolving from a swampy military camp and trading outpost into one of the country's greatest combinations of industrial and commercial power. In 1865, the city's southern boundary ended at Thirty-Ninth Street (Pershing Road); twenty-four years later, Chicago swallowed many of its suburbs in a massive annexation. Not the least of these annexations was that of the Town of Lake and its Union Stock Yard. In the years after 1886, the city's packing industry expanded and controlled the nation's supply of meat. During World War One, nearly fifty thousand people worked in the Union Stock Yard and Packingtown, and a quarter of million depended on the industry for their livelihood.

In the 1920s, the major packers began to decentralize in earnest and to mimic smaller independent midwestern packers and purchase livestock directly from producers, by-passing the Union Stock Yard. In the 1950s, Chicago's central location and railroad access no longer mattered to the major slaughterhouses that had long called the city home. Direct buying, the interstate highway system, and the refrigerated motor truck gave the packers more leeway to choose profitable locations. Changes in the way livestock were raised also encouraged the makeover. Eventually with that transformation came a tremendous readjustment in the industrial hierarchy that witnessed the decline of Armour, Swift, Wilson, and the emergence of other packers who came to dominate the industry. By 1960, Chicago's major packing plants had closed, and only small independent packers operated in

The Stone Gate continues to stand at its original location and presents a symbol of Chicago's industrial history while marking the entrance to the city' most successful industrial park. (Photograph by Johanna A. Pacyga.)

the area. When the Union Stock Yard celebrated its one hundredth anniversary in 1965–66, it had returned largely to its original role as a shippers' market. Five years later, the Union Stock Yard closed down and turned over its site for development to its sister organization the Central Manufacturing District.

Today Section 5 of the old Town of Lake is home to Chicago's most successful industrial park. This is largely the result of a public-private initiative in the form of TIFs and SSAs, along with innovative private sector investment and commitments. Perhaps more importantly, the Square Mile is again pointing to a new industrial future for the city with green industries increasingly taking the lead. The old CMD idea of an industrial incubator, providing jobs for workers and profits for companies, is alive and well. The Square Mile remains a center of innovation and even spectacle as tour groups visit the Testa Produce facility and The Plant to see what the future holds for food production and manufacturing in Chicago, America, and the world.

For historians, the Square Mile continues to tell the story of inno-vation and business development in an urban industrial setting. The Square Mile goes a long way toward explaining the development and impact of big business on the consumer society that developed in

America after the Civil War. Furthermore, it provides an account of ethnic and racial succession as well as of the worker struggle to unionize and insure the rights of those who labored and still labor in American industry. The story it will tell in the future is anybody's guess, but already the signs point to further innovation and even spectacle, although on a different scale, within the confines of the Square Mile.

Chicago's Agro-Industrial Past and Possible Locavore Future

In contrast to the nineteenth and twentieth centuries, the Chicago of the early twenty-first century seems chastened by violence, unable to deal effectively with postindustrial society or to educate or employ much of its population. Mired in its legendary corruption, it is no longer the city that felt it could be the number one metropolis of the United States. Chicago is now the nation's third city and perhaps soon to slip toward an even lower ranking behind the expanding cities of the South and West. Some Chicagoans look to a recently bankrupt Detroit and see the future. They are wrong, but it does seem Chicago has lost its way—at least momentarily.

Chicago sits in the heart of the Midwest, and it once served as not only the meatpacking center of the nation, but also the nation's lumberyard, granary, and potato market. The city still remains the heart of the futures trade. In the decades following the Vietnam War, manufacturing seemed to abandon the Midwest. Despite the loss of more jobs than some entire nations ever had, Chicago remains a producer of goods. It continues as a manufacturing center, one of the largest in the nation.

Over the last several years, the administration of Mayor Rahm Emanuel has attracted various corporations and businesses into the city; some are new, some have returned from their sojourn to the suburbs. It is time for Chicago to look clearly at its position in both the global economy and in the Midwest. Most observers see the future as an age of international investment and digital information, but many of the city's citizens are ill equipped to take advantage of those opportunities. Obviously, Chicago must continue to involve itself into the new economy, but it should not abandon its role as a manufacturer and as the great emporium. It might be time to revisit the history of the Square Mile.

The Chicago Mercantile Exchange and the Chicago Board of Trade still market the nation's heartland, but these valuable commodities have physically disappeared from the city. Yet Chicago still sits at the gate of the richest farmland in the world. The last ten years have seen the locavore movement emerge as a powerful force among a large segment of the population. Government regulations now call for meat products to list where the animals that they come from were born, raised, and slaughtered.[18] At one time, most people ate produce and other foods produced locally. Today the meat you buy in the local grocery is often raised, slaughtered, and packed far away, even overseas, and delivered to you in a plastic container. The same goes for vegetables and fruit. Locavores have attempted to reverse that process. The movement addresses concerns among livestock raisers, ecologically minded citizens, and those interested in providing opportunities on a local stage. This pressure group provides a chance for Chicago and for the thousands of unemployed to respond in innovative ways. It may also provide a way for Chicago to lessen its carbon footprint.

Midwest farmers still feed the country and the world. It makes sense for a city of over 2.7 million residents and a metropolitan region of over 9.5 million people to provide a market for locally raised and grown foodstuffs. If Chicago would once again establish a livestock market and attract local butchers to slaughter and pack meat products, it could support a large industrial base. This also goes for a large publicly run produce and poultry marketplace that could be an example to the nation. If the three were combined into a "Union Livestock, Poultry, and Produce Center" that would provide a place for local entrepreneurs to purchase livestock to be slaughtered locally, as well as poultry, fruit, and vegetables, the market could be an attraction for future investment. Chicago's population would benefit from hundreds, if not thousands, of possible jobs as well as from locally raised and slaughtered meat products, poultry, and vegetables. The city or a group of interested investors could engage forward-thinking architects to create a livestock facility based on the humane ideas of Temple Grandin as well as an attractive market for poultry and vegetables. Above all, a new marketplace could also cut down on the pollution caused by the transportation of prepared food products over thousand of miles.

The new market could be a tourist attraction as well, promoting Illinois and midwestern agriculture. In the early 1900s, some five hundred thousand visitors toured the Chicago Stockyards annually. The annual

International Livestock Exposition alone drew as many enthusiasts. Chicago could once again be a leading innovator in the food business, demonstrating the way forward.

The new market could be built on any number of vacant railroad lands, the old Packingtown site, or in the Calumet region, providing jobs and needed taxes to a city that has for too long ignored its place in the agro-industrial world. It must be ecologically sound and dispel the nuisances associated with Chicago's old marketplaces—especially the old Union Stock Yards. The new market would attract small businesses and provide jobs to a city that needs to employ its citizens in order to build a more stable social structure, a larger tax base for schools, and a brighter future. Chicago has a diverse, hardworking, and knowledge-able workforce; it is situated in the middle of a vast transportation network and serves as the gate to America's rich midwestern hinterland. With a little imagination and perhaps bravado, there is no reason it cannot regain its place as the great Emporium of the West and solidify its position among the other global cities. The Union Stock Yard may have been only the beginning.

ACKNOWLEDGMENTS

Many individuals have helped me with this manuscript. Family members and neighbors, especially my mother, the late Pauline Walkosz Pacyga, long ago told me their stories of working in the packinghouses. In the fall of 2011, I began to write this book thanks to the urging of Robert Devens, then a senior editor at the University of Chicago Press. Carl Smith and William Savage also counseled me and helped me to decide to explore the topic that has haunted me most of my adult life. In addition, Bill Savage, with his invaluable suggestions, has helped me make this manuscript more readable. I am indebted to Franco and Dennis Chiappetti for arranging a tour of their family's packing plant just outside the old yards. Brian Chiappetti walked me through the plant and permitted me to witness the spectacle of the kill floor. In addition, I owe a great debt to the men who worked with me in the stockyards more than forty years ago and who told me the stories and myths of their lifetimes—in particular, Steve Scanlon, Tom Hartnett, Walter Konkol, Ben Dees, and Charlie Brasil. There were others, but time has unfortunately clouded my memory and caused me to forget their names.

I wish to thank Kiki Bairaktaris of Park Packing Company, Inc.; Angie Brader, marketing coordinator for the Testa Produce Company; John Edel of The Plant; and Michael J. McMullin, program director, SSA # 7 and SSA #13; and the Back of the Yards Neighborhood Council. My good friend and colleague Ellen Skerrett, has, as always, helped in innumerable ways. John Corrigan lent me his invaluable collection of microfilms of the *Vindicator* and *Sun* newspapers. I would like to thank the staff of the Columbia College Chicago Library, the University of

Chicago Libraries, the Chicago History Museum, the Special Collections Department of the University of Illinois at Chicago, and the Special Collections Department of the Iowa State University Library. In addition, Rob Berkery and Joseph Kerzich lent key photographs. Suellen Hoy, Walter Nugent, Richard Fried, Perry Duis, and Robert Slayton each read versions of the various chapters of the manuscript and made helpful suggestions as to how to improve the final product. I am grateful for their time and patience. Dennis McClendon of Chicago CartoGraphics did his customary fine job of creating and making available a series of maps that have made the manuscript much richer. Columbia College's former interim provost, Louise Love; the former dean of liberal arts and sciences, Deborah Holdstein; and the chair of the Humanities, History, and Social Science Department, Steven Corey, all provided support for this project. My editor, Tim Mennel, along with Alan G. Thomas and Karen M. Darling of the University of Chicago Press, offered encouragement, friendship, and guidance well beyond the usual publisher-author relationship. For this I am most grateful. Nora Devlin assisted the project in innumerable ways. Mark Reschke did his usual thorough copyediting of the manuscript. I would like to thank the anonymous readers for their help in making this a much better book. Leo Schelbert, to whom this book is dedicated, has long been a mentor and friend. Most importantly, Leo is a prime example of a scholar-teacher. I can only hope to achieve a fraction of his brilliance and stubborn determination in discovering the story of the human condition.

My spouse, Kathleen Alaimo, herself a busy academic, has put up with tales of the Chicago Stockyards for all of the thirty plus years of our relationship. Our children, Johanna and Beatrice, have for too long listened to my ramblings about the stockyards. Johanna took photographs of today's Square Mile for chapter 6. As always, I have both heeded advice and disregarded it, and in the end I am solely responsible for the mistakes and shortcomings of the book.

NOTES

Preface

1 Tony Hiss, *The Experience of Place: A New Way of Looking at and Dealing with Our Radically Changing Cities and Countryside* (New York, 2010), p. xi; William H. Whyte, *City: Rediscovering the Center* (New York, 1988).

2 Louise Carroll Wade, *Chicago's Pride: The Stockyards, Packingtown, and Environs in the Nineteenth Century* (Urbana and Chicago, 1987); Robert A. Slayton, *Back of the Yards: The Making of a Local Democracy* (Chicago, 1986); Thomas Jablonsky, *Pride in the Jungle: Community and Everyday Life in the Back of the Yards Chicago* (Baltimore, 1993); James Barrett, *Work and Community in the Jungle: Chicago's Packinghouse Workers, 1894–1922* (Urbana and Chicago, 1987); Roger Horowitz, *Negro and White, Unite and Fight: A Social History of Industrial Unionism in Meatpacking, 1930–1990* (Urbana and Chicago, 1997); Rick Halpern, *Down on the Killing Floor: Black and White Workers in Chicago's Packinghouses, 1904–1954* (Urbana and Chicago, 1997); Rick Halpern and Roger Horowitz, *Meatpackers: An Oral History of Black Packinghouse Workers and Their Struggle for Racial and Economic Equality* (New York, 1999); William Cronon, *Nature's Metropolis: Chicago and the Great West* (New York and London, 1991); Robert Lewis, *Chicago Made: Factory Networks in the Industrial Metropolis* (Chicago, 2008); Sylvia Hood Washington, *Packing Them In: An Archaeology of Environmental Racism, 1865–1954* (Lanham, Boulder, New York, Toronto, and London, 2005); Charles J. Bushnell, *The Social Problem at the Chicago Stock Yards* (Chicago, 1902); Theodore V. Purcell, S.J., *The Worker Speaks His Mind on Company and Union* (Cambridge, 1954).

Chapter One

1 T. J. Zimmerman, "The Colossus of Business Organizations," *System: The Magazine of Business*, July 1904, pp. 165–66.

2 Zimmerman, "Colossus," pp. 168–69; *Chicago Tribune*, April 9, 1908.

3 Arthur C. Davenport, *The American Live Stock Market: How It Functions* (Chicago, 1922), pp. 30, 42–44.

4 Zimmerman, "Colossus," pp. 170–72.

5   *Chicago Tribune*, June 23, 1905.

6   Much of the following discussion of a visit to the packing plants comes from Swift and Company, *Visitors Reference Book* (Chicago, n.d.). The author's copy of the *Visitors Reference Book* is inscribed with the date October 28, 1910—perhaps the date of the visit to the plant. Other sources give the publication date as 1903.

7   Heller and Company, *H Secrets of Meat Curing and Sausage Making* (Chicago, 1922), p. 32; *Chicago Tribune*, June 23, 1905; John O'Brien, *Through the Chicago Stock Yards: A Handy Guide to the Packing Industry* (Chicago and New York, 1907), p. 58.

8   O'Brien, *Through the Chicago Stock Yards*, p. 60; George Wm. Lambert, *A Trip Through the Union Stock Yards and Slaughter Houses, Chicago, U.S.A.* (Chicago, n.d., ca. 1890s) pp. 21–24; F. W. Wilder, *The Modern Packinghouse* (Chicago, 1905), pp. 252–72; Louise Wade, *Chicago's Pride: The Stockyards, Packingtown, and Environs in the Nineteenth Century* (Urbana, 1987), pp. 102–3.

9   *Chicago Tribune*, June 23, 1905.

10 O'Brien, *Through the Chicago Stock Yards*, p. 68.

11 O'Brien, *Through the Chicago Stock Yards*, p. 72.

12 For a complete discussion of the cattle kill floor, see Wilder, *The Modern Packinghouse*, pp. 72–101; see also O'Brien, *Through the Chicago Stock Yards*, p. 46.

13 Wilder, *The Modern Packinghouse*, p. 411.

14 O'Brien, *Through the Chicago Stock Yards*, pp. 50, 69.

15 Swift and Company, *A Glance at the Meat Industry in America* (Chicago, n.d.), pp. 3–5, 19–20.

16 Swift and Company, *Visitors' Bulletin* (Chicago, 1933), pp. 2–3, 10, 15–16, 21–27; Armour and Company, *Seeing Armour* (Chicago, n.d.).

17 Robert Williams, ed., *The Chicago Diaries of John M. Wing, 1865–1866* (Carbondale and Edwardsville, IL, 2002), pp. xxiv–xxvii, 34–70; *Chicago Times*, September 18, 1865.

18 Jack Wing, *The Great Union Stock Yards of Chicago: Their Railroad Connections, Bank, and Exchange, The Hough House, Water Supply and General Features also, A Sketch of the Live Stock Trade and the Old Yards* (Chicago, 1865), pp. 4–5, 24.

19 *Chicago Tribune*, December 5, 1867.

20 *Chicago Tribune*, July 18, 1869.

21 *Chicago Tribune*, December 30, 1871, January 3, 1872.

22 *Chicago Tribune*, October 24, 1894.

23 *Chicago Tribune*, February 24, 1889, August 18, 1889, October 22, 1889; *Daily Sun*, December 30, 1891.

24 *Daily Sun*, May 28, 1892; Swift and Company advertisement in *The National Provisioner*, January 5, 1907, p. 18.

25 Lambert, *A Trip Through the Union Stock Yards*; O'Brien, *Through the Chicago Stock Yards*; Swift and Company, *Swift & Company Visitors Reference Book* , Swift and Company, *A Visit to Swift & Company, Union Stock Yards, Chicago* (Chicago, n.d.). The copy of *A Visit to Swift & Company, Union Stock Yards, Chicago* is postmarked February 15, 1917.

26 *Chicago Tribune*, July 29, 1910, August 19, 1902.

27 Sarah Bernhardt, *My Double Life: Memoirs of Sarah Bernhardt* (London, 1907), pp. 400-401. Quoted in Lawrence A. Scaff, *Max Weber in America* (Princeton and Oxford, 2011), p. 45; Rudyard Kipling, "How I Struck Chicago, and How Chicago Struck Me," in Bessie Louise Pierce, ed., *How Others See Chicago: Impressions of Visitors, 1673-1933* (Chicago, 1933, 2004), p. 259; *Chicago Tribune*, August 11, 1910, November 16, 1910, June 6, 1905, September 25, 1909, April 10, 1908, October 1, 1908, March 22, 1908, July 22, 1906, August 15, 1909. Lisa Krissoff Boehm, *Popular Culture and the Enduring Myth of Chicago, 1871-1968* (New York and London, 2004), pp. 81-82.

28 For an exhaustive discussion of the development of the stereopticon, see Laura Burd Schiavo, "From Phantom Image to Perfect Vision: Physiological Optics, Commercial Photography, and the Popularization of the Stereoscope," in Lisa Gitelman and Geoffret B. Pingree, eds., *New Media, 1740-1915* (Cambridge, 2003), pp. 113-38.

29 There are various websites dedicated to the story of the stereopticon. I have an extensive collection of the cards, and many of these have been used to illustrate this volume.

30 For the importance of postcards and Chicago's place in their history, see John A. Jakle and Keith A. Sculle, *Picturing Illinois: Twentieth-Century Postcard Art from Chicago to Cairo* (Urbana, Chicago, and Springfield, 2012). The authors deal with the stockyards on pages 63-65.

31 *Chicago Tribune*, June 23, 1905.

32 Stockyard memorabilia often appear for sale on the Internet, especially on eBay. Wood Brothers, *Ninth Biennial Edition of Facts and Figures of Chicago Live Stock Trade for Twenty-Four Years with Other Valuable Information* (Chicago, 1904).

33 W. Joseph Grand, *Illustrated History of the Union Stockyards: Sketch-book of Familiar Faces and Places at The Yards* (Chicago, 1896); Theodore Alexander Herr, *Seventy Years in the Chicago Stockyards* (New York, 1968); Larry Caine, *My City: The Great Chicago Stockyards, The International Amphitheater, The International Livestock Show, etc . . . etc . . . etc: An Autobiography* (2011).

Chapter Two

1 *Minutes of the Board of Directors of the Union Stock Yard and Transit Company*, December 20, 1865; *Chicago Tribune*, January 17, 1865.

2 William Cronon, *Nature's Metropolis: Chicago and the Great West* (New York and London, 1991), pp. 213-22; H. W. Brands, *American Colossus: The Triumph of Capitalism, 1865-1900* (New York, 2010), see chapter 7, "Profits on the Hoof"; *Third Annual Report of the Directors of the Union Stock Yard and Transit Company to the Stockholders, January 15, 1869* (Chicago, 1869), p. 6. For an account of the industry nationally, see Jimmy M. Skaggs, *The Cattle-Trailing Industry: Between Supply and Demand, 1866-1890* (Norman, OK, and London, 1973), and Jimmy M. Skaggs, *Prime Cut: Livestock Raising and Meatpacking in the United States, 1607-1983* (College Station, TX, 1986).

3 Elmer A. Riley, "The Development of Chicago and Vicinity as a Manufacturing

Center Prior to 1880" (Ph.D. diss., University of Chicago, 1911), pp. 22-23, 38-39; Howard C. Hill, "The Development of Chicago as a Center of the Meat Packing Industry," *Mississippi Valley Historical Review* 10, no. 3 (December 1923): 253-73; A. T. Andreas, *History of Chicago; From there Earliest Period to the Present Time: Volume One Ending with the Year 1857*, 3 vols. (Chicago, 1884), vol. 1, pp. 122, 153, 554, 560-63, 574; vol. 2, pp. 60, 334, 507; Arthur C. Davenport, *The American Livestock Market: How It Functions* (Chicago, 1922), p. 13; *Chicago Daily Tribune*, February 26, 1902; Board of Trade statistics in Joseph G. Knapp, "A Review of Chicago Stock Yards History," *University Journal of Business*, June 1924, p. 332; Robert Lewis, *Chicago Made: Factory Networks in the Industrial Metropolis* (Chicago and London, 2008), pp. 74-76.

4   For the impact of railroads on Chicago and the livestock industry, see Louise Wade, *Chicago's Pride: The Stockyards, Packingtown, and Environs in the Nineteenth Century* (Urbana, 1987), pp. 25-26.

5   The nine railroads were as follows: the Illinois Central, Michigan Central, Chicago, Burlington and Quincy, Michigan Southern, Pittsburgh, Fort Wayne and Chicago, Chicago and Alton, Rock Island, Chicago and Danville, and Chicago and North-Western. The original incorporators were John L. Hancock, Virginius A. Turpin, Rosell M. Hough, Sidney A. Kent, Charles M. Culbertson, Lyman Blair, M. L. Sykes Jr., George W. Cass, James F. Joy, John F. Tracy, Timothy B. Blackstone, Joseph H. Moore, John S. Barry, Homer E. Sargent, Burton C. Cook, John B. Drake, William D. Judson, David Kreigh, and John B. Sherman.

6   *Minutes of the Board of Directors of the Union Stock Yard and Transit Company*, March 2, 1865, March 4, 1865; A. T. Andreas, *History of Chicago*, vol. 1, pp. 155-56; vol. 3, p. 334.

7   For the development of Octave Chanute as an engineer, see Simine Short, *Locomotive to Aeromotive: Octave Chanute and the Transportation Revolution* (Urbana and Chicago, 2011). His work on the Union Stock Yard is described on pages 37-40.

8   Jack Wing, *The Great Union Stock Yards of Chicago: Their Railroad Connections, Bank, and Exchange, The Hough House, Water Supply and General Features also, A Sketch of the Live Stock Trade and the Old Yards* (Chicago, 1865), pp. 13-28; *Board of Directors Minutes, Union Stock Yard and Transit Company*, May 2, 1865, June 17, 1865; Wade, *Chicago's Pride*, p. 53; *Chicago Tribune*, November 18, 1865.

9   *Chicago Tribune*, December 27, 1865; *Chicago Evening Journal*, November 26, 1865.

10   *Annual Report of the Directors of the Union Stock Yard and Transit Company to the Stockholders, January 16, 1867* (Chicago, 1867), pp. 1-2, 7.

11   *Chicago Times*, December 29, 1865, December 30, 1865; Andreas, *History of Chicago*, vol. 3, p. 335.

12   *Chicago Tribune*, January 3, 1866.

13   Andreas, *History of Chicago*, vol. 3, p. 334; Wade, *Chicago's Pride*, pp. 56, 169.

14   *Chicago Tribune*, February 26, 1902; Wade, *Chicago's Pride*, p. 56; Andreas, *History of Chicago*, vol. 3, p. 335; *Minutes of the Board of Directors of the Union Stock Yard and Transit Company*, June 1, 1867; Joseph G. Knapp, "A Review of Chicago Stock Yards History," *University Journal of Business* 2, no. 3 (June 1924): 338.

15   Wade, *Chicago's Pride*, p. 56; *Second Annual Report of the Directors of the Union Stock*

Yard and Transit Company to the Stockholders, January 15, 1868 (Chicago, 1868), p. 1; Bertram B. Fowler, *Men, Meat and Miracles* (New York, 1952), pp. 41-42; Andreas *History of Chicago*, vol. 2, pp. 615-16; Nik Heyman, Maria Kaika, and Erik Swyngedouw, eds., *In the Nature of Cities: Urban Political Ecology and the Politics of Urban Metabolism* (New York, 2006), p. 80; Andrea Stulman Dennett, *Weird and Wonderful: The Dime Museum in America* (New York, 1997), p. 85; *Chicago Tribune*, October 31, 1866, November 12, 1899, January 17, 1900, June 16, 1867; John Wright, *Chicago: Past Present, Future* (Chicago, 1868), p. 282.

16   Andreas, *History of Chicago*, vol. 3, p. 335; vol. 2, p. 628; *Chicago Tribune*, November 25, 1873.

17   Wade, *Chicago's Pride*, pp. 65-66, 99; Andreas, *History of Chicago*, vol. 3, pp. 334-35, 451; *Chicago Tribune*, September 8, 1872.

18   Harper Leech and John Charles Carroll, *Armour and His Times* (New York and London, 1938), pp. 1-2, 102-3; Wade, *Chicago's Pride*, pp. 64-65, 99-100, *Chicago Tribune*, September 8, 1872.

19   Edward N. Wentworth, *A Biographical Catalog of the Portrait Gallery of the Saddle and Sirloin Club* (Chicago, 1920), pp. 162-63.

20   Wade, *Chicago's Pride*, pp. 28, 55, 66, 221; Wentworth, *Saddle and Sirloin Club*, pp. 182-83; Walter Roth, "Nelson Morris and 'The Yards,'" *Chicago Jewish History*, Spring 2008, pp. 1, 4-5.

21   Ralph P. Dainty, *Darling-Delaware Centenary, 1882-1982* (Chicago, 1981), pp. 34, 52, 56, 70, 125, 131; *Town of Lake Vindicator*, February 10, 1883; *Daily Sun*, July 21, 1891.

22   *Chicago Tribune*, June 15, 1866, February 22, 1873, July 26, 1879; Wade, *Chicago's Pride*, pp. 87-88.

23   *Drovers Journal Yearbook of Figures of the Livestock Trade for the Year 1922* (Chicago, 1923), p. 10.

24   *Chicago Tribune*, December 14, 1882.

25   *Board of Directors Minutes, Union Stock Yard and Transit Company*, June 21, 1872, June 27, 1872, January 15, 1873, September 1, 1873, May 17, 1875; Wade, *Chicago's Pride*, pp. 86-89; Commission on Chicago Historical and Architectural Landmarks, *Summary of Information on the Union Stock Yard Gate* (Chicago 1971), pp. 1-2.

26   Cronon, *Nature's Metropolis*, pp. 230-35; Lewis Corey, *Meat and Man: A Study of Monopoly, Unionism, and Food Policy* (New York, 1949), pp. 39-40; Wilson J. Warren, *Tied to the Great Packing Machine: The Midwest and Meatpacking* (Iowa City, 2007), p. 13; *Chicago Tribune*, August 4, 1882, October 13, 1882; *Town of Lake Vindicator*, February 10, 1883.

27   David Igler, *Industrial Cowboys: Miller & Lux and the Transformation of the Far West, 1850-1920* (Berkeley, Los Angeles, and London, 2001), pp. 160-67.

28   Wade, *Chicago's Pride*, pp. 103-9.

29   Sylvia Hood Washington, *Packing Them In: An Archaeology of Environmental Racism in Chicago, 1865-1954* (Lanham, MD, 2005), chapter 4.

30   *Chicago Tribune*, November 30, 1859, March 19, 1861, December 16, 1872; for a detailed discussion of the stench problem, see Wade, *Chicago's Pride*, chapter 8. For the role of DeWolf, see Margaret Garb, "Health, Morality, and Housing: The 'Tene-

ment Problem' in Chicago," *American Journal of Public Health*, September 2003, pp. 1420-30.

Chapter Three

1   I have discussed the growth of a communal and extra-communal responses elsewhere; see Dominic A. Pacyga, *Polish Immigrants and Industrial Chicago: Workers on the South Side, 1880–1922* (Chicago, 2003).

2   *Chicago Tribune*, December 29, 1865, May 25, 1866, May 25, 1873; *Daily Drovers Journal*, September 16, 1882.

3   Louise Wade, *Chicago's Pride: The Stockyards, Packingtown, and Environs in the Nineteenth Century* (Urbana, 1987), pp. 61-63, 70-71; Rev. Msgr. Harry C. Koenig, S.T.D., ed., *A History of the Parishes of the Archdiocese of Chicago Published in Observance of the Centenary of the Archdiocese, 1980* (Chicago, 1980), 2 vols., vol. 1, pp. 35-38, 145-51, 302-6, 438-41, 499-502, 654-59; Glen E. Holt and Dominic A. Pacyga, *Chicago: A Historical Guide to the Neighborhoods; The Loop and South Side* (Chicago, 1979), pp. 114, 133.

4   William Cronon, *Nature's Metropolis: Chicago and the Great West* (New York and London, 1991), pp. 228-30; Robert Slayton, *Back of the Yards: The Making of a Local Democracy* (Chicago, 1986), pp. 15-21.

5   For the evolution and domestication of pigs, see the following websites, accessed July 26, 2012: http://animals.about.com/od/mammals/p/hogspigs.htm; http://archaeology.about.com/od/domestications/ig/Animal-Domestication/European-Domestic-Pigs.htm.

6   Cronon, *Nature's Metropolis*; Ruggles quoted on p. 226, see pp. 225-28.

7   Heller and Company, *H Secrets of Meat Curing and Sausage Making* (Chicago, 1922), p. 34.

8   For the story of Mary the Apple Woman and Jack-Knife Ben, see W. Jos. Grand, *Illustrated History of the Union Stock Yards* (Chicago, 1896), pp. 102-4, 141-45; also *Daily Sun*, May 28, 1892.

9   F. W. Wilder, *The Modern Packinghouse* (Chicago, 1905), pp. 76-77, 118-19; "Wages and Hours of Labor in the Slaughtering and Meat-Packing Industry," *Bulletin of U.S. Labor Statistics* 252 (August 1917): 1077-78; John R. Commons, "Labor Conditions in Meat Packing and the Recent Strike," *Quarterly Journal of Economics* 19 (November 1904): 4-9; Floyd Erwin Bernard, "A Study of Industrial Diseases in the Stockyards" (M.A. diss., University of Chicago, 1910), pp. 11-16; Slayton, *Back of the Yards*, pp. 89 91-92.

10 John R. Commons, "Women in Unions, Meat Packing Industry," *American Federationist* 13 (May 1906): 82; Sophonisba P. Breckinridge and Edith Abbott, "Women in Industry: The Chicago Stockyards," *Journal of Political Economy* 19 (October 1910): 641-49; Commons, "Labor Conditions," p. 20; Mary Elizabeth Pidgeon, "The Employment of Women in Slaughtering and Meat Packing," *Bulletin of the Women's Bureau* 88 (Washington, DC, 1932): pp. 4, 18-19, 21-24; Mary E. McDowell, "Mothers and Night Work," *Survey* 39 (December 22, 1917): 335.

11 *Third Annual Report of the Factory Inspectors of Illinois for the Year Ending December*

15, 1895 (Springfield, 1896), pp. 10-11; *Fourth Annual Report of the Factory Inspectors of Illinois for the Year Ending December 15, 1896* (Springfield, 1897), p. 14; *Eighth Annual Report of the Factory Inspectors of Illinois for the Year Ending December 15, 1900* (Springfield, 1901), pp. 5, 7, 10-11, 21-22, 26-27; Florence Kelley, "The Illinois Child Labor Law," *American Journal of Sociology* 3 (January 1898): 492-95; Commons, "Labor Conditions in Meat Packing and the Recent Strike," *Quarterly Journal of Economics* 19 (November 1904): 24; Florence Kelley, "The Working Boy," *American Journal of Sociology* 2 (November 1896): 363; Howard Eugene Wilson, "Mary E. McDowell and Her Work as Head Resident of the University of Chicago Settlement House, 1894-1905," (M.A. thesis, University of Chicago, 1927), pp. 61-63; McDowell, "Summer on the Sidewalks" (typewritten manuscript), p. 27, in McDowell Papers, box 1, folder 3; *Chicago Tribune*, January 25, 1904.

12 *Chicago Tribune*, April 18, 1867, May 3, 1867, May 4, 1867, May 8, 1867, May 10, 1867, May 11, 1867; Henry Pelling, *American Labor* (Chicago, 1968), pp. 63-66, 71; Howard B. Meyers, "The Policing of Labor Disputes in Chicago: A Case Study" (Ph.D. diss., University of Chicago, 1929), pp. 162-72; Mary E. McDowell, "A Quarter of a Century in the Stockyards District," in Clyde C. Wilson, ed., *An Illinois Reader* (DeKalb, IL, 1970), pp. 336-37.

13 Wade, *Chicago's Pride*, pp. 114-20; Philip S. Foner, *The Great Uprising of 1877* (New York, 1877), pp. 145-68; *Chicago Tribune*, July 27, 1877.

14 *Chicago Tribune*, December 8, 1878; Wade, *Chicago's Pride*, pp. 122-23.

15 *Chicago Tribune*, November 15, 1879, November 16, 1879.

16 Wade, *Chicago's Pride*, pp. 124-26; *Chicago Tribune*, December 30, 1879.

17 See Craig Phelan, *Grand Master Workman: Terence Powderly and the Knights of Labor* (Westport, CT, 2000).

18 Wade, *Chicago's Pride*, p. 126.

19 For the Haymarket affair, see James Green, *Death in the Haymarket: A Story of Chicago, the First Labor Movement and the Bombing that Divided Gilded Age America* (New York, 2006); Paul Avrich, *The Haymarket Tragedy* (Princeton, 1986); Carl Smith, *Urban Disorder and the Shape of Belief: The Great Chicago Fire, the Haymarket Bomb, and the Model Town of Pullman* (Chicago, 2007).

20 *Chicago Tribune*, May 22, 1886, May 23, 1886, July 24, 1886; Wade, *Chicago's Pride*, p. 243;

21 *Chicago Tribune*, October 2, 1886; *Daily Drovers Journal*, October 6, 1886.

22 Wade, *Chicago's Pride*, pp. 246-47; *Chicago Tribune*, October 8, 1886, October 13, 1886, October 14, 1886; *Chicago Daily News*, October 8, 1886, October 9, 1886, October 11, 1886, October 12, 1886, October 13, 1886, October 14, 1886, October 18, 1886; *Daily Drovers Journal*, October 6, 1886, October 8, 1886, October 9, 1886, October 11, 1886, October 12, 1886, October 13, 1886; *Goodall's Daily Sun*, October 8, 1886, October 11, 1886, October 14, 1886.

23 Wade, *Chicago's Pride*, p. 247; *Chicago Tribune*, October 16, 1886.

24 Wade, *Chicago's Pride*, pp. 247-49; Phelan, *Grand Master Workman*, pp. 198-99; *Chicago Daily News*, October 19, 1886; *Chicago Tribune*, October 20, 1886, November 10, 1886; *Daily Drovers Journal*, October 19, 1886, October 20, 1886.

25 *Chicago Tribune*, October 27, 1886.

26   *Chicago Tribune*, November 3, 1886, November 9, 1886; *Daily Drovers Journal*,
     November 4, 1886, November 8, 1886, November 9, 1886, November 11, 1886,
     November 15, 1886, November 16, 1886, November 17, 1886; Wade, *Chicago's Pride*,
     pp. 249-53; Phelan, *Grand Master Workman*, pp. 199-201.

27   *Chicago Daily Sun*, July 3, 1894, July 5, 1894, July 6, 1894, July 9, 1894; *Chicago Daily
     News*, July 5, 1894, July 6, 1894, July 7, 1894, July 10, 1894, July 11, 1894.

28   Lloyd Lewis and Henry Justin Smith, *Chicago: The History of Its Reputation* (New
     York, 1929), p. 275; *Tenth Annual Illustrated Catalogue of S. E. Gross' Famous City
     Subdivisions and Suburban Towns* (Chicago, 1891), pp. 60-63; Henry Hall, ed.,
     *America's Successful Men of Affairs: An Encyclopedia of Contemporary Biogra-
     phy*, 5 vols. (New York, 1896), 3:354; *The Biographical Dictionary and Portrait Gal-
     lery of Representative Men of Chicago, Minnesota Cities, and the World's Columbian
     Exposition* (Chicago, 1892), p. 81. For a discussion of the nature of housing in Back
     of the Yards, see Pacyga, *Polish Immigrants and Industrial Chicago*, chapter 2.

29   Howard Eugene Wilson, "Mary E. McDowell and Her Work as Head Resident of
     the University of Chicago Settlement House, 1894-1904" (M.A. thesis, Univer-
     sity of Chicago, 1927), pp. 14, 17-19; Mary E. McDowell, "How the Living Faith of
     One Social Worker Grew," *Graphic Survey* 60 (April 1928); Mary E. McDowell, "A
     Quarter of a Century in the Stockyards District," in Clyde C. Walton, ed., *An Illi-
     nois Reader* (DeKalb, 1970), p. 327; Mary E. McDowell, "Civic Experience" (1914,
     typed manuscript), p. 3, in McDowell Papers, box 3, folder 14; Pacyga, *Polish Im-
     migrants and Industrial Chicago*, chapter 5. For a discussion of Mary McDowell as
     environmental activist, see Sylvia Hood Washington, *Packing Them In: An Archae-
     ology of Environmental Racism in Chicago, 1865-1954* (Lanham, Boulder, New York,
     Toronto, and Oxford, 2005), pp. 81-96.

30   Wade, *Chicago's Pride* pp. 256-58.

Chapter Four

1   Joseph G. Knapp, "A Review of Chicago Stock Yards History," *University Journal of
    Business* 2, no. 3 (June 1924): 338; George Wm. Lambert, *A Trip Through the Union
    Stock Yards and Slaughterhouses — Chicago, U.S.A.* (Chicago, n.d., ca. 1890s), pp.
    7-8; W. Joseph Grand, *Illustrated History of the Union Stockyards: Sketch-Book of
    Familiar Faces and Places at the Yards* (Chicago, 1896), pp. 10-12, 19, 24.

2   *Daily Sun*, September 26, 1891; Lambert, *A Trip Through the Union Stock Yards*, p. 8;
    Grand, *Illustrated History*, pp. 77, 79, 88-89.

3   *Chicago Tribune*, October 7, 1897, September 22, 1899; John O'Brien, *Through the
    Chicago Stock Yards: A Handy Guide to the Great Packing Industry* (Chicago and
    New York, 1907), pp. 30-32.

4   Charles J. Bushnell, *The Social Problem at the Chicago Stock Yards* (Chicago, 1902),
    pp. 4, 7; O'Brien, *Through the Chicago Stock Yards*, pp. 12-14, 26, 34.

5   Bushnell, *The Social Problem*, pp. 22-23; Grand, *Illustrated History*, p. 29; Arthur C.
    Davenport, *The American Live Stock Market: How It Functions* (Chicago, 1922), pp.
    53-58.

6   Louise Wade, *Chicago's Pride: The Stockyards, Packingtown, and Environs in the*

Nineteenth Century (Urbana, 1987), pp. 89-90; George T. Angell, *Autobiographical Sketches and Personal Recollections* (Boston, 1892), pp. 37-39; *Chicago Tribune*, September 17, 1871, April 27, 1873, May 17, 1874, May 6, 1877, May 4, 1879, October 10, 1879, April 6, 1880.

7 A. T. Andreas, *History of Chicago; From the Earliest Period to the Present Time: Volume One Ending with the Year 1857*, 3 vols. (Chicago, 1884), vol. 3, pp. 334-35; Wade, *Chicago's Pride*, pp. 84-85; *Chicago Tribune*, February 28, 1879, January 25, 1880, December 14, 1882.

8 *Daily Drovers Journal*, September 12, 1882, November 9, 1882, November 21, 1882, November 28, 1882, November 8, 1886.

9 *Chicago Sun*, August 12, 1891.

10 O'Brien, *Through the Chicago Stock Yards*, p. 26; *Wood Brothers Ninth Biennial Edition of Facts and Figures of Chicago Live Stock* (Chicago, 1904), p. 15; *Chicago Tribune*, October 10, 1904, November 29, 1908.

11 Alvin H. Sanders, *The Story of the International Live Stock Exposition: From Its Inception in 1900 to the Show of 1941* (Chicago, 1942), pp. 7-8; *Chicago Tribune*, January 18, 1900.

12 *Chicago Tribune*, November 23, 1902, November 30, 1902, December 1, 1902.

13 *Chicago Tribune*, December 1, 1904.

14 *Chicago Tribune*, December 15, 1905, November 17, 1907, December 1, 1907.

15 *Chicago Tribune*, November 4, 1909, November 29, 1909.

16 Sanders, *The Story of the International*, pp. 8-23; *Chicago Tribune*, November 24, 1899.

17 Sanders, *The Story of the International*, pp. 37, 59; *Chicago Tribune*, November 23, 1924. November 27, 1927.

18 *Report of the Commissioner of Corporations on the Beef Industry* (Washington, DC, March 3, 1905), pp. xxix-xxx, xxxiv, 21, 33, 46.

19 Arthur Cushman, "The Packing Plant and Its Equipment," in Institute of American Meat Packers, *The Packing Industry: A Series of Lectures Given under the Joint Auspices of the School of Commerce and Administration of the University of Chicago and the Institute of American Meat Packers* (Chicago, 1924), pp. 108-19.

20 *Drovers Journal Year Book of Figures of the Livestock Trade for the Year 1953* (Chicago, 1954), pp. 10, 12; *Report of the Commissioner of Corporations on the Beef Industry*, p. 55.

21 *Drovers Journal Year Book of Figures for 1953*, pp. 7, 10, 12.

22 Chapter 2 above deals with the formation of the Darling and Company. For the sale of the company to the Morris interests, see Ralph P. Dainty, *Darling-Delaware Centenary, 1882-1982* (Chicago, 1981), p. 70.

23 *Report of the Commissioner of Corporations on the Beef Industry*, pp. 22-23; Rudolph A. Clemen, *By-Products in the Packing Industry* (Chicago, 1927), pp. 7-8.

24 Clemen, *By-Products*, pp. 2-3.

25 Clemen, *By-Products*, pp. 12-16.

26 *Report of the Commissioner of Corporations on the Beef Industry*, p. 23; Clemen, *By-Products*, pp. 12-17, 21-22, 43; for a discussion of hide handling and tanning, see pp. 32-36.

27 Clemen, *By-Products*, pp. 74–76, 234–37.

28 Clemen, *By-Products*, see especially chapters 13 and 15; Alfred D. Chandler, *The Visible Hand: The Managerial Revolution in American Business* (Cambridge, MA, 1977), p. 398.

29 Much of the discussion on the organization of the packing industry in the late nineteenth and early twentieth century is derived from Chandler, *The Visible Hand*, pp. 391–402, and the *Report of the Commissioner of Corporations on the Beef Industry*.

30 *Daily Sun*, December 24, 1890; *Minutes of the Board of Directors of the Union Stock Yard and Transit Company*, February 2, 1891; Wade, *Chicago's Pride*, pp. 184–88.

31 Knapp, "A Review of Chicago Stock Yards History," pp. 339–44. For announced details of the 1891 agreement, see "The Chicago Stock-Yards Deal," *Chicago Tribune*, September 20, 1891.

32 *Daily Sun*, December 28, 1890, July 28, 1891, August 1, 1891; *Board of Directors, New Jersey Company Minutes*, July 9, 1890, July 10, 1890, May 2, 1891, July 15, 1891, July 27, 1891, July 30, 1891; *Opinions of Counsel in Reference to Agreement with Armour and Others*, July 10, 1891, in the Chicago Stockyards Collection, University of Illinois at Chicago Special Collections, box 1, folder 13. Henceforth referred to as Stockyards Collection; *Chicago Tribune*, March 2, 1892.

33 For the 1887 proposal, see "Lyons Transfer Yards," *Chicago Tribune*, September 14, 1887, November 22, 1890, October 2, 1892; *Chicago Inter Ocean*, March 10, 1892. For the deal with the small packers, see *Board of Directors, New Jersey Company Minutes*, October 9, 1891, July 6, 1892, December 10, 1892; *Special Meeting of Stockholders, New Jersey Company*, March 1, 1892, in Stockyards Collection, box 1, folder 13; Wade, *Chicago's Pride*, p. 187; *Daily Sun*, May 18, 1892. On the laws suit of the nonassociated packers, see, *The Court of Chancery, The Prerogative Court, and on Appeal, in the Court of Errors and Appeals of the State of New Jersey*, vol. 5 (Trenton, 1893), pp. 656–701. This is also reproduced in *Atlantic Reporter*, vol. 25, pp. 277–94.

34 *Daily Sun*, December 30, 1891; *New York Times*, April 7, 1899; *Chicago Tribune*, January 18, 1900, February 26, 1902; T. J. Zimmerman, "The Colossus of Business Organizations," *System: The Magazine of Business*, July 1904, pp. 166–67.

35 Lewis Corey, *Meat and Man: A Study of Monopoly, Unionism, and Food Policy* (New York, 1950), pp. 45–48; *Chicago Tribune*, January 3, 1912.

36 *Report of the Commissioner of Corporations on the Beef Industry*, pp. 26, 35.

37 *Official Journal of the Amalgamated Meat Cutters and Butcher Workmen*, March 1905, p. 27.

38 *Chicago Tribune*, January 16, 1905, March 16, 1905, March 21, 1905, April 9, 1905, April 11, 1905, April 19, 1905, May 5, 1905, June 16, 1905, July 2, 1905.

39 Corey, *Meat and Man*, pp. 51–52; *Chicago Tribune*, March 22, 1906.

40 *Chicago Tribune*, December 12, 1908.

41 *Chicago Tribune*, July 21, 1912; L. D. H. Weld, "The Packing Industry: Its History and General Economics," in Institute of American Meat Packers, *The Packing Industry: A Series of Lectures*.

42 For a description of how *The Jungle* became a best seller, see Christopher Wilson, "The Making of a Bestseller, 1906," *New York Times*, December 22, 1985.

43 Isaac F. Marcosson, *Adventures in Interviewing* (London and New York, 1919),

280-85; *Chicago Tribune*, May 5, 1906. For Sinclair's sources, see Louise Carroll Wade, "The Problem of Classroom Use of Upton Sinclair's *The Jungle*," *American Studies*, Fall 1991, pp. 79-101, For the Mr. Dooley quote, see Finley Peter Dunne, *Dissertations by Mr. Dooley* (London and New York, 1906), p. 249.

44 "Report of the Department Committee on the Federal Meat-Inspection Service at Chicago. April 5, 1906," in U.S. Department of Agriculture, Twenty-Third Annual Report of the Bureau of Animal Industry for the Year 1906 (Washington, DC, 1908), pp. 406-8.

45 *Chicago Tribune*, April 11, 1906, April 12, 1906.

46 Marcosson, *Adventures in Interviewing*, pp. 285-86; Wade, "Classroom Use of *The Jungle*," pp. 90-91.

47 Wade, "Classroom Use of *The Jungle*," p. 79; *Chicago Tribune*, June 27, 1906.

48 Wilder, *The Modern Packinghouse*.

49 For a timeline of history of the American Meat Institute, see http://www .meatami.com/ht/d/sp/i/232/pid/232 (accessed February 20, 2013); *New York Times*, May 22, 1922; Robert W. Bray, "History of Meat Science," American Meat Science Association, http://www.meatscience.org/page.aspx?id=182 (accessed February 21,2013); "Commerce and Administration: The Institute of American Meat Packers," *University of Chicago Magazine*, January 1924, pp. 102-3, 110; Institute of American Meat Packers, *The Packing Industry: A Series of Lectures*; Oscar Meyer, *Some Observations on the Economics of the Meat Industry* (Chicago, 1939).

50 Rudolph Alexander Clemen, *American Livestock and Meat Industry* (New York, 1923), pp. 697-98; Harry Rosenburg, "On the Packing Industry and the Stockyards" (n.d.), p. 10, in McDowell papers, box 3, folder 15; U.S. Congress, Senate, *Final Report and Testimony Submitted to Congress by the Commission on Industrial Relations*, S. Doc. 415, 64th Cong., 2nd sess., 1916, vol. 4, pp. 3514, 3521, 3464; "Wages and Hours in Meat-Packing, 1917," p. 61; John R. Commons, "Labor Conditions in Meat Packing and the Recent Strike," *Quarterly Journal of Economics* 19 (November 1904): 13, 16; Harold H. Swift, "Guaranteed Time in the Stockyards," *Survey Graphic*, November 1931, 122; Mary E. McDowell, "The Great Strike" (1904) (manuscript), in McDowell Papers, box 3, folder 15, p. 3.

51 Bert Crawford Gross, "Factors Affecting the Origin of Livestock Receipts at Chicago, 1923-27" (M.A. thesis, University of Chicago, 1929), pp. 14, 27-34; 1953 *Yearbook of Figures of the Livestock Trade* (Chicago, 1953), p. 14; J. C. Kennedy et al., *Wages and Family Budgets in the Chicago Stockyards District* (Chicago, 1914), p. 14; Breckinridge and Abbott, "Women in Industry: The Chicago Stockyards," p. 647.

52 For a description of the union's organization, see T. J. Zimmerman, "How the Stockyards Strike Was Managed," *System: The Magazine of Business*, July 1904, pp. 181-96; also David M. Brody, *The Butcher Workmen: A Study of Unionization* (Cambridge, MA, 1964).

53 Both James Barrett and I discuss the union movement and the strikes in the early twentieth century in some detail. See James R. Barrett, *Work and Community in the Jungle: Chicago's Packinghouse Workers, 1894-1922* (Urbana and Chicago, 1987), and Pacyga *Polish Immigrants and Industrial Chicago*. For the Irish women involved in the union movement, see Suellen Hoy, "The Irish Girls' Rising: Build-

ing the Women's Labor Movement in Progressive-Era Chicago," *Labor: Studies in Working-Class History of the Americas*, Spring 2012, pp. 77–100. For African Americans and the 1919 race riot, see Chicago Commission on Race Relations, *The Negro in Chicago: A Study of Relations and a Race Riot* (Chicago, 1922); William M. Tuttle Jr., *Race Riot: Chicago in the Red Summer of 1919* (New York, 1970); Dominic A. Pacyga, "Chicago's 1919 Race Riot: Ethnicity, Class, and Urban Violence," in Raymond Mohl, ed., *The Making of Urban America*, 2nd ed. (Wilmington, 1997), pp: 187–207.

54   Clemen, *American Livestock and Meat Industry*, chapter 32.

Chapter Five

1   John F. Hogan and Alex A. Burkholder, *Fire Strikes the Chicago Stock Yards: A History of Flame and Folly in the Jungle* (Charleston and London, 2013), pp. 58–69, 85; *Chicago Tribune*, December 23, 1910.

2   *Chicago Tribune*, December 23, 1910; Hogan and Burkholder, *Fire Strikes the Chicago Stock Yards*, p. 28.

3   Hogan and Burkholder, *Fire Strikes the Chicago Stock Yards*, pp. 123–38.

4   Arthur C. Davenport, *The American Livestock Market: How It Functions* (Chicago, 1922), p. 85.

5   Ira Nelson Morris, *Heritage from My Father: An Autobiography* (New York, 1947), pp. 252–53; E. M. Bakwin, *E. M. Bakwin: A Memoir* (Chicago, 2009), chapter 1; *The Armour-Morris Purchase: Its Benefits to the Public* (Chicago, 1923) in the Chicago Stockyards Collection, University of Illinois at Chicago Special Collections, box 1, folder 2. Henceforth referred to as Stockyards Collection.

6   Both the *Texas Live Stock Journal* and the *New Mexico News and Press* were quoted in the *Daily Drovers Journal*, September 16, 1882; *Lake Vindicator*, August 18, 1883.

7   *Drovers Journal Year Book of Figures of the Livestock Trade for the Year 1962* (Chicago 1963), p. 4.

8   Edward A. Duddy and David A. Revzan, *The Supply Area of the Chicago Livestock Market* (Chicago, 1931), pp. 1–3, 7–16, 19–27.

9   Edward A. Duddy and David A. Revzan, *The Distribution of Livestock from the Chicago Market, 1924–29* (Chicago, 1932), pp. 1–3.

10   Cronon, *Nature's Metropolis*, p. 259.

11   For the Armour affair, see the Chicago newspaper clippings file in the Chicago Stockyards Collection, box 1, folders 7 and 8.

12   For a complete description of the 1934 fire, see Hogan and Burkholder, *Fire Strikes the Chicago Stock Yards*, pp. 139–51.

13   Hogan and Burkholder have Means as a sixty-three-year-old supervisor of the feed dock, while the *Chicago Tribune* maintains he was a sixty-year-old watchman. It seems Means had held several jobs with the USY&T Company and may have been a supervisor earlier in his career. *Chicago Tribune*, May 22, 1934, May 22, 1934.

14   Hogan and Burkholder, *Fire Strikes the Chicago Stock Yards*, pp. 148–50; *Chicago Daily Drovers Journal*, May 21, 1934.

15   *Chicago Defender*, May 26, 1934; *Chicago Tribune*, June 15, 1934, November 11, 1934,

Chicago Daily Drovers Journal, May 21, 1934, May 22, 1934, May 23, 1934, May 25, 1934, May 26, 1934, November 11, 1934.

16   Furnishings List, Frederick H. Prince Memorial Room; correspondence from Arthur O. Fox to William E. Ogilvie, dated January 23, 1933; lists of various portraits, trophies, and other furnishings are also included in this file, all in box 1, file 3 in International Live Stock Exposition, MS 506, Special Collections Department, Iowa State University Library. Henceforth referred to as International Livestock Exposition Collection.

17   Lizabeth Cohen, *Making a New Deal: Industrial Workers in Chicago, 1919-1939* (New York, 1990), p. 164.

18   Cohen, *Making a New Deal*, see chapter 5.

19   Interview with Sophie Kosciowlowski in Les Orear, *Chicago Stockyards History, Interview Series* (Chicago, 1971), vol. 2, pp. 6-19.

20   *Chicago Daily News*, August 4, 1939; *The CIO News: Packinghouse Workers Edition*, April 1, 1940, April 15, 1940, June 10, 1940, August 5, 1940, October 28, 1940.

21   *The CIO News: Packinghouse Workers Edition*, February 1, 1941, May 12, 1941, June 9, 1941. For a history of the Back of the Yards Neighborhood Council, see Robert Slayton, *Back of the Yards: The Making of a Local Democracy* (Chicago, 1988), and Thomas J. Jablonsky, *Pride in the Jungle: Community and Everyday Life in Back of the Yards Chicago* (Baltimore, 1992).

22   *The Annual Report for Armour and Company's 76th Year, 1943* (January 7, 1944); Roger Horowitz, *Negro and White, Unite and Fight: A Social History of Industrial Unionism in Meatpacking, 1930-1990 (Urbana and Chicago, 1997)*, pp. 150-53.

23   Rick Halpern, *Down on the Killing Floor: Black and White Workers in Chicago's Packinghouses, 1904-1954 (Urbana and Chicago, 1997)*, pp. 193-200, 207-18.

24   Horowitz, *Negro and White*, pp. 168-69.

25   Theodore V. Purcell, S.J., *The Worker Speaks His Mind on Company and Union* (Cambridge, MA, 1954), p. 60; Horowitz, *Negro and White*, p. 170; Martin Millspaugh and Gurney Breckenfeld, *The Human Side of Urban Renewal: A Study of Attitude Changes Produced by Neighborhood Rehabilitation* (New York, 1960), pp. 193-94; Slayton, *Back of the Yards*, pp. 221-22.

26   Quoted in Horowitz, *Negro and White*, p. 175.

27   Leon Fink, Cindy Hahamovitch, Tera Hunter, Bruce Laurie, and Joseph McCartin, eds., *Encyclopedia of U.S. Labor and Working-Class History* (New York, 2007), pp. 1353-54.

28   Halpern, *Down on the Killing Floor*, pp. 228-31; Horowitz, *Negro and White*, pp. 184-89; Francis W. McPeek, *Labor Letter of the Industrial Council for Social Action, MAT Strike Bulletin*, March 20, 1948, p. 2.

29   Purcell, *The Worker Speaks His Mind*, chapter 7.

30   Alan Ehrenhalt, *The Lost City: The Forgotten Virtues of Community in America* (New York, 1996), p. 12.

31   *Chicago Tribune*, October 28, 1952, May 15, 1959.

32   Lloyd E. Slater, "Production-Planned Plant," *Food Engineering*, June 1952, p. 75.

33   *Chicago Daily Defender*, August 8, 1955; *Chicago Tribune*, September 13, 1955.

34   "Swift Uses Up to Date Techniques in Flexible Plant of Moderate, Capacity," *Na-*

tional Provisioner, May 23, 1959, p. 14; *Chicago Tribune*, January 24, 1958, May 15, 1959, October 4, 1959; *Chicago Daily Drovers Journal*, May 14, 1959; *Swift & Company, 1959* (Chicago, 1959), p. 6; *Swift & Company Year Book, 1960* (Chicago, 1960), p. 6; *Swift & Company Year Book, 1961* (Chicago, 1961), p. 7; *Swift & Company Year Book, 1962* (Chicago, 1962), p. 4.

35   *Chicago Tribune*, January 29, 1960, April 1, 1960, August 15, 1960; "Libby's Chicago Handling," *National Provisioner*, August 12, 1961, p. 16; *Swift & Company Year Book, 1961*, p. 12.

36   *The Annual Report for Armour, 1945* (January 4, 1946), in Chicago Stockyards Collection, box 1, folder 1; "What's New in the New Chicago Plant," *Armour Magazine*, May 1956; *Chicago Tribune*, May 20, 1954, March 4, 1956, July 11, 1959, October 7, 1960; *Chicago Daily Drovers Journal*, January 8, 1958, June 9, 1959; *Chicago Daily Defender*, July 6, 1959.

37   *Chicago Drovers Journal*, January 3, 1958.

38   *Chicago Drovers Journal*, January 30, 1958, July 22, 1959, August 4, 1959; *National Provisioner*, December 16, 1961.

39   *Chicago Drovers Journal*, May 14, 1959, June 9, 1959, June 12, 1959, June 16, 1959, August 4, 1959, August 24, 1959; *Chicago Daily News*, June 29, 1959.

40   *Chicago Tribune*, November 24, 1958, June 26, 1960.

41   *Drovers Journal Yearbook of Figures of the Livestock Trade for the Year 1953* (Chicago, 1954), p. 32.

42   *Chicago Tribune*, June 4, 1960, August 28, 1963; *Chicago Defender*, June 25, 1965, June 7, 1968, March 7, 1971.

43   *Chicago Tribune*, June 6, 1967.

44   *Chicago Tribune*, March 11, 1970, March 12, 1970; *Drovers Journal*, March 12, 1970, March 19, 1970.

45   *Drovers Journal*, May 7, 1970.

46   *Drovers Journal*, May 28, 1970.

47   Maureen Ogle, *In Meat We Trust: An Unexpected History of Carnivore America* (Boston and New York, 2013), pp. 94, 111, 113–14, 129–37, see quotes on pp. 138, 156.

48   *Chicago Tribune*, October 17, 1970.

49   *Chicago Tribune*, December 27, 1970.

50   *Chicago Tribune*, February 2, 1971.

51   *Chicago Tribune*, June 18, 1971; See Union Stock Yard Embargo and Closing Notices in Chicago Stock Yard Collection, box 4, folder 99.

52   *Drovers Journal*, July 29, 1971, August 5, 1971; *Chicago Tribune*, October 18, 1987.

53   *Chicago Tribune*, December 2, 1933; International Scrap Book Summary to January 1937, Memorandum to Mr. A. G. Leonard, January 4, 1937; Memorandum to Mr. O. T. Henkle, December 16, 1936; 1936 International Live Stock Exposition Press Publicity by States; 1935 International Publicity by States, all in International Live Stock Exposition Collection, box 3, file 6.

54   *Chicago Tribune*, May 15, 1942.

55   *A Review of the International Live Stock Exposition, 1946* (Chicago, 1946), pp. 7–9, 166; *Chicago Tribune*, October 27, 1946, December 8, 1946.

56   *Chicago Tribune*, August 27, 1984, December 7, 1987, August 5, 1999; *Encyclopedia of Chicago*, s.v. Amphitheater.

Chapter Six

1   For a thorough discussion of the development of the CMD, see Robert Lewis, *Chicago Made: Factory Networks in the Industrial Metropolis* (Chicago and London, 2008), especially chapter 7; Glen Holt and Dominic A. Pacyga, *Chicago: A Historical Guide to the Neighborhoods* (Chicago, 1979), chapter 2, "Stockyards/CMD"; Dominic A. Pacyga and Ellen Skerrett, *Chicago: City of Neighborhoods* (Chicago, 1986), pp. 453, 462–63, 472; Central Manufacturing District, *Speaking of Ourselves* (Chicago, ca. 1942); Mary D. Schoop, "50 Golden Years," *CMD Magazine*, June–October 1955; Executive Committee Meeting New Jersey Company, April 29, 1909, the Chicago Stockyards Collection, University of Illinois at Chicago Special Collections, box 1, folder 14. Henceforth referred to as Stockyards Collection.

2   The CMD's efforts to fill in a portion of Bubbly Creek is described in Sylvia Hood Washington, *Packing Them In: An Archaeology of Environmental Racism in Chicago, 1865–1954* (Lanham, MD, 2005), pp. 113–14. *Chicago Tribune*, June 25, 2011; *Crain's Chicago Business*, July 25, 2004; Metropolitan Water Reclamation District of Greater Chicago Press Release, February 7, 2012. For current efforts by the Army Corps of Engineers regarding Bubble Creek, see Medill Reports: Chicago, August 28, 2013, at http://news.medill.northwestern.edu/chicago/news.aspx?id=224 (accessed August 6, 2014).

3   The UFCW left the AFL-CIO in 2005 to help establish a new organization, the Change to Win Federation, but rejoined in August 2013.

4   See the UFCW website for the union's history at http://www.ufcw.org/about /ufcw-history/packing-and-processing/ (accessed June 28, 2013). See the History of the Saddle and Sirloin Club online at http://www.livestockexpo.org/ssclub.aspx (accessed June 25, 2013).

5   E-mail questionnaire filled out by Kiki Bairaktaris of Park Packing Company, Inc., on June 28, 2013. Also see the website http://www.parkpacking.com/ for Park Packing in Chicago (accessed June 17, 2013). Interview with Franco and Dennis Chiappetti on February 22, 2013. For Great Western Beef, see http://www.great westernbeef.com/about.aspx (accessed June 17, 2013).

6   Lori Healey and John F. McCormick, "Urban Revitalization and Tax Increment Financing in Chicago," *Government Finance Review*, December 1999, pp. 27–30.

7   TIF districts are one mechanism that are intended to promote economic development, but the City of Chicago also established other funds to keep Chicago competitive in attracting industrial development. In 1992, the city allocated $25 million from its larger citywide general obligation bond issue for economic development funding. This made it possible to attract large industrial companies in general to Chicago and in particular to the Chicago Stockyards Industrial Park.

8   *Chicago Tribune*, February 17, 1985; for the Stockyard TIF, see https://www.city ofchicago.org/city/en/depts/dcd/supp_info/tif/stockyards_industrial

commercialtif.html (accessed July 15, 2013). For the Southeast Quadrant, see http://www.cityofchicago.org/city/en/depts/dcd/supp_info/tif/stockyards_south easthquadranttif.html (accessed July 15, 2013). For the 1996 annex, see http://www .cityofchicago.org/city/en/depts/dcd/supp_info/tif/stockyards_annex tif.html (accessed July 15, 2013); *Crain's Chicago Business*, July 10, 1996; City of Chicago, *Stockyards Annex Tax Increment Financing Redevelopment Plan and Project, April 2005* (Chicago, 2005).

9   Lisa R. Jenkins, "CivicLab Research Alleges TIF Surplus in 11th and 12th Wards," *Gazette Chicago*, July 4, 2013, http://www.gazette chicago.com/index/2013/07 /civiclab-research-alleges-tif-surplus-in-11th-and-12th-wards/ (accessed July 15, 2013).

10 Ben Joravsky, "Mr. Big Spender," *Reader*, August 5, 2009; Ben Joravsky and Mike Dumke, "Shedding Light on the Shadow Budget," *Reader*, December 10, 2009.

11 *Northern Illinois Real Estate Magazine*, June 20, 2010, p. 10, http://digital.turn -page.com/issue/12355 (accessed June 28, 2013). Local Industrial Retention Initiative (LIRI) employment numbers for the Chicago Stockyards Industrial Park come from Michael McMullin in an e-mail dated June 27, 2013, and interview with Michael McMullin at the Back of the Yards Neighborhood Council offices on June 26, 2013. For Allen Brothers, see http://www.allenbrothers.com/allen-brothers-difference/history/ (accessed June 28, 2013).

12 Testa Produce Corporation, *Testa Produce, Inc.: Green by Nature . . . Greener by Choice* (Chicago, n.d.); *Chicago Sun-Times*, March 10, 2010; Testa Produce News Release, May 11, 2011, "Monkey Dish," accessed August 5, 2013, at http://www .monkeydish.com/id-report-news/articles/testa-produce-distribution-center -named-midwests-best-green-building-project. Interview with Angela Brader, marketing coordinator for the Testa Produce Corporation, June 25, 2013.

13 For the history of Peer Foods, see http://www.peerfoods.com/tradition.html (accessed August 7, 2013); CoExist at http://www.fastcoexist.com/1682763/inside -the-chicago-meatpacking-plant-being-turned-into-an-enormous-vertical -farm#1 (accessed August 7, 2013); KOMO News.com at http://www.komonews .com/news/business/In-an-old-Chicago-meat-plant-greens-and-fish-grow -146669355.html (accessed August 6, 2013); Delta SKY Magazine at http://delta skymag.delta.com/Sky-Extras/Favorites/Fish-Out-of-Water.aspx#.UcXBu V3Z4lM.facebook (accessed August 5, 2013); Skyygreens Press Release at http:// finance.yahoo.com/news/skyygreens-aquaponics-now-chicagos-first-182749517 .html (accessed August 6, 2013). For more on The Plant, see http://www.plant chicago.com/ (accessed August 7, 2013). Interview with John Edel on August 20, 2013.

14 Press release, City of Chicago, "Chemical Plant Will Rise in Stockyards through TIF, City Land Sale," October 3, 2012; City of Chicago, Department of Housing and Economic Development, "Staff Report to the Community Development Commission Regarding a Proposed Negotiated Sale of City-Owned Property and Designation of Developer," December 13, 2011.

15 For the CSIP, see http://bync.org/ssa-13-stockyards-industrial-park/ (accessed August 6, 2013).

16   *The Gate*, April 8, 2013; *Chicago Tribune*, February 17, 1985; SSA #13 Commissioners Meeting Minutes, October 17, 2012, Back of the Yards Neighborhood Council; SSA #13 Commissioners Meeting Minutes, August 15, 2012, Back of the Yards Neighborhood Council. For Stamp and Eat, see http://bync.org/category/special-events /stockyards-stamp-eat/ (accessed August 14, 2013).

17   For examples of the USY&T Company aiding packing companies to locate on their land, see New Jersey Company Director's Meeting Notes, June 6, 1899 (S&S Company), June 4, 1901 (Fowler Brothers Packing Company), November 27, 1901 (Hammond and Company), the Chicago Stockyards Collection, University of Illinois at Chicago Special Collections, box 1, folder 14.

18   David Pearson, "Meat Labels to Get Precise about Origin," *Chicago Tribune*, November 23, 2013.

INDEX

Page numbers in italics refer to illustrations.